MGA
A History &
Restoration Guide

Revised and Updated

MGA
A History & Restoration Guide

Revised and Updated

Robert P Vitrikas

Scarborough Faire

1151 MAIN STREET, PAWTUCKET, RHODE ISLAND 02860 USA 401-724-4200

TELEX: 710-384-8015 (A/B: SCARBORO PKET) - FACSIMILE: 401-724-5392

ISBN 0-9621881-1-5

Published by:

Scarborough Faire, Inc.
1151 Main Street
Pawtucket, Rhode Island 02860 U.S.A.

Contents

Foreword

When Robert Vitrikas first asked me if I would write this foreword I must confess that my instinctive reaction was "What? *Another* MG book?", because it seemed to me that, one way and another, there had been quite a few recently. But then I thought that, among all the facets of the MG scene, the MGA was probably the one model which deserved a book to itself. For, surely, the introduction of the MGA—which some called a 'courageous step' away from the square-riggers but which, to me, was inevitable—marked the dawn of a new era. And for the book to appear in this turbulent MG year of 1980, twenty-five years on from the date of the first MGA, is as nice a bit of timing as one could wish for.

A book which is both historical and technical must be very thoroughly researched. I am writing this foreword without having seen more than an outline of this one and must, therefore, take it on trust. But I *have* met the author and talked with him long and earnestly, an experience which leaves me in no doubt that the book will be as accurate and as authentic—and therefore as interesting and as informative—as any man could devise. I, for one, very much look forward to reading it.

John Thornley
Abingdon

Dedication

To the MGA factory workers who made this story possible.

Preface

For years the MGA has been the black sheep of the MG family. Everyone knew what a "B" was. They were in dealer showrooms, in advertisements and frequently seen on the road. Mention to someone you owned an MGA and a common response was, "Oh, yes, the one with the upright radiator and sweeping fenders." This usually led to a clarification trying to relate the shape of the MGA to the Austin Healey or some other fifties envelope-bodied sports car.

Well, now the situation has changed. Mention an MGA at a party and invariably someone will perk up and mention he or she owned one in college or had a friend who owned one. Interest in the MGA is visibly picking up as MGA registers are formed around the world, reproduction parts are being manufactured and the quality and number of MGAs is picking up at car shows. In many respects, the MGA is coming into its own in much the same way as the "T" types did in the mid-sixties.

With the growing enthusiasm for the MGA, it is notable that there is no single book dedicated to it. There have been books published recently which include the MGA in a discussion with the MGB and MGC which hopefully will have whetted your appetite for this book!

It is readily acknowledged by those connected with MG at the time of the MGA's introduction that if it had not been a success it could have spelled the end of MG. Fortunately, that was not the case.

As a longtime MGA advocate, I have fulfilled a longstanding ambition to spread the word on this important MG model. I started on this book two and one-half years ago, shortly after my wife, Bev, and I took over duties as historians for the North American MGA Register. When we began gathering material on the MGA it became apparent that there was a wealth of information available. As I started to consider the research necessary to write a meaningful book on the MGA, I realized that many of the personalities involved in the MGA story were still alive and could make a great contribution to the body of knowledge on the car. Encouraged by Dick Knudson, supported by my family and friends and with the cooperation and contributions of MGA people, my dream has become a reality.

As I am concluding this work on the MG model which launched MG into the world market in a big way and made it possible for so many people to enjoy MG motoring, the end of an MG era is at hand. A combination of economic difficulties and poor management decisions have led to the discontinuance of the MG marque as we know it and the closing of the MG factory at Abingdon.

Who are the real losers in this regretable situation? MG owners? Not really. We will still be able to get parts for our cars. The sheer number of cars and strong club organization will see to that. Prospective MG buyers? Perhaps, but they will have the option of some other make or perhaps a cobbled-up MG version of the TR-7 at some later date. The losers in this are the one-thousand-three-hundred MG factory workers who have devoted their lives to the manufacture of the MGs in Abingdon.

The timing of the announcement for the closing out of the MG marque was ironic. In celebration of the Fiftieth Anniversary of the MG factory at Abingdon in September 1979, the townspeople literally closed the town down for a week of festivities to mark the occasion. The celebration ended on Sunday. The announcement of MG's closing was made on Monday morning.

A deal with Aston Martin to continue production of the MG at Abingdon, which showed so much promise during the Spring of 1980, fell apart in August due to the lack of financial backing. The announcement was made that the plant at Abingdon would be closed in late September 1980.

What a different story it might have been if the Aston Martin deal had not fallen through. Aston not only had ideas, they had a working prototype which was offered with a clever body design which allowed the basic convertible model to be converted to a hardtop or estate car after purchase by the owner. This is the type of imaginative engineering the low to mid-price sports car market craves. The MG was one of the few sports cars in this end of the market.

Does this mean middle income enthusiasts will be relegated to second hand sports cars while craving a new model they know they never will be able to afford? I don't think so. The market is there. The MG enthusiasts are still there, waiting. Maybe someone, possibly even British Leyland, will come out with a simple, modestly priced, economical two-seat convertible, called MG.

Chapter 1

Roots of the MGA

In achieving the longest list of successes ever gained by any one make of machine, MGs have made motoring history. Their success is sustained by a coterie of clever technicians and engineers who adapt the knowledge won by racing men, building it into production models...Every MG victory is scored with a production model, never with a specially built car, except for record breaking...[1]

Cecil Kimber

What is An MG?

The story of the MGA sports car starts with the beginnings of the MG Car Company. People who own MGs are often asked what the initials MG stand for. They may jokingly respond with mighty good; but when pressed, the informed MG owner will reply Morris Garages. The initials MG do stand for Morris Garages, but with the passage of time they have become synonymous with the word sports car. In light of the key role MG has played in defining the word sports car, we might consider the question, "What is an MG?". An MG can take many forms. It can have two doors or four; four, six or eight cylinders; carburetors numbering one or two, supercharged or normally aspirated; convertible or hard top; one, two, four or five passengers; three or four speed manual or automatic or preselector gearbox; designed for track only, road use only or both. As varied as the specification of the MG has been, so also should our definition of the sports car provide a wide latitude within which the designer can work. Perhaps the definition arrived at by Colin Campbell, himself an automotive engineer for over 35 years, offers the best answer to our question. "A sports car is any road vehicle in which performance takes priority over carrying capacity." If this definition leaves you cold, the following thought on sports car driving taken from Sir Osbert Sitwell's book *Left Hand, Right Hand* describing motoring during the turn of the century will more colorfully describe the sensations many of

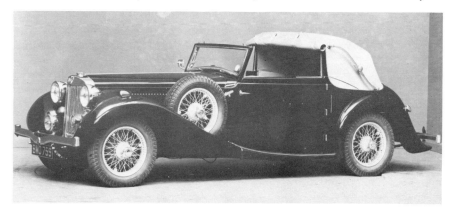

The magnificent WA Tickford drophead coupe. Introduced in late 1938, it provided elegant, sedate touring for up to five passengers with its 2.6 litre pushrod six cylinder engine. The WA was also offered with a four-door saloon body or as a tourer.

Surely the most complex road-going MG, the R-type would still be considered an advanced design today. Its specification included four wheel independent suspension, backbone central chassis (a la Lotus design), supercharged overhead cam four cylinder engine and a four speed preselector gearbox.

us enjoyed during our first drives in a roadster type sports car. Perhaps we were even lucky enough to have our girl friend along like the author did.

> *They would sit together, the two of them, the man at the wheel, the girl beside him, their hair blown back from their temples, their features sculptured by the wind, their bodies and limbs shaped and carved by it continually under their clothes, so that they enjoyed a new physical sensation, comparable to swimming; except that here the element was speed, not water. The winds—and their bodies—were warm that summer. During these drives, they acquired a whole range of physical consciousness, the knowledge of scents, passing from one into another with an undreamt of rapidity, the fragrance of the countless flowers of the lime trees, hung like bells on pagodas for the breeze to shake, changing into that of sweetbriar, the scent of the early mornings, and of their darkness, of hills and valleys outlined and. tinged by memory; there was the awareness of speed itself, and the rapid thinking that must accompany it, a new alertness, and the typical effects, the sense, it might be of the racing of every machine as dusk approaches, or the sudden access on a hot evening of cool waves of air under tall trees; all these physical impressions, so small in themselves, went to form a sum of feeling, new in its kind and never before experienced. Even the wind of the winter, at this pace snatching tears from their eyes, and piercing through layers of clothes, was something their fathers had not known.*[2]

The "M" in MG

Not only is the name MG indebted to William Richard Morris, (later Sir William Morris and later still, Lord Nuffield) but the marque owes its very existence to this ambitious, hardworking, level-headed man. Morris rose from ownership of a small cycle shop to head one of the largest automobile manufacturing companies in the world, giving away more than £27,000,000 to charities along the way.

William Richard Morris, founder of Morris Motors, worked his way up from a $1.00 a week job in a bicycle shop to head one of the largest corporations in the post-war era.

William Richard Morris was born on October 10, 1877, in Worcester, England, the descendant of a long line of Oxfordshire families who can date their ancestry back to 1278. Morris was nearly born in North America. His father, Frederick Morris, emigrated to Winnipeg, Canada, and served a time as a mail-coach driver in that country. Frederick Morris returned to his native England just before his thirtieth birthday and shortly after his return married Emily Ann Pether. Their's was not an easy life, only two of their seven children survived. Frederick Morris eventually came to work for his son William as an accountant at his first cycle and car shop and later held a staff position in the first Morris Garage on Longwall Street, Oxford. Young William Morris grew up in an exciting time during the 1890s when the world of transportation was discovering the bicycle. In those days of the Industrial Revolution and the romance of machinery, the best field for a young man to enter, next to medicine, was engineering which better suited Morris' middle-income family. Starting out as a fairly well paid apprentice at about $1.00 a week (inflation has had its effect on wages) with an Oxford cycle-maker, Morris quit after just nine months when his employer refused to grant his request for a raise and opened his own bicycle shop at No. 16 James Street, Oxford. From a humble beginning with a bicycle repair shop, Morris soon branched out into renting bicycles to the under-graduates at Oxford and later built, raced and won with his own bicycle design. Already the competition roots of the MG were beginning around the turn of the century. From bicycles, the next logical step was to motorcycles. In 1904, Morris put his hard earned knowledge from bicycles to good use in a sound and successful motorcycle design. Morris' appetite for motorcars was whetted by his trips to Europe picking up cars ordered by his wealthier motorcycle clients. Seeing a rich future ahead for the automobile, Morris decided to enter the automobile field in 1910. The first production Morris car, the Morris Oxford, was first driven on March 27, 1913. Walter Groves, editor of *The Motor*, gives us our first road test of a pre-production Morris Oxford on 17 December 1912.

We are able to illustrate the first finished car of those made by the W.R.M. Motors Ltd., of Longwall, Oxford, under the name of the

Morris-Oxford light car, and it will be seen that a very shapely external appearance has been obtained, the radiator being of the prow shape...Messrs. White and Poppe, the well-known engine manufacturers, are responsible for the power unit, which includes a four-cylinder, water-cooled engine of about 10 hp, being 60mm bore by 90mm stroke, a multiple-disc clutch, and gearbox giving three forward speeds...the radiator has no less then 340 feet of 3/16th inch copper tube. The rear axle is worm driven... The body is a two-seated, flush-side torpedo, painted pearl grey, upholstered in leather.[3]

This great granddaddy of the MGA sold for L175 and was available with various bodies, including a sporty single-seater listing for L220. This model boasted "a specially picked and tuned-up" chassis, disc wheels and mudguards, doing without such weather gear as a top and side-curtains.

In 1914 Morris was planning the production of a less expensive, mass produced follow-on to the Morris Oxford to be called the Morris Cowley. White and Poppe, supplier of the engines for the Morris Oxford, were working to capacity and could not provide additional engines for the Morris Cowley. Acting on the advice of his most trusted engineer, Hans Landstad, Morris contracted for 1,500 Red Seal engines from the Continental Motor Mfg. Company of Detroit. Additionally, transmissions, axles, Zenith car-

Cecil Kimber, the man who forged the MG legend that continues unabated today.

buretors and American Bosch electrical components were ordered from the United States. This American part in the manufacture of the predecessor to the first MG was of minor importance during World War I and died out shortly after the war's end when English suppliers could be found; however, the basic design of the engine in MG number one originated with the Continental Red Seal design. Several of the American equipped Morris Cowleys still exist today in the ranks of the Bullnose Morris Club. In fact, the door hinges could still be bought from the manufacturers in Detroit as recently as 1960. Morris contracted the firm of Hotchkiss et Cie (an English shadow company of the French firm) to produce the Red Seal engines in somewhat modified form; however, a problem arose concerning the production of American designed engines on metric standard French machine tools to fit British Whitworth standard spanners. A young employee of Hotchkiss by the name of Leonard Lord came up with the novel idea of fitting Whitworth heads onto the metric threaded bolts, thus solving the crisis. Lord became an employee of Morris Motors Ltd. when Morris purchased Hotchkiss in 1923, rising to Managing Director by 1933, then later resigning following a dispute with Lord Nuffield. Lord eventually went on to become director of Morris' arch-rival, Austin. When Austin and MG were merged in 1952, forming the British Motor Corporation (BMC), Lord assumed the head of the organization as Executive Chairman, a position from which he was to deal the MGA a stifling blow in 1952.

Cecil Kimber—The Soul of MG

If Lord Nuffield is to be considered the ambitious, hard working, level headed, business mind behind MG, then Cecil Kimber must be regarded as the personality and organizer behind MG.

Cecil Kimber was born in Dulwich, South London, the son of a printer. Kim, as he was known to his friends, tried working in the family printing business, but detested every minute of it and asked his father's permission to take up automobile engineering instead. His father disdained his request and as a result friction soon developed between them. Kim continued his interest in motoring, but unfortunately he was soon involved in a serious motorcycle accident in 1911 which nearly resulted in his right leg being amputated. Despite two years of treatment, he recovered from the accident with a limp. With part of the money he received as compensation for his injury, Kim bought his first car. His mother had taken ill while he was in the hospital and subsequently died of cancer. In the next three years, Kim's sister and brother

The Morris Garage on Longwall Street in Oxford was one of the first Morris Garages. It was acquired in 1911, the year before the first Morris car, the Morris Oxford, was constructed.

left home leaving him and his father with the printing business. The business began to falter and Kim's father asked him to contribute the remainder of the compensation from his accident to bloster the business. Kim had other ideas and asked for a raise instead so he could marry. This so infuriated his father that he cut Kim out of his life. Kim tried many times during his life to heal the wound between himself and his father, but never succeeded. This must have contributed to the dedication and resolve Kimber was to show in his future motoring endeavors. In 1914, he took his first job in the motor business with Sheffield-Simplex. Having at last achieved a measure of financial independence, Kimber married Irene Hunt in 1915. Kimber quickly gained recognition as an organizer with Sheffield-Simplex, later transferring to AC Cars then E.G. Wrigley, a component manufacturer. However, when E.G. Wrigley was in danger of closing down in 1922, Kimber moved to Morris Garages, where he was given the position of sales manager. When the General Manager suddenly resigned the following year, Kim was promoted to the position of general manager at the age of 34.

Just what sort of man was Cecil Kimber? His organizational abilities have already been mentioned. Kim was an avid sportsman with a real zest for competition, as evidenced by his motorcycle and automobile racing exploits. His style of driving was legendary, seemingly with no concern for his own safety, he actually kept to his slogan of "Safety Fast" and seldom had an accident. His only serious crash occured while driving his wife and mother-in-law in a factory experimental car which had a new type front suspension fitted. The suspension failed and the resulting crash broke Kimber's nose, but he somehow got the damaged car back to Abingdon, picked up another and continued the journey. Kim never reported the accident because he feared that those responsible for the suspension design might be blamed for the accident. A writer for *The Autocar* gives us this account of a ride in 1937 with Kimber in the then new 1-1/2 litre MG.

> *Many times I have made that run from Havre to Rouen, but never have the 55 miles seemed so short. Maybe Kimber was relieving his feeling after the 30 mph limits of England, for he travelled fast, but it did not seem to be fast, since the new 1-1/2 litre must be about the most comfortable car of its size in existence, and quiet as well. We were cruising at 60 most of the time, and on one grade we exceeded 60 in third. 'Not bad, eh?' querried Kimber. "Quite good,' I replied. 'But don't break the thing. We've only just started.'[4]*

Kim's second love was sailing and he was often to be found on his boat *Fairwind*. Kim was also an avid fisherman and despite a heavy work schedule, he always managed to get away for Derby Day, but not to watch the horses but rather to fish, claiming, "It is the best day of the year for the may-fly and on that day nothing under 2 lb came out of the water!"

Kim acquired a love of art from his mother who was a painter. His appreciation for art was realized in his neat geometric designs, the most famous and lasting of which is the MG octagon. The octagon symbol first appeared in an ad in the May 1924 issue of *The Morris Owner*. The octagon symbolized the enclosure of a large area within a small space, hence the "quart in a pint pot" slogan of the early MG days. In 1927, the octagon was adopted by Kimber as the symbol of MG. His infatuation with the octagon led to the inclusion of octagons on every imaginable place on earlier MGs; octagonal sidelamps, radiator caps, dipstick handles, instrument faces, panel knobs, camcover breather holes and even gearshift knobs. The Kimber family even has a service of octagonal dinnerware for special occasions.

The Morris Garages trade name was established in 1927, and in the spring of 1928 the name was changed to the now familiar MG Car Company.

Kim was a generous man, often giving elaborate parties for his friends

Octagon mania! Can you find the nine octagons in this interior photo of a WA Saloon?

...or the eight octagons on this N-type Magnette?

and outwardly living a luxurious life, although he was not exceptionally well paid, and actually maintained a close hold on his private funds. Kim enjoyed his position with MG and often rankled his contemporaries at Morris Motors with his ability to "twist the old man's tail harder than anyone else." Long diligent hours in his Tudor style office in Abingdon complimented his hard play off the job.

As General Manager of the Morris Garages, Kimber was busy trying to keep the rapidly expanding business organized and running smoothly. Despite this hectic activity, Kimber still found time to compete with Morris Cowley Chummy specials, achieving a gold in the 1923 London-to-Lands End Trial. Kimber learned in the late summer of 1924 that the Morris Cowley built Chummy was to be priced lower than the Morris Garages built Chummy, and that sporting style bodies would no longer be available from Morris. This was the deciding factor in Kimber's decision to go ahead with

Old Number One, registered FC7900, is generally regarded as the first true MG although this has been the subject of much discussion!

The care and craftsmanship that the Abingdon work-force puts into their product is no better illustrated than in this 18/80 Mark I. The body covered these beautiful "MG" brackets, so most proud owners didn't have the opportunity to admire them! This particular car was prepared for a motor show. MGs have always reflected painstaking preparation for their public appearances, be they for show or competition.

In September 1929 the MG factory was moved from Cowley to Abingdon where sufficient "elbow room" was available to accommodate an ever growing need for more factory space. At Abingdon MG was to find a home in this historic village where the Thames and Ock rivers join.

The two K-3s, Eyston and Lurani on the right and Howe and Hamilton on the left, check into a control point on the Mille Miglia.

Pushing the new K-3 to its limit, Captain George Eyston and Count Lurani won the 1100 c.c. class in the 1933 Mille Miglia. Their team mates, Earl Howe and "Hammy" Hamilton finished second in class, garnering the team prize for MG. This marked the first time a non-Italian team had won the coveted award.

an MG sports car design which borrowed somewhat from the Morris standard line, but also utilized original designs with performance taking precedence in such components as the engine and chassis. With this philosophy in mind, the first MG was registered on 27 March 1925 as "11.9 hp, owner Cecil Kimber. Colour, Grey, Reg. No. FC 7900." This first MG established the competitive prowess of the MG marque by winning a gold on its first outing at the 1925 London-to-Lands End Trial. The glory days of the MG lasted from 1925 until 1935 when a management decision to stop factory participation in competition was made. The achievements during this period are best summed up by Kimber himself.

> In achieving the longest list of successes ever gained by any one make of machine, MGs have made motoring history. Their success is sustained by a coterie of clever technicians and engineers who adapt the knowledge won by racing men, building it into production models...Every MG victory is scored with a production model, never with a specially built car, except for record-breaking. The best of British drivers have handled MG cars, and Continental racing men have at times abandoned the product of their own countries in order to gain success on this all-British machine. Tazio Nuvolari was hailed as

Italy's leading driver when he took his MG Magnette to victory in the 1933 Tourist Trophy race. The 1934 racing season concluded with MG receiving a signal honour—Rafaele Cecchini, who had driven his Magnette with consistent success throughout the year, was awarded the 1,100 cc championship of Italy...Every race in the British calendar has been won at some time by an MG, except the Mannin Moar, but including the BRDC's 500 miles event, admitted to be the hardest and fastest of all long-distance races. That is why MG cars are supreme. Every lesson learned by the racing drivers is employed by factory engineers to make the production car still better.[5]

The stark economic realities of the depression dictated the MG factory's withdrawal from racing, also forcing Lord Nuffield to sell the assets of MG to the Nuffield Group. The official statement read, "The directors have decided that, at all events for the present time, racing for the purpose of development has served its useful purpose."

The R-type marked the end of the era of ever more complex and sophisticated MGs. The economic realities of the times put an end to these engineering master-pieces. Note that this is not an overhead shot. The chassis has been turned on its side and is resting on the knock-offs!

The end of the mechanical extravaganza of six cyclinder, overhead camshaft, supercharged MGs was at hand, forcing a return to more mundane "corporate components." John Thornley, who followed Kimber's steps as General Manager, tells it this way.

Between 1930-35 in the intensely and ridiculously expensive period when we had made four new models each year, year after year, ever more complex, further away from what was then practical reality, we had been casting bread upon the waters. We had spread the name of MG around the world at the expense of going fairly severely into the red every other year so that Kimber had to go along to Lord Nuffield and say, 'Please to keep going, I want some more money.' And it was about 1935 that Lord Nuffield got a bit fed up with this and...cut.

One of the last racing teams sponsored by the MG factory was a six woman team which competed in the 1935 Le Mans 24 hour race. It would be 20 years before another MG, the MGA prototype EX 182, would break the factory's absence from racing at Le Mans. The withdrawal from racing marked the beginning of the end for Kim; and with the advent of World War II the production of the MG was suspended in 1939 with the TB model. In the early months of the war Kimber negotiated an important contract for MG to make war material which ran counter to the on-going negotiations the Nuffield Group was conducting with the War Cabinet. The ensuing furor resulted in Kimber's resignation from his beloved MG. In tragic contrast to his "Safety Fast" lifestyle, Cecil Kimber died in a freak 4 mph train accident on February 4, 1945. (Cecil Kimber was succeeded as General Manager by Jack Tatlow, with John Thornley taking over in 1952.)

Post War Transition

The cessation of World War II was quickly followed by the production start of the MG TC. The TC was basically the same car as the TB which was in production prior to World War II, and was the car which launched the MG Car Company into the American market and thence to the forefront of the world sports car market. Following World War II, steel was strictly allocated according to export sales. "Export or die" was the byword of the day. It was this policy that encouraged MG to expand its American market, and expand it did. Production swelled from 280 cars a week to 1380. After the TC caught on, MG had to sell about ten TCs in America in order to get the steel to build one Y-type for domestic sales. It is a great credit to workers at MG that this increase in production was achieved with little additional labor, no extra shifts, and no expansion of the factory. A moveable assembly line and a little ingenuity certainly helped. As a result of the rebuilding programs after the war, many companies were given the opportunity to start with a clean sheet of paper on the drawing board, their imaginations fired with unfulfilled ideas nurtured during the lapse of car production and fueled by the new found knowledge gained during the frantic technical research and development done on war machinery.

Public attitude also changed following the war. People had been through the hard times—now they were ready to enjoy life—and the automobile was a prime source of their enjoyment. The late forties and early fifties marked a change in public taste away from the rough riding, drafty, leaky, noisy, cramped sports cars of the thirties toward an automobile which delivered sporty performance—perhaps more than before—but with the practicality which would allow use of the sports car as a second car with no more fuss than the family sedan. The sports car was beginning to move from being the plaything of the master of the house on weekends and holidays, to a second car which had to work for its living during the week, often at the hands of the wife of the house, running to the store for a loaf of bread, taking the children to school and other chores. Designers concentrated on the refinement of suspension and chassis designs. The experience gained from the aircraft industry during the war led to increased awareness of the benefits of aerodynamic styling.

The men of MG, John Thornley, Cecil Cousins, Sidney Enever, and Alec Hounslow to name just a few, knew that they would have to respond to the changing times if MG was to remain prosperous in the years ahead. There would be no resting on their laurels, no matter how numerous or how great they may have been, for the car buying public is a demanding one and at times maddeningly hard to predict. MG had established itself as a maker of small, reliable, well-built cars sold at a modest price noted for their fine handling and performance, an attribute demonstrated on race tracks all over the world. The list of world class drivers who got their start driving MGs competitively is quite impressive: Phil Hill, Stirling Moss, Carroll Shelby, Briggs Cunningham, Jack Brabham, Ken Miles, Roger Penske, Denny Hulme, Richie Ginther and John Fitch to name a few. In responding to the challenges of the late forties and early fifties, the British sports car industry, and MG in particular, established themselves as the leaders in the mass produced sports car field during the fifties.

An Idea Takes Form—UMG 400

Building on their competition experience, development of the MGA embraced the concept that "racing improves the breed." From its very inception, the MGA was rooted in competition development as few cars have been. George Phillips, a photographer for *Autosport*, was one of the more successful MG racing drivers during the late forties and early fifties. Phillips and London garage owner Dick Jacobs were known around the MG factory

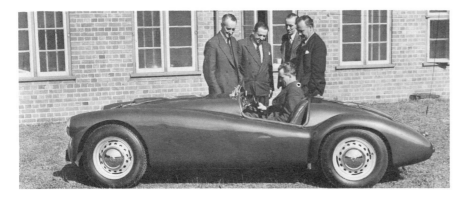

as the "heavenly twins" because they were constantly seen around the factory looking for parts and information to help them continue their winning ways. In 1950, Jacobs and Phillips were closely involved with the factory in developing the TD Mark II, which became a production success.

Phillips and his co-driver, Winterbottom, campaigned at TC in the 1950 Le Mans race, finishing a creditable eighteenth overall and second in class. Having made this good showing and thus being qualified for the 1951 Le Mans race, Phillips approached John Thornley, the MG works manager, for assistance in preparing a car for the 1951 race.

What the T-Series really needed for a high speed race like Le Mans was a better streamlining. Syd Enever already had an idea for a streamlined body and so it was decided to build a one-off body and mount it on the newly designed TD chassis, which incorporated independent front suspension. It was thought that this envelope body would also help to soften up the MG market for the streamlined body which must inevitably come. The project was given the designation EX 172, the earliest EX number in the MGA family tree. Drawing on his experience with "Goldie" Gardner's EX 135, Enever began to adapt the design to a road racing car. Apparently the work on EX 172 was done without the full knowledge of S.V. Smith, then Nuffield Director. George Phillips recounts MG's surreptitious shufflings. "I seem to remember Smith visited Abingdon every Tuesday and when he was coming they'd wheel the car out into the field where he couldn't see it. Eventually it came to the showdown day and they didn't know if they'd have a job or not if Smith didn't like it. Anyway, it seems he did because they ran the car

for me and they all stayed on."[6]

Like so many MG designs which would follow, the EX 172 body shape was tested as a quarter scale wooden model in the wind tunnel at Armstrong-Whitworth. Framework for the body was constructed of 16 gauge square section (5/8 inch) tubing. These were shaped along the plan data lines of the body drawing (every ten inches). Wooden forms were also placed along these data lines and the aluminum body panels were formed over them. The body panels were attached to the square section framework by rivets and the entire bodywork was attached to the chassis using rubber mounts. The body was designed to be easily removeable for access to the chassis. Because the chassis was of the old parallel rail design, it was not possible to place the driver's seat between the rails; therefore, a driving position not unlike that of

The problem of fitting the traditional MG grill onto an envelope body was nicely handled and set the general pattern for the production MGA grill. The hood scoop was for the carburetors, not the driver, as was the case on later MGA competition cars. Sitting up and out of the car in the wind stream probably eliminated the driver cooling problem!

The interior is nicely finished off with fitted carpets, crash pad around the cockpit and even a telescopic steering wheel. Notice the tool box on the passenger side and the snap fasteners for the passenger tonneau cover. A portion of the square section tubing to which the body panels were attached can be seen just in front of the tool box.

John Thornley, Assistant General Manager of MG at the time, talks with MG Director S.V. Smith about the evolutionary EX 172.

pre-war race cars was adopted with the driver sitting well out of the car. A blister windscreen was used to deflect the air stream up and over the driver. In order to test the efficiency of the streamlining, a stock TD and EX 172,

Despite being an "under the counter" special, UMG 400 was beautifully finished. Note the faired in license plate lamp and quick release fuel filler cap. The passenger has no door. The driver's door is thoughtfully indented to accommodate the driver's elbow.

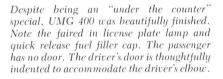

Wind tunnel testing played a big role in the development of the MGA shape to maximize its efficiency at speed. Many car manufacturers today are re-discovering the importance of aerodynamic efficiency.

now registered as UMG 400, were driven out to the South Oxford by-pass where a practical test took place, as described by Henry Stone, a factory mechanic working in the experimental shop at the time. "We took a TD and UMG 400 onto the southern bypass around Oxford. We whacked them both up to 80 miles an hour and lifted the foot off. UMG 400 just went on and on

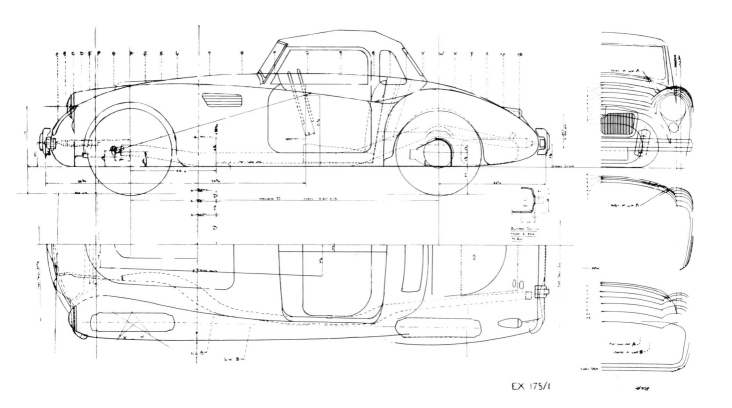

EX 175/1

and on and on and on out of sight and of course the standard TD just pulled itself up."

Clearly the design change was a great step forward in high speed efficiency, resulting in a nearly 30 mph increase in top speed over the stock TD (UMG 400 was timed at 116 mph on the Mulsanne Straight in Le Mans). Development of the body went smoothly, though there was a problem with where to place the cold air intake for the radiator. With the streamlined body shape a boundary layer of still air formed around the car which required careful study regarding placement of the air intakes, as well as outlets. Short pieces of yarn were taped to the body and the action of the yarn was observed at speed. The boundary layer of still air was indicated where the yarn lay flat against the body. Where the yarn fluttered indicated areas of high or low pressure turbulence. This method was used to determine placement of the grill, as well as the hood scoop used to ram cool air into the engine compartment. The engine used in UMG 400 was a TD XPAG unit with which Phillips had much experience. He felt that the engine was strong enough to withstand hard use during the race despite factory reservations.

In pursuit of a class win and the index of performance, Phillips drove the car hard from the start of the long 24 hour race in 1951; and as a result, a valve broke after only three hours, retiring the car. John Thornley recalls his premonition before the race. "I was afraid that (engine failure) was going to happen because in talking with George beforehand, he was so utterly convinced of the complete indestructability of the power unit that I knew in my bones that with the improved aerodynamics, he was going to overcook it." Despite the mechanical retirement, Enever was very pleased with the car's performance and began to consider changes which would make the car a production reality.

As to the fate of UMG 400; the car was offered for sale to Phillips after Le Mans, but he declined. It is presumed the car was subsequently cut up by the factory.

At this point the stage was set for MG's whiz kid, Syd Enever, to assert his considerable talent in the complete ground-up design of a new MG sports car known as EX 175. Perhaps this would be a fitting place to characterize Mr. Enever's career and abilities while at MG. John Thornley, long time friend and co-worker of Syd's for nearly 50 years provides this account.

I am perfectly satisfied in my own mind that Sydney Enever is a genius. What he achieved is the more remarkable because he achieved it with the absolute minimum of formal education. He left school when he was 14. He joined Morris Garages and was virtually a messenger boy delivering spare parts and this sort of thing, riding a bicycle with a plate hanging below the crossbar with 'Morris Garages Oxford' painted on it. He was completely self taught; taught by observations, taught by practice, trial and error. In practice, he got it right. He was equally at home in arguing with chaps whose speciality was airflow in combustion spaces and with chaps whose speciality was air flow over body surfaces, or for that matter, strength of materials, strength of gears. He was an instinctive engineer of the W.O. Bentley type who could look over a con rod and say, 'Well, that isn't strong enough, we want a little bit more on here and there.' And often enough events would prove him right. He was an unsung genius. He deserves far more plaudits than he has received.

This wooden model was used for wind tunnel testing of the EX 175 shape. The hood blister was necessary to clear the taller XPAG engine of the TD. The double hump cowl which dates back to the early 1930s was not continued on the MGA. The knock off ventilated disc wheels look remarkably similar to those used on the Twin Cam.

Perhaps as a result of his self-taught knowledge, Syd had a profound belief in the basics and a disdain for designers who felt they were above them. In a conversation with John Thornley before the war, Syd provided this insight. "These high falutin' chaps writing these days about the finer points of suspension. They completely lose sight of the basics. The basics are in here (pointing to a huge volume on the design of railroad locomotive suspension written about 1896). If you can get 50 tons of railway locomotive to stay on a pair of railway rails at 80 miles per hour, you've got to know something about suspension."

Pursuing the development of UMG 400, Enever designed an all new chassis with the project designation EX 175, which featured wide spacing of the side frame rails to allow seating, thus making a lower wind cheating profile possible. Box section construction provided an extremely rigid chassis, quite in contrast to the previous flexible design of the TC. Independent front suspension of the TD and Y-type, employing coil springs with Armstrong lever action hydraulic shock absorbers, was retained. Two of these chassis were built and one was clothed in a smooth wind cheating shape which was very pleasing to the eye while retaining the basic shape of UMG 400, albeit with a slightly more aggressive shape as a result of a longer wheelbase and somewhat heavier fender treatment. At this time, MG didn't have a design shop of its own and body construction was done by BMC's Bodies Branch at Coventry. Eric Carter, who played a large role in MG body construction through the years, was head of the design office there and recalls the EX 175 project.

> *Syd visited us at Quinton Road with a sketch of a proposed style for the outside shape plus some proposed details for a chassis. We made a start the following day with a full-size drawing and on the third day, details were issued to our experimental department in the form of tracings or slip sheets to start work on preliminary wooden formers to produce the panels. Within three months that prototype was finished. Bodies Branch being a small company with a maximum of 1200 employees and cooperation between its various departments being first class, no time was wasted. Syd was a regular visitor during the building of this body when cooperation was absolutely essential to marry the body and chassis together while they were being built at different plants. In fact, on receipt of the chassis from MG we had no trouble...with the mounting.*[7]

The body was nicely detailed with bumpers let into the front and rear bodywork and a license plate holder blended into the rear bodywork. Originally, the windshield was a fairly upright design, but this was later changed to a more rakish angle. A vent was originally intended for the upper portion of the front fenders, between the door and front wheel arch, but this was discarded in favor of the unusual cowl vents which have since become a

This rear view of the EX 175 model shows the faired in license plate holder and recesses in the rear fenders to allow a closer fitting bumper. Both of these were dropped on the production models because they were too costly.

symbol of the MGA to many owners the world over. The convertible top was designed as a three window model which was later adopted on the Twin Cam and 1600 models. EX 175 was nicely finished off with a telescopic steering wheel providing three inches of travel, wire wheels, a radio and a luggage carrier. A TD XPAG engine, transmission and rear axle were fitted and the car was registered as HMO 6. The second chassis was put aside to play its own special part in MG history later.

At about this same time, 1951, an important change in the business structure of the company took place which was to have a profound effect on the future of the MGA and HMO 6 in particular. In 1952, the Nuffield Group of which MG was a part, merged with Austin Motor Company to form the British Motor Company (BMC). The merger with Austin, a long time rival of MG, was not taken well at Abingdon. Additionally, MG lost its design office with H.N. Charles and George Cooper being transferred to the Central Design Office at Cowley; leaving MG with a small but dedicated development department principally consisting of Syd Enever, Alec Hounslow and Henry Stone. John Thornley describes the operation like this, "Sydney Enever would draw his ideas on the back of an old envelope and Alec Hounslow and Henry would beat it into shape." As part of the agreement, Lord Nuffield gave policy control to Sir Leonard Lord, the head of

Austin Motors and a former MG employee. Shortly after the merger, a proposal for production of the MGA in the form of HMO 6 was presented to Lord. John Thornley had just been appointed General Manager of MG at that time, and John 'puts the events in perspective.

> *George (Phillips) started it all but there were two other aspects. One that MG, as part of a larger combine (part of the Nuffield organization to start with and then from 1952 on as part of British Motor Corporation) was such a small element of the overall picture that it tended to get neglected. It was only we who lived in Abingdon and worked in Abingdon, beavering away, that produced in succession the TD and TF and the TF 1500 and then finally the MGA. We being very substantially ahead of out time in that the portotype MGA was in existence in 1952. We showed it with great pride to our then new boss Sir Leonard Lord. We were three days too late in that Donald Healey had been at him with the 2-1/2 litre 4 cylinder; what came to be known as the Austin Healey 100 which was produced at Longbridge. To him, one sports car was very much like the other and there was not room for spending a lot of money on two, the MGA and this thing that he had bought off Donald Healey. We were disappointed, obviously. We knew we were right. We knew it would come to the surface in the end. It was just a question of how long we would have to wait. We knew perfectly well it wasn't the end of the MGA. After this we kept chipping away at Lord. It wasn't purely the desire to produce the MGA, it was to save the MG market in the states again which was not being replaced by the Austin Healey. The TR 2 was intruding into the TD/TF market. We always said that if we had been given the go ahead with the MGA when we first put it up, to wit two years earlier, the Triumph would never have got into the states at all.*

HMO 6 later did duty with Lockheed as a test bed for disc brakes which were subsequently introduced on the MGA 1600. Following this, HMO 6 met the same fate as its predecessor UMG 400 and was cut up.

HMO 6 Dimensions

Wheelbase	*95 in.*
Track, front	*47 3/8 in.*
Track, rear	*50 in.*
Length	*155 3/16 in.*
Height	*50 in.*

An Interlude—The TF

Following this setback, the picture of MG dimmed further with the declining sales of the TD. TD sales fell 40% in 1953 and this precipitated

With sales of the TD plummeting and the EX 175 design rejected, a new model had to be found. This 1953 mock up was one of the designs tried before arriving at the TF.

development of the TF. The TF was designed literally on the garage floor by Cecil Cousins, Alec Hounslow, Syd Enever and a panel beater by the name of Billy Wilkens. The TF prototype was built in two weeks by these gifted men and then turned over to the design office to draw up the plans. The TF is now regarded as one of the most beautiful of all the square-rigged MG's; however, when it was introduced at the 1953 Motor Show it was derided as indicative of a company which had lost its impetus and ability. As if to rub salt in the wound, the highly successful TR 2 was introduced the same year.

In 1954 the second EX 175 chassis, clothed in a sleek streamliner body, was tested at the Bonneville Salt Flats in an attempt on the Class F records in the sprint and duration categories. The engine for the special was derived from the XPEG engine of the TF 1500. The body design was inspired by Goldie Garnder. This special, designated EX 179 by the factory, with its well drilled MGA prototype chassis, was driven by Captain Eyston to new US and international records in the Class F sprint category at a speed of 153.69 mph; and with Eyston and Ken Miles driving established new records for the six hour duration category at 121.63 mph and for the 12 hour category at 120.87 mph.

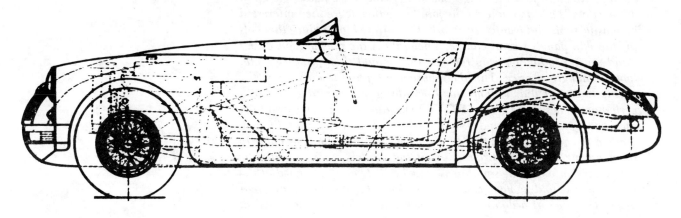

EX 182, the dawning of a new era. This blueprint shows the full undertray designed to reduce air drag at speeds over 100 mph caused by wind turbulence between the underside of the chassis and the road. The larger gas tank and repositioned spare tire can also be seen.

A Star Is Born—EX 182

With the realization that the TF was to be a stop-gap measure against eroding sales, the work on the new MG was given a belated go ahead in June 1954. Syd Enever tells it like it is, "We had been sitting on the thing for two years and suddenly it was all panic and scurry. Huh! Management..." The old plans which had been lying on the shelf for two years were dusted off and the further development of HMO 6 was given factory designator EX 182. An introduction date of April 1955 was set, just under a year away. Plans were also made to enter a team of factory cars in the 24 Hours of Le Mans in June of that year, breaking an absence of 20 years from factory participation in that race. Born out of competition experience of UMG 400 and EX 179, the new MG was to make its debut on the race track to demonstrate to the world that racing does in fact improve the breed. With the introduction date only ten months away, a crash program was begun to ready the new MG for her introduction. This was an incredibly short time to develop a production car. Fortunately, the ground work had been well established with HMO 6. In an interview with Doug Nye, Eric Carter, who was charged with translating Syd Enever's drawings into a production reality, recounts the development.

> *A new full-size sheet of paper was put up on Friday and was squared up with ten inch squares. Syd dropped by and told me of the changes from the prototype. They weren't much at all, only larger bonnet and trunk lids, the deletion of the rear number plate mounting and slightly slimmer front wings—though this later change was hardly noticeable. The following day, Saturday, we started on the skin lines, and on Tuesday tracings and prints were beginning to be issued to the experimental*

The EX 182 prototype nearly completed. The wind-screen has not been attached, the vent in the rear of the hood has not yet been cut and the cowl vents are missing. The exceptionally clean lines of the MGA are readily apparent.

shop to start work on producing wooden formers, metal edged, to make the first few production body sets on. Next day, Wednesday, a delegation from Pressed Steel Company at Cowley arrived, headed by the late director of engineering , Bob Robertson. They had come up to discuss details and to quote on the job. Since they were then interested in 'plastic' tools and wanted the work, they offered to produce the tools for the skin panels free of charge. They said if the plastic tools didn't stand up to production requirements they would then produce metal tools at an agreed price. This they subsequently had to do because the plastic tools just didn't stand up. Everything was compressed into a very short time span to get the MGA into production. Just one example, the seats were designed and drawn up in one day using a totally new method of construction at that time; and no modification was made to them during the whole production of the model, except to suit the coupe version when the squab was raised a little and narrowed at the top. Then the folding hood caused some headaches due to the long rear deck. The idea of a double fold to tuck under the deck occurred at about eight o'clock one evening and an hour later the scheme was roughed out on paper and turned out to be a neat and acceptable solution, with the side curtains stowed in front of it.[8]

The problem of what to name the new MG was a challenge, since the gamut of the alphabet had been run and in fact could be said to have started all over again with the introduction of the ZA. The company didn't want to continue along with the TC, TD, TF model designation which lent itself to being recognized and understood only by the true MG enthusiast. This was particularly a problem in view of the expanding international market in which MG found themselves competing where product identity was very important. The name arrived at, MGA, was uniquely suited to these requirements. As John Thornley logically explained, "It compels the use of the name MG whenever reference is made to it; what is more, twenty-five further models can be produced before this same problem recurs!"

Syd Enever, MG's chief engineer, was given overall responsibility for the design of the MGA, alias EX 182. Alec Hounslow, whose long career with MG included work on the TA and TF development, was chosen to oversee the construction and development of the EX 182 Le Mans team cars. Alec's experience with racing machinery is extensive. He is probably best known for his exploits as riding mechanic with Tazio Nuvolari in the legendary MG victory in the 1933 Tourist Trophy Race, during which his patience and nerves, as well as mechanical abilities, were pressed to the limit. The problems the volatile Nuvolari encountered with the unfamiliar Wilson preselector gearbox used in the K-3 are described by John Thornley, "Yes, the score on the very first lap was three complete gyrations in the square, a rearward visit to within inches of the famous butcher's shop in

Comber, and an excursion up the escape road at the Dundonald hairpin. Otherwise the lap passed off without incident!"[9]

Alec Hounslow recounted his experience to Kenneth Ullyett in *The MG Companion.*

> *Who can blame Tazio for taking time to get the hang of the box? He soon understood about preselection, and snicked the lever back to third, but then forgot to press the pedal. The result was we arrived much too fast at most turns. I began to wonder what I had let myself in for. And I knew no Italian. Luckily we got hold of Hugh P. McConnell, whose fluent Italian enabled him to give Tazio a short technical dissertation on the Wilson system of preselection and how to do it!*[10]

Alec spent nearly all of his career at MG working in the racing, experimental or prototype shops. His experience in preparing cars for European endurance racing included the C, J, and K-types, so his job of preparing EX 182 for Le Mans team was not an unfamiliar one.

With worn tires and bearing scars on its bodywork from the 1933 Ulster Tourist Trophy race, the winning K-3 draws an admiring look from Lord Nuffield. The indominatable Tazio Nuvolari flailed his mount around the course breaking the lap record seven times in the process and providing his MG riding mechanic, Alec Hounslow, with a few anxious moments as well! The fiery Italian, Nuvolari, was so impressed with the MG victory earlier that year in the Mille Miglia that he asked to drive an MG in the Ulster race.

The development of the chassis and body were well established by the EX 179 and HMO 6 projects; however, the question of a suitable powerplant for the MGA had not been settled. The recently introduced powerplant of the TF 1500, the XPEG, was decided against in favor of the robust "B" series engine which was one of the first designs to find common use within the fledgling BMC. The transmission and rear axle were also standard BMC parts, leaving only the front suspension as a carry-over from the TF. Clearly this new MG was designed to be a complete break with the past with respect to both outward appearance and internal mechanical specification, beginning a new era of MG development and design. The former autonomy enjoyed by MG under the Nuffield Group was at an end and the economic realities of being a part of a larger organization would be felt in the future in having to make full use of readily available components from other makes within the organization. The adoption of the BMC "B" series engine, transmission and rear axle were the beginnings of this reality.

The development of the engine to transform it from a family sedan powerplant to a free revving, high performance sports car powerplant, coupled with delays in the body tooling resulting from the unsuccessful experiment with plastic dies, were quickly seen to take longer than originally estimated and production would not be able to commence in time for their entry at Le Mans under the production sports car category. A request was submitted to Automobile Club de l'Ouest, promoter of the Le Mans race, for the cars to be entered under the sports prototype category. The request was approved.

Syd Enever called in British engine developer Harry Weslake to suggest modifications to the "B" series cylinder head to improve its high speed breathing, despite the fact that this would mean the cylinder heads would no longer be interchangable with the other "B" series engines. Weslake substituted larger valves and carburetors, as well as enlarging the cylinder head around the valves. A new camshaft which boosted the horsepower and extended the engine rev range was employed. The "B" series cylinder head employed a heart-shaped combustion chamber, which when combined with the higher compression ratio of the "B" series engine, had the unpleasant characteristic of being prone to dieseling or running on if anything less than 97 octane gasoline was burned. This running on is due to the hot spot created by the point of the heart-shaped combustion chamber and has been the bane of tune-up specialists and backyard mechanics ever since.

As production of the MGA neared, prototypes for final testing were built. This particular prototype is fitted with a competition windshield. A radio antenna is mounted, however there is no radio. The oval cowl vents are lacking the "MGA" center section.

Further development of the HMO 6 chassis and body design resulted in several changes, primarily to ease production difficulties. The chassis was shortened by one inch, reducing the wheelbase an equal amount. The front track was slightly wider and the rear reduced somewhat. Some realignment of the chassis rails was also necessitated. As for the body, the front fenders were given a slightly reduced cross section while the rear fenders were reduced considerably in cross section. The distance between the rear of the front wheel arch and the leading edge of the door was reduced by one inch to conform with the reduced wheel base. The bumpers front and rear were given a lighter, less ponderous look and the overriders no longer echoed the stepped design of the bumper face bars. The rear fenders were no longer indented to allow the rear bumper to blend into the body work as on the front. This was done to reduce tooling costs for the fenders. The front bumper was also slightly lowered. Rear lamps were of different design, no doubt to take advantage of the widely used design common to the TR 2/3, Morgan, etc. The tail lamps were also mounted lower on the fender. A concession to the variously shaped license plates which would be mounted at the rear meant the nicely shaped license plate holder had to go in favor of a more versatile fixing. Front parking lamps were of a different design and were mounted lower on the fender. Due to the reduced height of the "B" series engine, the hood bulge could be discarded; however, the forward portion of the bodywork between the fenders was made fuller, probably to accommodate the radiator. The trunk area was also increased by making the bodywork around the truck lid fuller. The hood and trunk lid were reshaped, as were the doors, to ease entry and exit. The original drawing of HMO 6 shows a windscreen less steeply raked than that on the MGA. Interior room was virtually unchanged; however, the top was of a different design with smaller side curtains and a single window convertible top. Lastly, the gas filler pipe was moved to the right side from the left.

Development of the Le Mans cars continued under the watchful eye of Alec Hounslow, culminating in the completion of four cars; two main race

Part of the team who designed and built the Le Mans team cars stand proudly with their stable just prior to the team's departure for Le Mans. Alec Hounslow is fourth from the left and Syd Enever is fourth from the right. The newly modified service van is behind them.

entries, one back-up race car and a test car. The main race cars were registered LBL 301 (number 42 in the race) and LBL 304 (number 41 in the race). The back-up car was registered LBL 303 (number 64 in the race). The specifications for the cars were as follows:

Engine

Displacement	1,489 cc (90.8 cu. in.)
Bore	73.025 mm (2.875 in.)
Stroke	89.0 mm (3.5 in.)
Compression	9.4:1
Main Bearings	3, lead bronze
BHP	82.5 @ 6,000 rpm
Torque	115 lb/ft @ 4,500 rmp
Max BMEP	142 lb per sq in. @ 4,500 rpm

Transmission and rear axle

Clutch: 8 in. single dry plate

Overall gear ratios:

1st	9.555:1
2nd	6.318:1
3rd	4.945:1
4th	3.900:1

Rear axle ratio: 3.9:1 (originally 3.7:1 prior to race)

mph per 1,000 rpm in top gear: 19.7

Chassis

Wheels and tires: Dunlop 60 spoke wire wheels with alloy rim

Front tires:	5.50 x 15
Rear tires:	6.00 x 15

Electrical equipment: 12 volt positive ground, 37 ampere hour battery

Fuel system: 20 gallon tank, twin high pressure SU fuel pumps

Dimensions

Wheelbase	94 in.
Track, front	47 7/8 in.
Track, rear	48 3/4 in.
Length	150 in.
Height	41 in.
Ground clearance	6 in.
Weight (dry)	1,596 lb

Did you ever wonder, as the octagonal enthusiast you undoubtedly are, what it would be like to have your own personal guided tour around a brand new MG race car design, culminating with a test drive on the track? Come with me then as we go on an imaginary trip backward in time to the spring of 1955, shortly before the Le Mans race in June, and explore this new offering from MG.

Arriving at the MG factory engineering department, known to many enthusiasts under the old name of Experimental Shop, we are at once impressed by the orderly, business-like appearance. Images of pre-war trial and error development obviously have no part here. It is evident that the lessons learned during the war with regards to orderly scientific investigation and development under controlled conditions have been applied to the development of this latest MG product.

We are introduced to Syd Enever, MG's chief engineer and man in charge of the EX 182 project. Syd exudes an air of confidence and discipline with his neatly combed wavy hair, piercing eyes, firm set jaw and dapper double-breasted business suit. Syd explains that he is no newcomer to the MG family, having worked as a shop boy in 1920 with the Morris Motors Ltd. garages, later becoming a fitter in the repair shop and finally transferring to the experimental department where he has risen to the top of the newly named Engineering Department.

Syd recounts how the design for the EX 182 body originated with an under-the-counter special built for George Phillips to run in the 1951 Le Mans race. Syd explains that this design should have been ready two years ago, but prototype development was delayed for two years by BMC corporate decision. He is obviously pleased to be getting on with the project and justifiably proud of his work. Calling over Alec Hounslow, Syd politely excuses himself to return to his office.

Alec is an established racing mechanic who has worked his way up the ladder of experience to head the team of mechanics preparing this latest creation from MG for Le Mans. Alec has a purposeful air about him, dressed in a white lab coat and tie, his dark hair combed straight back as if to keep it from getting in the way of more important work. His good natured disposition quickly shows as he jokes about his earlier exploits with MG racing teams. Alec reminds us of the family nature of the experimental shop key personnel, explaining that he, Syd Enever and Cecil Cousins all "grew up" in the MG Experimental Department together.

John Thornley, another old MG hand, was the originator of the Le Mans project. The MGA was to be the first high volume sports car produced by MG and its market penetration was vital to the survival of MG. John thought that by running the car at Le Mans a great deal of free publicity could be had before the motoring world, especially the American market.

Taking us over to a workbench, Alec shows us one of the Weslake designed cylinder heads for the "B" series engine. We are told that the production MGA will use a similar head; however, the unusual right or left carburetor mounting arrangement of the prototype head will not be used. In place of the 1-3/4 in. SU units used on the racing engine, 1-1/2 in. SU carburetors will be adopted. Bearings used for the connecting rods and crankshaft will be of the lead-bronze type in place of the white metal bearings of the Magnette engine due to the greater stress created by higher engine speeds. The production MGA will utilize lead-indium bearings. The cylinder head employs no head gasket, but rather the faces of the cylinder block and head are scraped and lapped to eliminate the possibility of head gasket failure with the employment of a much higher compression ratio on the competition engine. Alec assures us with a grin that this unusual technique has been thoroughly tested on the engine test bench. All engines were run for 24 hours on a test bed, torn down, inspected, and reassembled to assure reliability.

We mention how different the engineering department appears from what we were expecting, with all the modern test equipment in evidence. Alec proudly responds that things have certainly changed since the old days of surreptitiously testing new designs on public roads with occasional daring "continental tours" to determine suitability for other markets. Today new designs are tested on specialized test rigs with the finest instrumentation available. Cambridge stylus-on-tape recorders are employed to allow design team members to leisurely examine experiment results in detail. As for road testing, the use of the military proving grounds in Surrey and the Motor Industry Research Association (M.I.R.A.) track at Lindley proving grounds are available. Chassis tuning is also done at Dunlop's skid pad. Engine and chassis dynamometers are employed to measure performance characteristics under varying conditions simulated by environmental chambers.

Following our tour of the engineering department, Alec asks us to accompany him to another area where one of the Le Mans cars awaits our eager inspection.

The modified B series engine used in the EX 182 on the test bed. The carburetors are shown with velocity stacks mounted.

The right side of the engine used in the Le Mans cars displays several interesting design features. The carburetor balance pipe can be seen between the number one and four sparkplugs. This design was too expensive and unnecessarily complex for production. Its location made the dipstick very hard to get to. The cooling passages in the cylinder head and block are connected by the hose seen at the rear of the engine. Engine block freeze plugs were secured by bolting bars across their faces. Even the nuts holding the bars were drilled and wired in place to prevent loosening! The oil filter is removed for mounting in front of the car along with an oil cooler.

Despite all the modern test equipment at the factory, the continental road test was not abandoned. Here two factory testers pause in the French Alps near Val d'Isere with LJB 370, a prototype MGA.

Arriving at an unlit work area, Alec throws a switch, bathing the latest creation of the MG works in light. Standing quietly aside like a proud father, Alec allows us a moment to take in the object of his labors of the past few months.

The smooth, flowing lines of the new model are very pleasing to the eye. Elegant one might say. The sparing use of chrome is evident from our side view where even the door handles are absent, a refreshing change from the 1955 offering from Detroit. Walking around the car, the overall integrity of the design and the high level of finish are apparent. The car looks purposeful in its British Racing Green color, accentuated by the subdued sparkle from the alloy wire wheels and the stark green interior. The lowness and aerodynamic shape are enhanced on the Le Mans cars with the employment of a racing windscreen and driver surround combined with a metal tonneau over the passenger compartment which allows the smooth rounded sweep of the nose to extend over the hood and passenger compartment, trailing off over the rear deck. The attention to aerodynamics is evident elsewhere in the faired-in rear view mirror and full underpan. The visual break with the past square-rigged style is striking and the feeling is that this long awaited new design from MG will be a success, having to make up for lost time against such makes as the TR 2, AC, Jaguar and the Austin Healey 100 which have already adopted the streamlined envelope body style.

Alec comes over to the car and begins to point out the differences between the Le Mans cars and the standard production models announced at the London Auto Show in May. The aluminum bodies for the Le Mans cars were built from drawings by Bodies Branch, Conventry as production bodies were not yet available. In the interest of lightness, always important on a competition machine such as this, the body and fenders are made of 18 gauge aluminum, as is the transmission tunnel. Hood, doors and trunk lid remain aluminum as on the standard production models. Also in the interest of lightness, the bumpers are omitted and a single 12 volt 37 ampere hour battery fitted instead of two six volt units. Aluminum alloy wheels help reduce the unsprung weight and improve handling.

Additional cooling considerations are handled by an oil cooler air intake build into the front valence panel and an air intake is built into the rear of the hood with an internal scoop to route cool air into the engine compartment. Wire wheels aid in cooling the drum brakes which will take quite a beating on the Le Mans circuit. Additional cooling is provided by drilling holes in the brake drums and backing plates. Consideration for the driver's comfort is not forgotten with the provision of a fresh air intake mounted on the nose of the car between the grill and right fender. This intake leads to a duct which routes the fresh air to an outlet on the firewall directing fresh air onto the driver's feet and legs. Alec explains this modification was made

A beaming Ken Wharton seems pleased with the testing of EX 182 at Silverstone in preparation for Le Mans. Note the absence of the driver's air intake next to the grill.

after a test session at Silverstone on the recommendation of Ken Wharton.

In the interests of safety, the hood is secured with two leather straps at the front and a single high-power driving lamp is mounted in the right half of the grill to assist visibility during the night driving at Le Mans. A larger gas tank of 20 gallons capacity and twin SU high pressure fuel pumps are required for the long high speed race ahead. A large quick release filler cap is provided in the center of the trunk lid to speed pit stops. Steel bars are welded between the chassis, side members, front and rear, to provide jacking points for the lever-type jacks used in the pits. Dzus fasteners provide ready access through the aluminum underpan to the underside of the car.

Lifting the hood, Alec points out the radiator header tank mounted on the shelf above the firewall to insure an adequate supply of cool water in the cylinder head during the race. Velocity stacks are used in place of air cleaners to increase air flow into the carburetors. The remote mounting of the oil filter up front with the oil cooler is noted as is the tubular exhaust manifold with its additional extractor effect over the standard MGA exhaust manifold. In addition to the standard Armstrong hydraulic shock absorbers, Andrex adjustable friction dampers are mounted in the front to reduce body roll and increase high speed stability. Slightly larger 6.00 x 15 Dunlop racing tires are fitted to the rear in contrast to the 5.50 x 15 tires in the front to improve handling. A 3.7:1 rear axle ratio (later changed to 3.9:1 for the actual race when it was discovered that the hairpin at the end of the Mulsanne straight would require downshifting to first gear with the 3.7:1 ratio axle) is substituted for the standard MGA 4.3:1 ratio, allowing a higher top speed down the Mulsanne straight. In place of the standard gearbox ratios of the MGA production model, a close-ratio gearset is fitted allowing the drivers to keep the engine in the peak of the horsepower and torque curves during the thousands of shifts which lie ahead during the race. We are told that the alloy 60 spoke wheels, oil cooler and close-ratio gearbox will be offered on the production MGA as competition accessories. Alternative rear axle ratios will also be offered.

The interior is predictably spartan. The two bucket seats are deeply contoured to limit lateral movement and the driver's seat is angled rearward slightly. The outline of the standard instrument panel is embossed into the fascia; however, the placement and type of instruments is different than on the standard model. Switch knobs are octagonal in shape, having been borrowed from the TF. The steering wheel is standard MGA with no MG crest center boss. The car is right hand drive and the shift lever, with a standard MGA knob, is at the driver's left. Detail differences between the race car and the MGA are an aluminum flap over the transmission dip stick hole in place of the standard rubber plug, an oval-shaped handle for the trunk lid release instead of the standard round handle, a longer throttle

Working out an electrical problem. The tachometer shown was later replaced with a larger five inch unit.

pedal is fitted to improve heel-and-toe downshifting and the MGA motif is missing from the center of the cowl vents.

To complete the racing team operation, a large van will accompany the team. The van is very complete, providing storage for spares, hand tools, machine tools, pull down bunks and even a kitchen. An ingenious set of ramps which pull out from beneath the bed of the truck are employed as a service rack.

Despite the seemingly long list of changes from production MGAs, the changes really aren't all that major, especially considering their entry in the prototype category. Alec points out that MG's original intention was to enter stock production cars and they have carried this philosophy over to these prototype entries.

Having completed our inspection of the Le Mans car, we are driven to a nearby racetrack where another of the gleaming British Racing Green team cars awaits us. As we prepare to climb into the driver's seat, one of the mechanics present reminds us to observe a rev limit of 6,000 rpm and cautions us not to overdo it as this car, LBL 301, will be one of the main entries at Le Mans. (LBL 301 was involved in an early hour crash at Whitehouse Corner, seriously injuring the driver, Dick Jacobs; the car was a complete write-off.)

On entering, we notice the narrow door makes entry awkward, but upon settling into the seat we find ample leg room available. The seats are very comfortable, offering good lumbar support as well as restricting lateral movement, both very important qualities in a race as long as Le Mans with its many high speed turns. The long bottom cushion provides good thigh support. The thin rimmed steering wheel is placed a comfortable distance away to allow a near straight arm driving position, if desired. The short gearshift with its typically short MG pattern is as close to the wheel as practical and very conveniently located. The pedals are of the pendulum type, that is suspended from the firewall, and with the additional length of the accelerator pedal, allow easy heel-and-toeing. Immediately in front of the driver is a large tachometer, flanked by a water temperature/oil pressure gauge on the left and an ammeter on the right side. A fuel gauge is located on the far side of the radio speaker.

The newly created BMC Competition Department acquired a van suitably modified to better support the competition effort away from the factory. Shown here are the driving compartment and the kitchen area complete with sink, stove and refrigerator.

The rear of the van showing the workshop area. The ramps could be raised with the car inside the van and the car then backed onto the ramps to provide an elevated working position.

At long last the magic moment has arrived. We're ready to experience this new era of MG motoring on the track. No choking is required as the car has been recently run and carburetors are set a bit rich. The engine fires instantly, eagerly, and seems anxious to get on with the task at hand. With a feint toward second to help align the gears, the lever snicks precisely into first. Remembering the close-ratio gearbox, we pick the revs up to 2,500 rpm (don't want to embarrass ourselves by stalling), slowly engage the clutch and we are off. Amazingly enough, the clutch is light and smooth, although the close-ratio box could easily lead to stumbling on take-off. Getting the feel of our new mount and warming the drive train up to running temperatures, we drive leisurely the first few laps, shifting at 4,000 rpm. The car has excellent steering characteristics at these lower speeds, being light, precise and quick, quite in keeping with its MG heritage. At lower speeds similar to those encountered in town driving, the suspension rides roughly over small surface irregularities; however, as the speeds approach those normally encountered on open road motoring, the ride smooths out and is actually quite comfortable. The engine is noticeably smooth and flexible, even in its present race tuned form, being content to trundle along at 1,500 rpm in top gear and then accelerate smoothly up to road speed. Predictably, the noise level in this race prepared car is high and the heat from the engine and transmission is beginning to make itself felt. Sitting much lower in the car, the buffeting from the wind is comparatively mild, the perspex windscreen assisting the airflow over the driver's compartment.

It is quite a change to be sitting *in* rather than *on* a car as one does in the T-series MGs. The drivetrain seems to be sufficiently warmed up and it is time to press this car to its limit, the very conditions for which it has been so carefully prepared. Bringing the car to rest at the beginning of the straight, we engage first gear, pick the revs up to 3,500 rpm and quickly engage the clutch while pinning the accelerator to the floor. Wheelspin is easily produced, accompanied by mild wheel hop with this brutal technique and the tack eagerly races to the red line of 6,000 rpm; quick shift into second and again wheel spin is produced; shifting into third a faint "chirp" is heard from the back wheels. Sliding the lever into fourth, we are passing the magical 100 mph point with the tach reading only 5,000 rpm. We make a mental point to check the top speed on the next lap as the turn at the end of the straight is rushing toward us. Applying the drum brakes hard, we are impressed with the powerful action from this high speed. Drifting the car through the 50 mph corner, the larger tires on the rear give the car near neutral handling characteristics. When adhesion is finally lost, the rear wheels gently let go first and when in a slide the car is perfectly manageable, even at amazingly large drift angles which we inadvertently find ourselves at times while trying out the handling. This is a very forgiving car and ought to provide a safe, fast training vehicle for the many beginning sports car enthusiasts who will undoubtedly become MGA owners.

Our earlier observations on the ride at Speed are proven out as the ride is pleasantly firm and controlled at the high speeds we are now encountering. The Andrex dampers keep the car level, even on the most extreme corners, and high speeds are taken with confidence with no tendency for the front suspension to become light and wander. Coming down the straight, we register a top speed of nearly 120 mph at 6,000 rpm. Very impressive for a car of only 1.5 litres and 82.5 bhp. The car seems most at home on a series of frequent, fast sweeping turns linked by short straightaways. The brakes are holding up superbly, with no tendency to fade despite frequent hard use. The engine is ideally mated to the handling characteristics with excellent acceleration in the mid-range. This should be an ideal combination on the types of roads normally encountered in highway driving.

Having had our fun, we reluctantly head for the pits. Switching off the engine, she chugs a couple of times, as if wanting to get back to the track. Our body still tingling from the vibration and wind of high speed motoring, we reluctantly extract ourselves from the cockpit and stand there in the afterglow of an experience we know will be remembered fondly in years to come. We have the feeling that this car must be a winner, not only on the track, but in the showrooms where the real battles for supremacy in the production sports car market will be fought. The combination of good looks and the technical sophistication we have just experienced should make this new chapter in the history of the MG the most successful yet.

The Proof Of The Pudding—Le Mans

The three team cars were driven to Le Mans and acquitted themselves well. LBL 304 (number 41) finished 12th overall, driven by Ken Miles and Johnny Lockett. These two drivers were to combine their skills again the following year when they would break 16 international records in EX 179 at the Bonneville Salt Flats in Utah. LBL 303 (number 64) finished 17th overall, driven by Ted Lund and Hans Waeffler. Number 64, it will be remembered, was the backup car on the team. LBL 301 (number 42) was involved in a serious accident early in the race and later scrapped. Its driver at the time, Dick Jacobs of "heavenly twins" fame, was seriously injured, but made a full recovery afterward. Jacobs' co-driver was Joe Flynn. The Le Mans race of 1955 was marred by a terrible Mercedes crash which resulted in the death of over 80 people. The publicity from the crash overshadowed the achievements of the MG team and was a very unfortunate turn of events as the Le Mans effort had been designed to give the MGA world-wide publicity. As a result of the adverse notoriety racing received from this incident, MG resumed a low profile regarding active factory participation in racing, leaving private entries, albeit with some under-the-counter support from MG, to carry on the racing exploits of MG.

A Taste Of Things To Come

Production of the TF ended in May 1955. Because of delays in delivery of body panel dies, the production of the MGA was not begun until September 1955. In the interim, only the MG Magnette saloon was produced. During this period, the factory fitted the Le Mans cars with standard rear axle ratios, standard ratio gearboxes and proper weather equipment and made the cars available to the motoring press for road testing, giving them a taste of what was to come. An *Autosport* test of LBL 304, which finished 12th overall at Le Mans, resulted in the following performance figures. Testing was done with the top folded and side screens stored, worst possible conditions for high speed tests.

0-30	4.0 sec
0-40	6.4 sec
0-50	10.0 sec
0-60	12.8 sec
0-70	17.0 sec
0-80	23.5 sec
SS 1/2 mile	18.4 sec

Speeds in gears: (4.3:1 axle)

1st	30	mph
2nd	48	mph
3rd	78	mph
4th	104.6	mph

Fuel consumption: Hard driving—22 mpg (Imperial gallons)

An *Autocar* test of the Le Mans backup car, LBL 303 (number 64) which finished 17th overall, resulted in the following figures. Testing was done with a passenger, 16 gallons of fuel, top folded and side screens stowed.

0-30	6.2 sec
0-60	13.8 sec
0-80	25.8 sec

Fuel consumption: Hard driving—23.8 mpg, normal driving—28 mpg (Imperial gallons)

Speeds through the gears with the Le Mans 3.9:1 axle ratio and close-ratio gearbox resulted in the following maximum speeds:

1st	48 mph
2nd	73 mph
3rd	93 mph
4th	118 mph

When Autosport writer John Bolster tested EX 182 LBL 304 in July 1955, he proclaimed it "...by far the best car that has ever come out of Abingdon."

Whatever Happened To EX 182?

What of the Le Mans cars after the race? A steel bodied car, which was taken from an early production run, was constructed along the lines of the EX 182 cars to replace the EX 182 destroyed in the Jacob's crash. The team of three cars was to have been entered in the Alpine Rally, but because of bad publicity from the Le Mans race, the Alpine was cancelled. The team was used in the interim for journalists to road test and then they were entered in the Tourist Trophy Race at Dunrod later that same year. Following the race at Dunrod, BMC withdrew from factory participation in road racing and the EX 182 cars were put to other uses such as running test beds for experimental brake and engine designs. Of the three original all aluminum bodied cars, one was written off in the Jacob's crash in the 1955 Le Mans race and the others made their way across the Atlantic to the US. LBL 304, number 41 in the race, was sold by the factory in 1959 to an American who shipped the car to the States. During the servicing prior to delivery, the engine oil drain plug apparently wasn't sufficiently tightened and less than 100 miles from the dealer the plug fell out on the Pennsylvania Turnpike and all the oil was lost with the subsequent engine seizure. Following an unsuccessful argument with the dealer over responsibility for the mishap, the car was put up for sale in 1960. George Lehsten, taken by the car's appearance and wishing to divest himself of his lumbering Buick, bought the car not knowing the true value of his purchase. In order to pass New Jersey regulations, the fuel tank had to be converted back to stock as did the bumpers. For convenience sake, the steering was switched from right hand to left hand drive. Following an accident in 1965, George discovered the peculiarity of the aluminum body work upon attempting to replace a fender. An appeal for help from England was successful and an aluminum fender was obtained. Could this have been one of the extra stampings that were originally made up? Following a frame up restoration which took five years, EX 182 is resplendent in its black lacquer paint and red interior, regularly winning trophies at car shows in the Denver, Colorado area.

LBL 303 was retained by the factory as a test bed for future changes to the MGA line, such as disc brakes for the front and eventually on all four wheels. LBL 303 also served as a test bed for the development of the twin cam model MGA. Following its use as a test bed by the factory, Ted Lund, the primary driver of the car at Le Mans, purchased the car. Lund later sold the car while on holiday to a wealthy jockey who lived in Canada. The jockey then sold the car to a purchaser in Brantford, Ontario, who in turn sold it to a collector of American cars in Berford, Ontario, who wanted to use it for his daughter's transportation to and from teacher's college.

Somewhere along the line LBL 303 acquired a modified 1600 cc engine, four wheel disc brakes, twin coils, a 4.55:1 rear axle ratio, and a competition clutch. Needless to say, this car was not well suited for commuting much less at the hands of a young lady. The daughter drove the car only once after which it sat in a field with grass growing through its now stationary wire wheels.

Word began to spread about this "funny looking MGA" sitting forlornly in the field; and two curious MGA enthusiasts in the area went to have a look. One of the two, Gordon Whatley, immediately recognized the car as one of the EX 182 Le Mans team cars. The owner of the car didn't fully realize what he had; but knowing that it was indeed a rare type MG, he was asking a considerable sum for it. Deciding to postpone any action, the two enthusiasts returned home. Three years passed and word spread that a pilot from England was considering purchasing the car. Gordon and his friend decided that they had better seize the opportunity and purchase the car or it would return to England in the hands of the pilot. Gordon's friend had just completed restoration of a lovely MGA and didn't wish to purchase the car, so Gordon went back to have another look and wound up purchasing it. Considering the age and history of the car, it was in good shape, sporting a fresh red paint job. Gordon decided to drive the car for a summer to see how it ran before beginning restoration. Gordon describes the car as a "bear to drive around town," commenting that the close-ratio gearbox makes stop and go driving a real chore. The engine in the car is a modified 1600 unit and in combination with the 4.55:1 axle gives very brisk performance. Heat thrown back into the passenger compartment from the engine and transmission made driving very uncomfortable, especially in the hot days of summer. After driving the car for two summers, work was started on the restoration, but was soon set aside because of other projects and to allow more time to thoroughly research the car to insure authenticity. Reflecting on the restoration of a unique racing car, Gordon indicated that a great deal of research was necessary to insure authenticity; however, due to various modifications made during the years, a certain degree of latitude was available. Additionally, on a car intended for racing, such things as a 25-coat hand-rubbed lacquer job was not needed. The stark interior and absence of bumpers and other trim items also reduced the labor and cost of restoration. Gordon put LBL 303 back on the road in Le Mans trim during the summer of 1979, complete with aluminum fenders, racing tires, driver surround, racing windscreen, metal passenger compartment tonneau, etc. Regretably the engine for the car as originally installed cannot be located, and as a result the 1600 engine currently installed will be used. Gordon is a member of a vintage racing club in Canada, and plans to compaign the car in vintage races, bringing the life cycle of this milestone car full circle some 25 years after the MGA story opened.

The MGA Pedigree

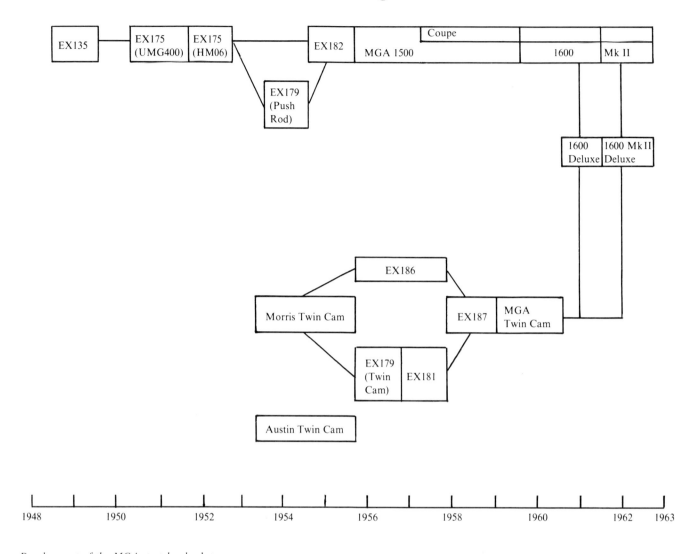

Development of the MGA stretches back to 1948 and was heavily steeped in competition as this diagram illustrates.

Chapter 2

The MGA 1500

The most complete, most extensive design change in twenty years. Early enthusiasm for its appearance can now be augmented by the knowledge of its very surprising performance.[1]

Road and Track

Dawning Of A New Era

The introduction of the MGA 1500 was a long awaited event by both the motoring public and press. MG had been among the last of the major sports cars to forsake the traditional shape of the pre-war era for the smooth, streamlined shape pioneered during the late thirties. Among sports car manufacturers, only Morgan would remain true to the old style. The early fifties were exciting, as well as frightening times for the auto manufacturers. While the technological progress had been rapid, so had the attrition of respected makes which had failed to keep pace during the post-war boom. Names like HRG, Bugatti, Frazier-Nash, Lea-Francis, and Singer all met their demise during the fifties. The public acceptance of the new MGA was crucial to the continued existence of the company. It was against this

backdrop that the curtain rose on this newest offering from MG; and its creators surely must have anxiously awaited the initial road testers' opinions and the public reaction, which would be closely tied to the testers' reports. They were certain of the merit of their labors and had complete faith in the judgement of Syd Enever; but widespread public acceptance would be necessary to support the mass production they were gearing up for. The initial introduction date was to have been June 1955; however, problems with the plastic body tools necessitated a delay while the conversion was made back to steel dies. The first MGA chassis was begun on May 16, 1955. It carries the chassis number 10,101, taking up where the TF 1500 had left off at 10,100. This first MGA was painted Tyrolite green with wire wheels, but interestingly enough it wasn't the first MGA dispatched from the factory. That honor belongs to chassis number 10,106, an orient red car with black interior and wire wheels which was started on May 27, 1955 and dispatched on July 13, 1955 to its North American destination. 10,101 was not dispatched until July 27, 1955.

The debut of the MGA was made at the Frankfurt Auto Show on September 22, 1955 where it literally got off to a flying start, as *The Motor* describes. "This car arrived in dramatic circumstances with the aid of Lockheed; not in this case the brake constructors but the makers of the Constellation aircraft, to the belly of which the car was slung for the journey from England to Germany."

Mating of engine and chassis is much easier without the body in place!

Another milestone is reached. The 100,000th MG rolled off the line on 16 May 1956. Just six years later that figure would be nearly doubled.

Several road tests had been conducted on the Le Mans cars while production lines were gearing up; however, the road tests could not be regarded as representative of the final product. At last the comments began to flow in.

Autosport . . . *"The racing car of today is the touring car of tomorrow." How true are those oft-quoted words when applied to the new MG. Its appearance excited universal admiration wherever I went, and the more discerning were quick to remark that it was beautifully made. Above all, at a base price of L595, it represents remarkable value. . . . This is a jolly good little sports car; if you want one, hurry up and queue!*[2]

The Motor . . . *. . . enthusiastically as it was everywhere received. The famous slogan of the factory (Safety Fast, ed.) has indeed never been better applied . . . . will undoubtedly be greeted as a worthy bearer of the famous radiator badge . . . . sold at the highly competitive price of L595.*[3]

Road and Track . . . *The most complete, most extensive design change in 20 years. Early enthusiasm for its appearance can now be augmented by the knowledge of its very surprising performance. Anybody who likes anything about sports cars will be more than pleased with the new MG. How are they going to supply enough cars to meet the demand?*[4]

Autocar . . . *If I earned my bread and butter as a MGA car salesman at home or abroad, I would expect there to be a jam on it most days of the week. I should also expect to find big smiles on the faces of customers when they checked in for routine service.*[5]

Sports Car Illustrated *(now* Car and Driver, *ed.) . . . . . . basically safe, friendly, likeable car—a genuine, wellbuilt sports machine at a price that can't be considered anything but reasonable and fair.*[6]

From the above comments, the motoring press felt the wait for the MGA had been well worthwhile. The car buying public obviously also agreed, for they were to make the MGA the most popular sports car ever produced by the time it went out of production. The total sales of the MGA were to reach 101,081 units by the time the last MGA rolled off the production line in June 1962.

Just what was it that created all this enthusiasm? Let's take a closer look at this new product from Abingdon.

After a long awaited delivery, the MGA quickly made a succession of appearances at auto shows in Frankfurt, Paris and New York where it was enthusiastically received.

Engine

The engine is very similar to that used in the Le Mans cars, with some detuning to make it more tractable on the road. The displacement remains unchanged at 1489 cc. Dual SU 1-1/2 inch carburetors are retained; however, the peculiar extension of the intake passages to the spark plug side of the cylinder head have been eliminated on the production engine and the balance pipe which was mounted on the spark plug side of the engine has been mounted on top of the intake manifold. This was simpler and less expensive with little loss of efficiency. This balance pipe is used to assist in the even distribution of the fuel-air mixture to the cylinders and increase part-throttle performance. Air cleaners used on the carburetors are of the oil wetted type and do not silence the air flow into the carburetors to a great degree. The sound produced by the inrushing air is music to most enthusiasts who buy this type of car; however, with the hood up the constant moaning can get tiresome after a while. The exhaust manifold is a more efficient design than normally encountered in a production car, utilizing a three-branch design to achieve some scavenging effect. Because the cylinder head is not of a cross-flow design and the intake and exhaust ports are siamesed, there is little chance of putting the more sophisticated forms of intake and

Probably the weakest part of the engine, the cylinder head had points where carbon was prone to collect and contribute to a tendency to run on. Siamesed exhaust ports between the second and third cylinders caused a hot spot which often resulted in a cracked head. A cross-flow head would have been ideal and in fact an after-market version was offered.

The B series engine shared most parts with other BMC products using the 1500 powerplant but was modified for increased performance in the MGA.

exhaust ram tuning to good use without resorting to a crossflow head first. The compression ratio of the EX 182 engine has been reduced from 9.4:1 to a more moderate 8.3:1. Even at this reduced compression ratio, the engine still insists on running on after the ignition is switched off on all but the highest octane fuels. The camshaft has been revised to give a lower horsepower peak speed as well as a lower torque peak speed to give the engine more flexibility, an important factor with the standard ratio gearbox. Horsepower is reduced somewhat from 82.5 @ 6,000 rpm to 68 @ 5,500 rpm. This figure was soon raised to 72 hp @ 5,750 rpm. The basic "B" series engine with a slightly reduced output is shared with the Austin A-50, Morris Oxford and ZA Magnette, insuring that parts for the three main bearing engine should be readily available all over the world.

The engine starts readily, even under the most extreme conditions and warms up quickly. The idle is rough at about 850 rpm, but the engine is willing to rev smoothly right up to the redline of 6,000 rpm, although it seems somewhat strained above 5,500 rpm. The pleasant raspiness of the exhaust

As would be expected, minor improvements were made in the development of the production models from prototypes. Compare the photo on the left (MGA-17-2-5) which shows a right-hand drive production model, with the photo on the right (MGA-17-2-6) which shows a left-hand drive prototype model. Differences include the placement of various cables, fuel lines and wiring. A heat shield was added on the production model between the exhaust manifold and the carburetors. The radiator flange for holding the hood prop is reshaped as well. Interestingly, the cowl vent center piece reads "1500" instead of "MGA."

1500 Engine Horsepower & Torque Curves

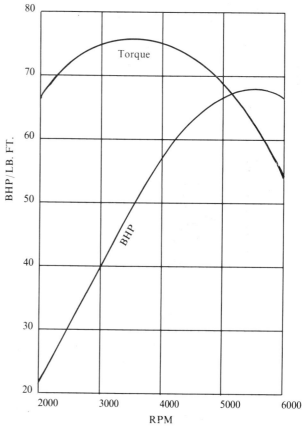

The 1500 c.c. engine provided a reasonably flat torque curve which gave brisk acceleration through the gears. The horsepower peak was well matched to the standard rear axle ratio giving a top speed of nearly 100 mph.

note upon lifting the accelerator foot is a real treat to the enthusiast who enjoys the mechanical music of a sports car, and remains a characteristic of the MGA in the minds of many owners. The output of the engine is healthy for its size and the torque curve is flat enough to permit high gear acceleration from as low as 20 mph.

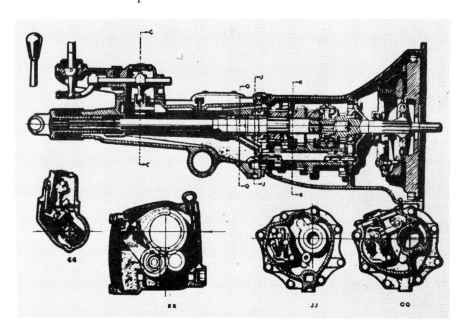

The Magnette gearbox was a reasonably good match for the MGA engine. The remote gearchange gave a compact, precise shift pattern.

Gearbox

The gearbox in the MGA is the same as the Magnette gearbox. Third gear is chosen to allow passing speeds up to 68 mph, enabling good use of the gear ratios for highway performance. A close-ratio box with ratios as per the Le Mans cars is available as a factory option. Synchromesh on the top three forward gears is provided. A remote gearchange is incorporated which allows very precise changes to be made with no shift levers to get out of adjustment. The use of a semi-enclosed gearchange also prevents ice and dirt from fouling the mechanism, especially during the winter months. A very close shift pattern is used in combination with a short lever providing an ideal combination for precise, quick shifts. Reverse has been repositioned from the TF pattern and a spring lockout is provided to make engagement of reverse, positioned to the left and back, difficult. However, due to the narrow gate between second and third, it is possible to attempt to engage reverse while downshifting from third to second. The synchromesh is unbeatable, allowing full-throttle power shifts to be made with confidence.

Selecting first gear from rest is sometimes difficult and it is best to feint toward second to get the gears aligned and then engage first gear. Some whine is noticeable from the indirect gears, though this is by no means objectionable on a car of this type. First gear seems overly low, giving a top speed of only 26 mph at 5,500 rpm, second gear is not much better giving 42 mph at 5,500 rpm, while a rather large gap exists between second and third resulting in a versatile third gear top speed of 68 mph at 5,500 rpm. Fourth gear provides 17 mph per 1,000 rpm or 93.5 mph at 5,500 rpm. While much criticism has been leveled against the choice of ratios, there is merit to the selection offered. A low first and second gear, closely spaced, provide ideal ratio for gymnkhana and autocross club events where speeds requiring third gear are rarely encountered. The closeness of third and fourth provide an excellent combination for highway passing situations. If the car is to be used on a race track, the option of a close-ratio gearbox is available.

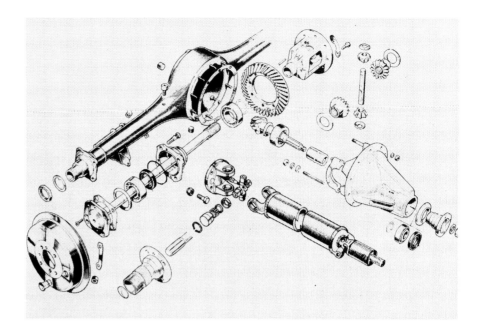

The rear axle was a standard BMC unit which was offered with several optional ratios. A rugged unit, the rear axle seldom gives trouble.

Rear Axle

The rear axle is a standard BMC unit. It is of 3/4 floating design incorporating a standard ratio of 4.3:1 hypoid bevel gears. Alternate ratios of 3.7, 3.9, 4.1 and 4.55:1 are available. Cruising at 3,500—4,000 rpm on trips makes one wish for a lower numerical ratio axle or overdrive, as the excellent streamlining of the body reduces load on the engine at speed.

The rugged box section frame contributed to the exceptional strength and rigidity of the MGA as compared to its contemporaries. The outward sweep of frame is very evident in this overhead shot.

Chassis

The frame for the MGA is made up of two parallel box-section side members and six cross-members which combine to provide excellent torsional rigidity. The channel section frame had long been popular with designers because of the flexibility it provided. The springing effect was utilized to increase traction on rough roads where the chassis flexibility contributed to the effective spring rate on a single wheel without affecting, to any significant degree, the springing rate if the front or back wheels encountered a bump simultaneously.

The incidence of single bumps is much greater than that of double bumps, which affect both front or rear wheels simultaneously. With a beam type axle, as used on the TC and previous production MG designs (the revolutionary R-type being the most notable exception), this frame flexing resulted in appreciable "bump steer" requiring quick driver correction to keep things on an even keel. With the advent of independent front suspension on the TD and TF models, a design which was carried over into the

MGA, the camber angles of the front suspension are determined by the positioning of the upper and lower wishbones. The designer is able, therefore, to engineer the exact camber angles he desires at all positions of wheel deflection. If the frame twists, then the settings of the wishbones change, thus disturbing the hard won camber angle settings, a situation which is intolerable. With the incorporation of independent front suspension, the utilization of a stiff chassis became a necessity. Pound for pound, the box section chassis member has 500 times the torsional stiffness of the channel section frame member.

In the case of the MGA, the utilization of an open cockpit eliminated the additional rigidity provided by a roof so an extremely strong truss section was built under the scuttle. This additional bracing led to a rather narrow door making entry awkward.

Further forward, the independent front suspension is attached to a box section cross-member. The Y/TD/TF front suspension design utilizes unequal length wishbones, coil springs and Armstrong lever-action hydraulic shocks. This suspension design originated with Alex Issigonis and Jack Daniels of the Morris design staff. It was to have been introduced on a Morris at the 1939 Auto Show; however, the war forced its postponement until 1947 when it was incorporated in the Y-type saloon. Simplicity and the use of rubber bushes keep the number of grease points to six. Shortly after production was started, it was discovered the front springs were too soft.

The front suspension of the MGA was a design shared by MGs from the 1947 Y-type to the MGB. The flange mounted on the front cross member has a hole in it to guide the hand crank toward the crankshaft pulley nut. The hand crank, provided with the tool kit, is very convenient for turning the engine when adjusting the valves.

After a period of hard use, the springs would deteriorate to the point that during hard cornering the oil pump pickup would be uncovered, resulting in a momentary loss of oil pressure. Stiffer front springs were introduced at chassis number 15,152.

The rear axle is located and suspended by semi-elliptic springs utilizing Armstrong lever action shock absorbers to dampen suspension movement. Before the first thousand cars had been built, an error was discovered in the specification of the rear axle hub bearing nut. The left-hand hub had a right-hand thread, the same as the right-hand hub, which resulted in the hub bearing nut working itself off as the car was driven. MG wasn't the first to make this mistake, nor the last. Triumph made a similar error with the knock-off nuts on early model Spitfires.

The sides of the chassis are swept outward to permit lower seating and provide additional protection for the passenger compartment in the event of

This detail of the rear axle shows the battery hold-down clamps which are often missing on present cars. The strap just to the rear of the axle limits its travel during rebound.

a side collision. Simple though the design may be, the details have been carefully worked out to provide a good combination of road holding and riding comfort. With the exception of some lightening holes and deepening of the chassis side rails, the chassis used in the MGA is nearly identical to that used on EX 179, an MG record breaker which achieved a speed of 170.145 mph in 1956. Syd Enever insisted on making the chassis of 14 gauge steel rather than the standard 16 gauge. His reasoning for using this heavier gauge steel was that "You can rust away two gauges of metal and still have a motorcar!" Perhaps those of us who are restoring an MGA chassis should thank Mr. Enever for his foresight! The weight penalty of the heavier chassis is off-set by the lighter engine, gearbox and rear axle. In comparison to the TF, the result is only a small weight gain.

Body

The body of the MGA has several endearing characteristics for the enthusiast. It was the last MG to be built using a separate chassis and body design which permits complete dismantling of the body off the chassis for a thorough restoration. The use of aluminum doors, trunk lid and hood preclude rusting of these panels. Unlike some of its contemporaries such as the Austin Healey, the problem of corrosion between butted aluminum and steel panels doesn't occur.

Thanks to the separate body and chassis of the MGA, it is possible to keep your MGA looking as good as new, when this period shot was taken.

Don Hayter, who came to the design department from Aston Martin around the time of the MGA's introduction, explained that the use of aluminum for hinged panels reflected a desire to keep the weight of the production car as close to that of the EX 182 cars as possible. Their dedication to lightness is commendable in view of the high cost of aluminum (three times that of steel) and the extensive hand finishing necessary to produce a good job. The MGB also started out life with aluminum hinged panels, but the use of aluminum has been cut in order to keep costs down.

Doors, fenders, hood and trunk lid all unbolt leaving the center section of the body in one piece. Inner fenders and bulkhead are spot-welded in place and add strength to the center structure which carries the weight of the fenders and moveable panels. Because of the rigid frame design and the separate body, the panels do not carry any load and as a result there is no evidence of body panels "working" even when driven hard over rough surfaces.

The style of the body has a timeless simplicity of line. There are few protrusions to arrest the smooth flow of the eye over the gently curved body. The absence of chrome decorations, even to the lack of door and trunk lid handles, is

This interior view of a prototype model is true to the production models except for the octagonally shaped light switch which was round on production models. Notice the lack of a clip in the center of the windscreen top frame. This was added on the 1600 model. The instruments are the early type.

The MGA was the first two seat MG to have a trunk. Restorers take note of the tool roll attachment atop the spare. The hand crank was held by clips on the bulkhead just above the tool roll. This left-hand drive model is probably destined for Europe as indicated by the long, narrow license plate holder. The adjustable Lucas license plate lamp accommodated several different shaped license plates, an important consideration in a world market car.

very effective on a car as small as this, resulting in an air of elegance and integrity of line out of proportion to its size. From the performance figures, the aerodynamic efficiency is high, giving an increase in top speed of 15 mph over the TF with no increase in horsepower. In fact, 60 mph can be maintained with only 16 horsepower. The car looks handsome from any angle and unlike many roadsters, it looks equally attractive with the top up.

The interior of the car is well appointed with comfortable Conolly leather covered seats, carpeting and well laid out instruments. The use of door panels incorporating large openings for storage within the doors is very useful for stowing odds and ends on trips, especially in view of the lack of a glove box. With the top erected there is also room for storage behind the seats. The incorporation of a trunk, a first for MG in a car this size, is a welcome addition, however small it might be. There is a surprising amount of room available, if one packs in soft bags. Just don't try to fit any suitcases in the trunk.

Much of the room in the trunk is taken up by the spare tire which is no longer carried outside the car as on the TF. A large tool roll is strapped on top of the spare tire. The tool roll is incredibly complete containing items for every conceivable roadside debacle. Also found within the trunk is an engine starting crank clipped above the spare tire on the bulkhead. A hole is fitted in the front bumper and valence panel to allow the use of the crank. The

The MGA 1500 bullet-style front parking lamp lens. Subsequent lighting regulations necessitated a change in the lens for each MGA body style.

trunk is opened with a pull-handle located deep within the bowels of the storage area behind the seats. At first some amount of hand waving may be necessary to locate the handle, especially when the top is stowed. With a little experience, however, it is readily found.

The hood release is also a pull-handle located under the scuttle on the left side. The hood itself is equipped with a secondary safety latch. The hood opening is fairly small and presents a problem in reaching the air cleaners and windshield wiper motor. Replacement of the clutch requires removal of the engine and checking the hydraulic fluid level in the rear shock absorbers requires their removal to perform the operation. The batteries are buried under a panel behind the seats which makes checking their water level a bothersome chore, especially when the top is stowed. Removal of the batteries requires the patience of Job and the body control of a contortionist. The single battery of the TC/TD/TF was mounted in the engine compartment. The last MG to have dual batteries mounted behind the seats was the TB of 1939.

Getting into the car through the narrow doors is an awkward job, but the strength of the frame is worth it. The top is constructed of a smooth plastic material rather than the coarse canvas of the TF and provides a good fit in combination with the side curtains. The single window in the top provides good visibility to the rear, important in a car this low; however, rear quarter vision is limited. A triple window was added on later models, eliminating this problem. The side curtains are designed to clip onto the windshield frame, preventing them from bowing away from the windshield at speed. The lower hinged portion of the side curtains is convenient for signaling; however, snaking one's hand through the narrow opening to the door pull from the outside is awkward. The lack of sliding panes makes the interior unbearably stuffy, especially during summer rainstorms. The stowage of the top requires some dexterity and is best done with two people. The top stows very neatly behind the seats under the body, where it is completely hidden from view, a la Corvette. A drape separates the top from the passenger compartment and includes pockets for the stowing of the side curtains. Together the top and side curtains provide decent weather protection and their neat stowage is commendable. Remarking on the quality of body construction, *Sports Car Illustrated* said, " 'A' is a very attractive car from any angle and downright beautiful from some. Its look and feel of quality closely approach those of some cars costing twice as much. The body feels and is very substantial. The quality of the painted finish is good, there is no skimping on the instrument panel and the reinforced bumpers are very adequate."[7]

Driving Position and Controls

Upon entering the car, one is immediately struck by the low seating position, particularly in comparison to the TF. The placement of an armrest between the two seats adds to the feeling of coziness and security the interior provides. The seats provide good lateral location and support the shoulders well; however, support in the small of the back is lacking and the backrest is a bit upright for some tastes. A lack of thigh support is also felt on long trips. The seats and armrest are nicely covered in leather, some with contrasting piping. Sufficient shoulder and hip room is provided, and leg room, especially for the passenger, is generous. The steering wheel is somewhat close, making straight arm driving difficult. However, a telescoping steering wheel is available as an option. The rim of the wheel is thin by today's standards, but was common in the fifties. The use of spring spokes imparts a feeling of flexibility which some don't enjoy and the inevitable cracking of the rim hasn't pleased anyone. A comfortable driving position is achieved by stretching out the left leg under the clutch pedal and cocking the right leg against the transmission tunnel with the foot on the accelerator.

An early 1500 model with the single window top and 1500 standard side curtains. The optional luggage rack is seen on this example.

The style and construction of the MGA body were appreciated by the motoring press in their road tests. Many of the tests were conducted in the autumn, insuring the weather protection came under close scrutiny. Despite the lack of roll-up windows, a reasonably snug fit was provided.

Being a good high speed cruiser, especially in view of today's 55 mph speed limit in the U.S., a light foot is required on the accelerator, which can lead to discomfort in the shin area after a long trip. The placement of the pedals doesn't allow comfortable heel-and-toe downshifting, requiring the use of the side of the foot to operate the accelerator. The accelerator pedal travel is great, which also adds to the difficulty. The routing of the accelerator linkage is tortuous but it seems to work even in left hand drive cars where the routing is especially complex. The pedals are closely spaced and people blessed with large feet may find themselves hooking their accelerator foot on the brake pedal or hitting the accelerator pedal when trying to brake, a potentially embarrassing situation. It should be noted that the MGA is not alone in this area, as most British cars also suffer from this malady. The placement and feel of the shift lever is ideal, allowing quick, precise selection of gears. The transmission does require 6-8,000 miles to loosen up when new, however.

The car is definitely more at home with the top down, (taking on a more relaxed atmosphere as the rattles and squeaks from the top disappear). The full length tonneau is a valuable accessory which enables prolonged top down motoring. The lower seating position enables the driver, even a tall one, to remain below the top of the windscreen and thus out of the wind blast. Wind turbulence around the sides of the screen is minimal and the cockpit is remarkably quiet with the top down, actually quieter than with the top up, enabling normal conversation at highway speeds. With the top erected, there is plenty of head room. Noise from the top fabric and side curtains is excessive, especially at high speeds. The center of the front cross piece over the windshield tends to lift at speeds over 90 mph and a clip to cure this problem was later fitted. This obviously doesn't present a problem for most of us these days! Visibility through the curved windshield is good, with no distortion visible. The lower seating position does limit forward visibility to a small degree. The optional heater/demister does an acceptable job in clearing the windshield, but the low blower speed has trouble keeping pace with the really cold winters often experienced in the U.S. The bakelite heater control panel is very susceptible to breaking and few MGAs have survived with their's intact. Self-parking wipers are fitted with only two speeds, on or off; or if you prefer, too slow and too fast.

Large, easy to read white on black speedometer and tachometer are situated in front of the driver with the fuel and combination oil pressure/water temperature gauges flanking the centrally located radio speaker grill. The numbers on the tach and speedometer were marked at wide intervals on earlier MGA 1500s but this was later changed to the more conventional marking every 10 mph and 500 rpm. Right hand drive cars had the oil pressure/water temperature gauge mounted next to the tachometer where the driver could keep on eye on these important readings. On left hand drive cars the gauges were not switched, that is the fuel level gauge was next to the driver and the oil pressure/water temperature gauge was awkward to see on the other side of the radio speaker, and often was covered by the ignition key. It is a popular conversion on left hand drive models to switch the position of the gauges.

The early model 1500s had these style instruments with wider markings. The oil pressure/water temperature gauge on this left-hand drive exmple is mounted where it can conveniently be seen. Unfortunately, production left-hand drive models had the gauge mounted to the right of the radio speaker. A popular conversion is to switch the fuel and oil pressure/water temperature gauges on left-hand drive models. The steering wheel center boss is a pre-production item.

A separate ignition and starter switch, the latter requiring a good stiff tug to engage, are reminders of the way things were before the days of starter solenoids. In the case of the MGA the separate starter circuit was put to good use by incorporating a remote starter switch in the engine compartment which facilitated setting of valves and ignition timing. When delivered new, the spare ignition key was screwed to the inside of the firewall. A horn button finds its unusual placement in the middle of the dash, just under the radio speaker grill. The remainder of the controls are scattered around the dash, provided with a single letter to designate their function. A fog lamp switch is provided on all cars and is wired up to the wiring harness, should a fog lamp be fitted at a later time. The fuse box doesn't present the labyrinth of assorted sizes and types which accost the driver of today's electronic marvels of automotive engineering. The MGA uses just two fuses, 35 amperes each, and is thoughtfully provided with storage space on the fuse block for two spare fuses. The dimmer switch is inconveniently located high on the firewall, above the clutch. A map reading light is conveniently placed on the passenger's side to aid the intrepid navigator during night-time rallies. The placement of the fly-away handbrake on left hand drive models, on the right side of the driveshaft tunnel near the passenger's legs, provided a convenient ice-breaker on dates. The hidden placement of the door pull inside the door allowed many an amorous owner to have his passenger at his mercy until the secret location was revealed. In any event, reaching across to demonstrate proper opening of the door (and closing for that matter) presented its own interesting opportunities!

Handling

The new MGA offered many improvements in the handling field over its predecessors. Its successful introduction at the 1955 Le Mans race is a testament to the quality of the handling, especially when one considers that the Le Mans cars used basically the same suspension set-up as the production cars with the exception of the Andrex friction dampers on the front suspension. It is difficult to view the progress of automobile design through the mist of nostalgia; however, the progress since the pre-war era was such that the MGA could lap the tortuous Nurburgring track faster than a pre-war supercharged racing car. The Nurburgring has a reputation of being the supreme test of driver and automobile, incorporating every imaginable trial in its 14-1/2 mile long course.

MGA handling was among the best in its class and it soon became a favorite among club racers.

Offering a combination of good handling and ride is always a compromise for the designer and rarely does a car do well at both. The MGA leans a bit too much on the race track, a product of somewhat soft springing compared to most race cars. This condition can be alleviated by the addition of an anti-roll bar on the front which was offered as an option on later models. On the highway, the MGA exhibits a stiff ride over the smallest bumps at low speed. As the speed increases, the ride begins to smooth out, exhibiting good stability at high speeds. Resistance to cross-winds is better than many contemporary sports cars.

Designed to be a car suitable for the weekend autocross racer as well as the weekday commuter, the MGA is most at home on medium speed twisty roads with short straights. The combination of quick, precise rack and pinion steering and light weight make the car very easy to drive either in the city or on the open road. The advantage of a 28 foot turning circle is greatly appreciated in tight city driving, especially when parallel parking. With the standard tire inflation pressures, the car feels slightly spongy in hard cornering, accompanied by loud squealing of the tires at the slightest provocation. Increasing the pressure to 26 psi all around results in a more precise feel in the steering, an absence of tire squeal and no noticeable deterioration in ride. The car exhibits a near neutral handling characteristic; (the rear wheels loose traction gradually and with ample warning, slightly ahead of the front, making the car very easy to control in a drift). The forgiving nature of the handling makes this an ideal car for the beginning enthusiast to learn on. The live rear axle makes rough road cornering less than enjoyable, with the hard sprung rear end "walking" toward the outside on bumpy curves. On a smooth surface the cornering power is impressive.

Whether driving in the city or on a twisty country road, the MGA seems to be an ideal size; just right for picking your way through heavy traffic, utilizing the excellent gearbox and good indirect acceleration to advantage, or winding down that favorite country lane early on a Saturday morning. Acceleration may not be of the kick-in-the-back variety, but rather more refined, demanding a measure of expertise on the part of the driver to extract the performance which is available, creating more of a challenging, and thus rewarding, situation. The car transmits a unified feeling to the driver, especially with the top folded, resisting rattles and squeaks on all but the roughest roads. The factory recommends a cruising speed of 89 mph, a figure which feels a bit strained in the 1500 model. Prolonged driving at this speed will inevitably result in dropping oil pressure unless an oil cooler is fitted.

Brakes

The brakes are unchanged from the Le Mans cars and are commendably free from fade, exhibiting excellent stability and power when stopping the car from high speed. A brake test conducted by *Sports Cars Illustrated* resulted in an unusually high deceleration figure of 0.86 g, and over a ten-stop test the brakes lost only 9.3 of their braking efficiency. For those desiring greater braking efficiency, wire wheels were available to aid in cooling and a harder brake shoe, Feredo BG95/1, is recommended for added resistance to fade. The four wheel drum brakes have a 10 inch diameter resulting in a swept area of 134 square inches and were designed by Lockheed.

Clutch

The clutch is hydraulically operated and is of the single dry plate type. The action of the clutch pedal is positive and smooth, resulting in some slippage under brutal treatment in the higher gears. For competition work a stronger clutch would be recommended.

Coupe

Slightly more than one year after production of the MGA began, a white MGA coupe was displayed at the London Auto Show in October 1956. The introduction of a coupe model was a rarity for MG. With the exception of the custom bodied models, such as the Arnolt TD which utilized a Bertone body fitted by S.H. Arnolt of Chicago and a single Airline coupe body fitted to a TA, coupes had been absent from the MG sports car line for more than 20 years.

The MGA coupe offered style, comfort and weather protection a cut above that of the roadster.

The introduction of the coupe must be regarded as a sign of the times when enthusiasts were demanding greater comfort at speed and added protection from the elements in the "Grand Touring" tradition.

The coupe closely resembled the roadster with the optional hardtop fitted. This similarity is more than coincidental. The coupe is indeed designed from the removable hardtop which was introduced shortly before the coupe in the late summer of 1956. Deluxe perspex sliding sidescreens were also available with the hardtop to compliment the added weather protection. The fiberglass hardtop owes its origin in turn to the aluminum hardtops fitted to the works team in the Alpine Rally. These tops allowed the cars to be entered in the GT category.

The coupe was done in very short time (8-10 weeks) at Bodies Branch, Coventry in the experimental department. Its progress was hurried along by Eric Carter, Syd Enever and Jimmy O'Neil. Production was designed to allow the roof panels and side pillars to be hand shaped over forms and then welded to a modified roadster body. When first designed, a chrome bead was to run from just behind the head-lamps along the tops of the front fenders and continuing over the rear fenders; however, this was not incorporated in normal production coupes. Weight of the coupe was up only 65 pounds from the roadster; however, a corresponding increase of four horsepower, which applied to roadster and coupe, offset the weight penalty when performance was compared with the earlier 1500 roadster. The improved aerodynamics of the coupe body resulted in the MGA at last breaking the magic 100 mph barrier in stock form.

Price of the new coupe was £59 over the introductory price of the 1955 roadster. For this extra money the coupe owner received roll up windows, vent windows, outside door handles, inside door pulls, special upholstery on the seats and door panels, map pockets forward of the doors, carpeted storage space behind the seats, referred to as a "doggie seat," and a vinyl covered instrument panel with chrome trim. For added distinction, a special dark blue color, "Mineral Blue," was offered on the coupe only. The door latches were of an ingenious design which pulled out away from the body by

A considerable amount of hand work went into the construction of the coupe. Here the final touches are being applied on the production line at Bodies Branch, Coventry.

The door handles added an elegant touch to the coupe.

means of a lever located high on the door in such a way as to be nearly invisible from a distance. Despite the redesigned seat upholstery, the complaint of not enough thigh support continued and the car suffered from drafts around the doors and windows. The added complexity of roll up windows resulted in more chances for rattles to develop and at high speeds or rough roads even a new car's windows shook. Noise level of the coupe was better than that of the roadster with the top erected, aided by a polyurethane foam plastic sound deadner applied behind the dash. However, it was by no means silent, requiring the driver and passenger to raise their voices to carry on a conversation at speed. That old bugaboo of heat around the pedals was still making itself felt on the driver's feet. The large rear window and curved glass windshield provided excellent all-round visibility; however, the windshield does exhibit distortion in the extreme corners. Offering a greater measure of comfort and elegance for the enthusiast wishing to move into something more civilized, the coupe provided a concession to the movement away from the open roadster, which would eventually lead to the near extinction of all open sports cars by the mid-1970s.

The MGA coupe continued in production until June 1962.

A Comparison With EX 182

The automobile market is a highly competitive one in which makes are inevitably compared to each other. Whenever a new model is introduced, the natural instinct is to compare the latest offering with its predecessor. Because the Le Mans EX 182s were made available to the motoring press during the interim between the TF and the MGA, we have a reasonable bank of knowledge to draw a comparison from.

Comparing the MGA and the EX 182, *The Autocar* reported in its September 1955 issue, "...road holding, braking and steering are unaffected and in these respects the MGA recalls very intimately the Le Mans car." It can easily be seen that the body of the MGA is virtually identical to the EX 182, although the interior is more luxuriously appointed. Road testers of the day remarked on the negligible loss of power compared to the competition model which utilized a much different engine from the production MGA. The testers were pleasantly surprised to learn that the road holding, brakes and steering were relatively unchanged from the Le Mans cars, giving the new model demonstrably superior handling as compared to most road-bred sports cars. Reduced heat, noise and wind in the passenger compartment added the icing on the cake. The overall impression was that the MGA lost little regarding performance in transition from the EX 182 and gained much regarding comfort in the passenger compartment. There are very few cars today, or yesterday for that matter, who can boast such a close resemblance with the racing prototype, and most of these exotic machines come with price tags and temperments to match.

The development of the MGA had much in common with sports cars of the twenties and thirties which could lay claim to a direct heritage with their racing brothers, being able to provide reliable transportation for their owners to the track, and with little more than taping the lights, removing the spare, etc., put in a creditable performance on the track. The EX 182 echoed this philosophy when the three race cars were driven from the factory to the 1955 Le Mans race.

A Comparison With The TF

The MGA design marked a break with previous traditions regarding both style and engineering developments as few new models have done. Retaining little in common with the TF except the independent front suspension, it is remarkable that the two cars share virtually identical wheelbase, track, weight and horsepower measurements. The gain in straight-line acceleration the MGA enjoys over the TF is especially impressive when one considers the higher numerical rear axle ratio of the TF which should enhance acceleration in view of the nearly equal weight. The gain of the MGA over the TF becomes more pronounced as the speed rises due to its improved aerodynamics. In the area of road handling, an important characteristic of MGs in particular, the MGA was clearly the favorite of the two, although the ride seems to be much the same as the TF, perhaps explained by the common front suspension and similar rear suspension arrangement.

The MGA is more difficult to enter due to the reinforced bulkhead; however, a more conventional front hinged door is utilized as opposed to the rather old fashioned rear hinged door of the TF, which echoed its outdated chassis design. Once inside, the driver is aware of sitting much lower in the car, described as sitting *in* rather than *on* the cars. This is due to two improvements: the MGA is 2-1/2 inches lower than the TF and the outswept frame side rails enable the seats to be set lower between them. There is increased room around the pedals, especially the accelerator, though still not adequate in many cases. The shift lever retained the crisp, short throws of the TF but the relocation of reverse was cheered as a "tremendous improvement" by *Road and Track*. The replacement of the rough canvas top of the TF by the smooth plastic one of the MGA was welcomed as being less susceptable to rot and easier to clean.

No comparison road test would be complete without a comparison of statistics, in this case for both relative sizes as well as performance. A comparison of physical dimensions follows.

	TF	MGA
Displacement	1,466 cc	1,489 cc
Horsepower	68 @ 5,500 rpm	68 @ 5,500 rpm
Weight	1,854 lb	1,988 lb
Wheelbase	94.0 in.	94.0 in.
Track, front	47.4 in.	47.4 in.
Track, rear	50.0 in.	48.8 in.
Tire size	5.50 x 15	5.50 x 15
Bore and stroke	72 x 90 mm	73 x 89 mm
Axle ratio	4.875:1	4.3:1
Price	$1,995	$2,195

A *Road and Track* comparison between the two cars resulted in the following performance figures.[8]

	TF	MGA	% Improvement
0-30	4.8	4.6	4.2
0-40	7.1	6.8	4.2
0-50	11.0	10.2	7.3
0-60	16.3	14.5	11.0
0-70	24.7	19.9	19.4
SS 1/4 Mile	20.7	19.6	5.3
Top speed	85 mph	95 mph	12.0
Total drag @ 60 mph	119 lb	94 lb	21.0
MPG cruise 65/75 mph	25	30	20.0

The following pages contain a summary of pertinent technical information on the MGA 1500, including a listing of production changes introduced during the model run by chassis and engine serial number order. These production changes are extracted from the *MGA Workshop Manual* and are included to illustrate the many production changes introduced during the life of an automobile, especially one so radically different from its predecessor. The production changes will also aid restorers in maintaining originality.

Acceleration Curve Comparison

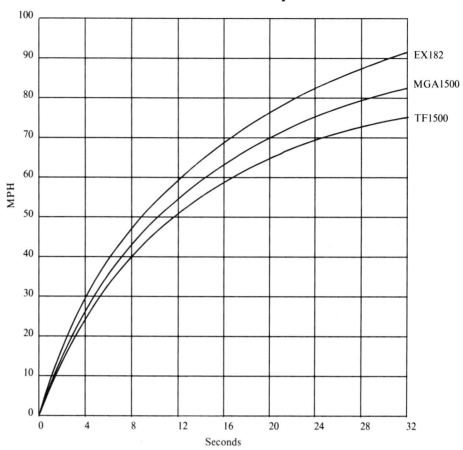

EX182

MGA1500

TF1500

The MGA 1500 offered a significant improvement in acceleration over the TF 1500, especially as the speeds increased.

Specifications:

Introduced:
     Roadster—May 1955
     Coupe—October 1956
Production dates:
     Roadster—September 1955 to May 1959
     Coupe—December 1956 to May 1959
Total production: 58,750 (roadster and coupe)
Chassis numbers: HD 10,101—68,850
Engine numbers: 15GB, 15GD
Price:
     Roadster—$2,195 ($L$844)
     Coupe—$2,750 ($L$1,049)
Engine:

Displacement	1,489 cc (90.8 cu. in.)
Bore	73.025 mm (2.875 in.)
Stroke	89.0 mm (3.5 in.)
Compression	8.3:1
Main bearings	3, steel backed white metal
BHP	68 @ 5,500 rpm (later 72 @ 5,750 rpm)
Torque	77.4 ft/lb @ 3,500 rpm (later 80.2 ft/lb @ 3,850 rpm)

Red line   5,800 rpm
Valve float   6,000 rpm
Transmission/rear axle:
    Clutch: 8 in. single dry plate
    Overall gear ratios:
        4th   4.3:1
        3rd   5.908:1
        2nd   9.520:1
        1st   15.652:1
Rear axle ratio:
    Standard—4.3:1, optional—3.7, 3.9, 4.1, 4.55:1
MPH per 1,000 rpm in top gear:
    17.3 w/ 4.3:2 axle
    21.0 w/ 3.7:1 axle
    19.7 w/ 3.9:1 axle
    18.3 w/ 4.1:1 axle
    16.8 w/ 4.55:1 axle
Chassis:
    Wheels and tires: 48 spoke wire wheels optional, perforated steel disc
    wheels standard, alloy rim 60 spoke wire wheels competition option.
    Tire size 5.50 x 15 with disc wheels, 5.60 x 15 with wire wheels.
    Electrical equipment: 12 volt positive ground, 51 ampere hour battery
    (two six volt batteries in series)
    Fuel system: 12 gallon (US) tank with single high pressure SU electric
    fuel pump
    Dimensions:
        Wheelbase   94 in.
        Track, front   47-1/2 in. w/ disc wheels, 47-7/8 in. w/
                            wire wheels
        Track, rear   48-3/4 in.
        Length   156 in.
        Height   50 in. (roadster and coupe)
        Ground clearance   6 in.
        Weight   1,988 lb roadster (curb weight)
                            2,107 lb coupe (w/ 5 gallons of fuel)
        Turning circle   right: 28 ft 3 in.
                            left: 30 ft 9 in.
    Colors:
        Exterior: Black, Orient Red, Tyrolite Green, Ash Green, Glacier
            Blue, Old English White, Mineral Blue (coupe only)
        Interior: Black, Red, Green, Grey

The MGA 1500—dawning of a new era.

Production Modification:

The following is a listing, in numerical order, of those modifications made to the MGA 1500 during the production run. The listing is divided into two parts, chassis and engine modifications.

Chassis Modifications

Chassis number 10,917 (disc wheels) or 11,450 (wire wheels) onward—modified rear axle hub bearing nuts: The left-hand hub bearing nut on the rear axle now has a left hand thread and is turned clockwise to unscrew. The right hand hub nut is unchanged and retains the right hand thread.

Chassis number 15,152 onward—modified front coil springs: Modified front coil springs are introduced at car number 15,152. The new springs (part no. AHH5546) are interchangeable on earlier cars in pairs only.

Chassis number 16,101 onward—sealing hood seams: Commencing at car number 16,101, a new hood is introduced with the seams stitched, lapped, and welded. On cars prior to this commencing number trouble may be experienced with water seeping through the stitch holes. These hood seams can be sealed with stitch sealing solution (part no. 17H9663), available in one pint tins.

The solution must be applied in a well-ventilated place and a dry atmosphere is essential. Normal fire precautions must be taken as the solution is inflammable.

The hood seams should be painted both on the inside and outside with two thin coatings of the solution, with ten minutes drying time allowed between each coat. The hood should be left for 24 hours after the application of the solution before it is used.

Chassis number 24,954 onward—accelerator return spring: On later cars, an additional accelerator return spring is introduced as a safety precaution and the original return spring is replaced by a new spring.

The new parts may be fitted to earlier cars as a set as follows: Remove the original accelerator return spring and fit the new spring (part no. AHH5621). Remove the accelerator cable and replace the anchor pin with the new anchor pin (part no. AHH5625). Fit the anchor bracket (part no. AHH5623) to one of the accelerator cable guide screws and fit the auxiliary return spring (part no. AHH5624).

Chassis number 58,918 (Europe less France) or 60,340 (France) onward—modified European light unit: Cars exported to Europe are not fitted with the new European-type headlamps. These lamp units are fitted with special bulbs and front lenses giving an asymmetrical beam to the right hand side. Access to the bulb is gained in the same way as described in Section N. 16 of the *Workshop Manual*. The bulb, however, is released from the reflector by withdrawing the three-pin socket and pinching the two ends of the wire retaining clip to clear the bulb flange.

When replacing the bulb, care must be taken to see that the rectangular pip on the bulb flange engages the slot in the reflector seating for the bulb.

Replace the spring clip with its coils resting in the base of the bulb flange and engaging in the two retaining lugs on the reflector seating.

The appropriate replacement bulbs are listed in Section N. 25 of the *Workshop Manual*. They are not interchangeable with those used in conjunction with the Continental-type headlamps previously fitted. (Illustration available on page N. 18 of the *Workshop Manual*.)

Chassis number 61,504 (15GD engines) onward—modified power unit: A new power unit, having the type designation 15GD, is fitted from car number 61,504 and to certain earlier cars. The engine incorporates the various modifications made to the 15GB unit and has the starter motor placed higher on the gearbox mounting plate.

Modifications have also been made to the gearbox, to the propeller shaft, to the gearbox cover, and to the right hand toe-board, so that neither the engine, the gearbox, nor the propeller shaft is interchangeable with those previously fitted. The above changes involve alterations to the procedure for power unit removal and replacement.

Follow the instruction given in Section A. 18 of the *Workshop Manual*, but note that the propeller shaft need not be disconnected from the rear axle flange. When the floorboards, toeboards, gearbox cover, and propeller shaft have been removed, mark the propeller shaft and gearbox flanges and disconnect the propeller shaft from the gearbox.

Modified gearbox: The main gearbox casing has been modified to accommodate the new high position of the starter motor on the engine. The gearbox extension has also been changed to suit the new gearbox third motion shaft. The propeller shaft is now bolted to a flange which is splined to the gearbox third motion shaft and secured by a nut and spring washer. This arrangement supercedes that of the splined sliding joint for the propeller shaft on the third motion shaft. The new gearbox is not interchangeable with that previously fitted.

Modified propeller shaft: The new propeller shaft incorporates a splined sliding joint at the front end. In addition to the nipples fitted to each universal joint, a nipple is also provided on the sleeve yoke for the lubrication of the sliding joint splines. This nipple must receive attention every 3,000 miles (5,000 km) with the gun filled with the appropriate lubricant.

Instructions given for the servicing of the earlier propeller shaft apply, in the main, to the modified propeller shaft. The following points, however, should be noted:

(1) In order to remove the propeller shaft, it is necessary to remove the four nuts and bolts securing the front universal joint flange to the gearbox flange, as well as those securing the rear flange to the rear axle flange.

(2) Check the sliding splines for wear by attempting to turn the splined sleeve yoke in relation to the splined shaft. If excessive circumferential movement is present a reconditioned propeller shaft assembly will be required.

(3) When fitting new universal joints, it will be found helpful to separate the two parts of the propeller shaft at the sliding joint.

(4) Before refitting the splined sleeve yoke to the shaft, push the threaded dust cover, the metal washer, and the felt washer over the splines onto the splined shaft. When assembling the joint, ensure that the trunnions of the front and rear universal joints are in line. This can be checked by observing that the arrows marked on the splined sleeve yoke and the splined shaft are in line.

(5) Fit the propeller shaft to the car with the sliding joint at the gearbox end.

Engine modifications

Engine number 15GB487 onward—windowless yoke dynamo: A dynamo without brush gear inspection windows (part no. 11G220). Access to the brush gear in these dynamos is gained by undoing the two through-bolts and withdrawing the commutator end bracket. Every 12,000 miles (19,000 km) the unit should be partially dismantled for the inspection of brush gear and commutator. To check the brush spring tension, the yoke should be completely withdrawn from the armature and the commutator end bracket refitted to the shaft.

When reassembling a windowless yoke dynamo the brushes must first be held clear of the commutator in the usual way, i.e. by partially withdrawing the brushes from their boxes until each brush is trapped in position by the side pressure of its spring. The brushes can be released onto the commutator with a small screwdriver or similar tool when the end bracket is assembled to within about 1/2 inch (13 mm) of the yoke. Before closing the gap between the end bracket and yoke, see that the springs are in correct contact with the brushes. Coil steady plate, (part no. 11G221) should always be used with dynamo, (part no. 11G220).

Engine number 15GB3289 onward—modified gearbox mounting plate: The gearbox mounting plate has an oil escape recess and groove machined in the front face to relieve the air depression around the rear main bearing oil seal and prevent oil being drawn into the clutch housing. The plate is interchangeable and retains the same part number.

Engine number 15GB5504 onward—modified tappets and push-rods: The ball ends of the push-rods and the seats in the tappets are increased in spherical diameter. The tappets and push-rods are interchangeable in sets and the new part numbers are:

Tappet	1H822
Push-rod	11G241

Engine number 15GB5682 onward—piston rings with chrome periphery: The top compression ring on the piston is superseded by a piston ring with a chrome periphery to improve the life of the piston ring and to improve oil consumption. The later piston ring is interchangeable with the old.

Engine number 15GB6615 onward—modified crankshaft: Originally the diameter of the oil return thread on the crankshaft was 2.139/2.1405 in. (54.33/54.37 mm), but at engine 15GB6615 this was reduced to 2.138/2.1385 in. (54.305/54.32 mm). For the correct functioning of the oil return thread it is imperative that it should be concentric with the bore of the housing and have between .003 and .006 in. (.075 and .15 mm) clearance measured from the crest of the thread to the housing. This may be checked with the aid of a long feeler gauge and a mandrel.

Engine number 15GB6625 onward—Ignition vacuum pipe fuel trap: A modified ignition vacuum pipe (part no. 1H830) is fitted. A small trap containing a fine mesh gauze incorporated in the pipe which will prevent fuel entering the vacuum control unit. The modified pipe may be fitted to earlier vehicles.

Engine number 15GB7981 onward—modified gearbox front end cover: Commencing at engine no. 7981, and a few earlier gearboxes, a modified gearbox front end cover is introduced. The new cover is fitted with an oil seal to prevent the possibility of oil leaking into the clutch housing. There is also a venting duct in the cover necessitating modified fork rods. The part may not be fitted to earlier cars. The new part numbers are:

Gearbox front end cover	1H3137
Gearbox cover oil seal	1H3138
Reverse fork rod	11G3137
First and second fork rod	11G3079
Third and fourth fork rod	11G3140

It is essential that the front cover should be concentric with the first motion shaft in order to avoid oil leaks. This is effected as follows:

Mount the cover, less oil seal, onto the gearbox, and push right home on the studs. Ensure that the cover is free to move in all directions on the studs. If not, the points at which the holes bind on the studs must be relieved until the cover is free to "float." Remove the cover and refit the oil seal, using service tool 18G134 with adaptor 18G134Q. Fit service tool 18G598 to the bore of the front cover, and push it in until it is tight. Lightly oil the seal and carefully fit the front cover, retaining the centralizer 18G598 firmly in position. Fit all spring washers and nuts and tighten them finger tight only. Using a suitable socket spanner, tighten all nuts by diametric selection one half turn at a time until the nuts are fully tightened. Remove the centralizer.

Engine numbers 15GB26661—15GB26700 and 15GB26933 onward—modified oil filter: A new oil filter is fitted. The element may be removed from a later type oil filter without disconnecting the oil pipe. Tecalemit and Purolator filters are used, and the elements, which are interchangeable, bear the BMC part no. 8G683 (Tecalemit and Purolator).

Engine number 15GB38484 onward—modified piston and gudgeon pin: A new piston (part no. 1H1114) with a modified gudgeon pin having a reduced internal diameter to give increased strength. The later pistons and gudgeon pins are interchangeable with the originals, but only as a complete set.

Engine numbers 15GB39365—15GB39526 onward—modified water pump: A new water pump (part no. 1H1149) which incorporates a one-piece bearing is fitted. The pump is interchangeable with the original, but only as a complete unit.

Engine number 15GB40824 onward—modified pistons and rings: New pistion assemblies with compression and oil control rings of increased radial thickness are introduced. The compression ring grooves are of reduced diameter. These changes have been made to reduce oil consumption.

The piston assemblies complete with gudgeon pins and rings are interchangeable in sets with those previously used. The new and old oil control rings are also interchangeable in sets and the earlier type compression rings may be used with the later type pistons. It is not permissible, however, to fit the new type compression rings to the old type pistons.

Engine numbers 15GB46045—15GB46100 and 15GB46342 onward—modified oil pump and strainer: On later engines a modified oil pump (part no. 1H1191) and an oil strainer assembly of simplified construction (part no. 1H1192) are fitted. The oil suction pipe position is now moved forward towards the front of the engine to eliminate any possibility of oil starvation during cornering or braking. The new units are interchangeable as complete assemblies with the oil pumps and strainers previously used. The three oil pump to crankcase studs, however, have been lengthened to accommodate the greater thickness of the oil pump bottom cover, their part number now being 51K267.

The Twin Cam MGA

The MGA Twin Cam model had as tortuous a development as any MG produced, as well as one of the shortest production runs. Prior to the Twin Cam, the last MG to use an overhead cam engine was the PB in 1936. Since then MG has been forced to use a more pedestrian unit, mildly modified for their use. The problem with these engines was they sacrificed performance for ease of production, low cost, and reliability. Invariably this meant an unsophisticated engine design. John Thornley expresses the company's frustration. "We had soldiered on for so long with these silly heads where gas came out the same side that it went in. Moreover, the pushrods were down the same side as the ports. I can't think of anything more ridiculous!" What was the impetus for the design of the Twin Cam engine? Some say the engine was designed to test bearings. If this is so, then why such a costly and complicated design? Indeed, why were two twin cam engines designed. Perhaps the bearing test story was fabricated to cover up the real reason the twin cam engine was developed. As simply put by John Thornley, "We had wanted this purely for competition purposes. Not because of any trouble but because we wanted a really sporting engine for competition."

The Twin Cam was developed for a very select market, as John explains, "We did aim at a limited market. This was really the undoing of the Twin Cam. We wanted to make 25 a week. Then we could steer them around to those enthusiast people who would know how to handle them throughout the world." After nearly two years of pleading and cajoling, J.W.T. got his wish and George Harriman, then head of BMC, conceded, "All right you can do it, but you've got to use the existing cylinder block." It was this decision to keep the original cylinder block that may have spelled the doom of the twin cam engine, as J.W.T. bemoans. "I heaved a great sigh and said, 'Yes sir.' and came away and I knew bloody well that before we were a fortnight into design there would be a hole that we didn't want or a box that we did and we would have an independent block. And if we were going to have an independent block, we ought to have been able to design the engine with a clean sheet of paper and having a bore/stroke ratio of our own selection. I think it was remarkable that the engine was as good as it was." Work was begun on the twin cam design in March 1953, and by the time the engine was put into production about the only thing in common

The Austin twin cam engine was a "clean sheet" design and should have been superior to the Morris design. A smooth running performer, it couldn't quite match the power output of the Morris engine. In this view the modified master cylinder on the left side of the firewall is for the Girling front disc brakes. The header tank for the radiator is seen on the right and is not connected to the cylinder head. The radiator is not installed either. The large pipe passing in front of the engine is for air, not water.

with the "B" series block was the bore centers! The original design was conceived by Gerald Palmer and development was done by Eddie Maher and Jimmy Thompson, all at Morris Engines Branch, Cowley.

I suppose it was only appropriate that MG's arch-rival, Austin, would figure in the twin cam story. While the Morris twin cam design was being developed, an Austin design was also being considered. Both engines were to make their debut at the Dunrod Tourist Trophy Race on September 18, 1955. The Morris design utilized a head with valves inclined at 80° while the Austin design had its valves set at an angle of 66°. The Morris design was based on the "B" series block while the Austin design was unique.

Marcus Chambers, Competition Department Director for BMC at the time, surmises that the Austin engine was a scaled up version of the famous Murray Jameson twin cam Austin design of pre-war fame. There is a strong resemblance in the cam cover design. The Austin unit was very smooth and fit well in the MGA; however, it was down on power and revs. The Austin engine was installed in the EX 182 which had finished 17th at Le Mans. A bulge in the hood was necessary to clear the taller engine and Girling front disc brakes were fitted. The Morris twin cam design was fitted into the Ex 182 which had finished 12th overall at Le Mans. The car was also fitted with

Girling front disc brakes. Additionally, the front fenders were modified for better air penetration, the headlamps being lowered and replaced with Riley parking lamps. It didn't matter that they were useless at night because the Tourist Trophy race was run during the day. A third car was also entered, being built to EX 182 standards from a production body.

The "droop nosed" EX 182 sported a Morris design twin cam engine and Girling front disc brakes. The design improvements enabled the MG to mix it up with the Porsches, however, mechanical problems forced a withdrawl from its one and only race, the Dundrod Tourist Trophy in September 1955.

The cars were prepared just before the race and preliminary road tests indicated both models were plagued by fuel starvation on cornering with the two twin choke Solex carburetors fitted. Additionally, the maximum rpm for the Austin engine restricted its performance to nearly that of the standard Le Mans car. In a little known, but fateful decision, a factory report on the race states, "It was therefore decided, as there was little prospect of being able to correct both engines in the time available, to substitute a further Le Mans (EX 182) engine for the 66° (Austin) engine, and to pursue correction of the carburation difficulties on the 80° (Morris) engine." The decision was made the night before the departure of the team for Belfast, site of the Tourist Trophy race. Tommy Wellman, mechanic on the Austin engined car, had finished preparing the car at eight that night. Having just finished his supper and looking forward to a good night's sleep before rising at six to drive the car to Belfast, he received a call at ten that night directing the Austin engine be replaced with a standard Le Mans engine. Needless to say, that was a long night! The switch was completed at four in the morning and the team departed at six, without the Austin engine. The Austin twin cam design was never heard from again.

While the team was enroute to Belfast, Eddie Maher of Engines Branch was working overtime himself fabricating an intake manifold on which to mount two Weber carburetors. It was hoped the Webers would cure the fuel starvation problem. The manifold was completed in time and sent by air to Belfast. While the team was sitting down to supper the night before practice started, the manifold arrived. Calling on the reserve of infinite patience and determination that every racing mechanic carries in his tool box, the mechanics set out to install the new manifold and carburetors that night, working virtually all night at the old Belfast airport to complete the difficult task in time for practice on Friday. The car went well enough in practice; however, during the race it began misfiring when hot. When running right, the car showed good promise, lapping at 79.46 mph, enabling the MGA to mix it up with the Porsches. Persistent misfiring led to the withdrawal of the car on lap 34, midway through the race. Subsequent examination revealed a hairline crack had developed in the intake manifold which caused the mixture to go weak when the manifold heated up. The standard EX 182 car, driven by Ted Lund and J.R. Stoop, retired on lap 8 with a split in its experimental alloy fuel tank. The tank had been tested prior to the race; however, a particularly nasty hump in the course appropriately called "Deers Leap" sent the car airborne each lap, putting an unexpected strain on the tank which resulted in its splitting. The other entry with the standard Le Mans engine in place of the Austin twin cam, ironically, was the only car of the three to finish the race. J.E.G. Fairman and P. Wilson drove the car to a fourth place finish in its class behind three Porsches and ahead of all the works Triumphs. Its fastest lap was 77.39 mph, over two mph slower than the Morris twin cam.

The twin cam engine design was later utilized in the EX 179 and EX 181 record breaking projects. The EX 179 project employed an unblown version of the twin cam engine in establishing 16 Class G international records in August, 1956 with Ken Miles and Johnny Lockett driving. The EX 181 project utilized a supercharged version of the twin cam engine producing 280 bhp @ 7,300 rpm, while the back-up engine produced 303 bhp. In August, 1957, EX 181 established several Class F international records, including a run of over 245 mph.

The development of the new MGA Twin Cam model was given the project designation EX 187. Despite the fact that the engine had been under development since 1953, considerable work was still necessary to adapt the engine for use on the road. The use of domed pistons created an uneven combustion pattern which was cured with the use of a penthouse roof design. The engine had previously been fitted with a simple sine-wave cam lobe pattern which didn't allow smooth running under 2,000 rpm, so new camshafts with a compound sine-wave pattern were developed giving good low speed flexibility while retaining the high peak power output. Fifty degrees of valve overlap did result in a small amount of lopping at idle.

Just when it seemed everything was ready for production, the American

The start of the Dundrod TT. Number 36, in the foreground, was the only car of the team to finish the race. Number 35 trails two cars back with a pushrod engine substituted for its Austin twin cam. Presumably the Morris twin cam is past the camera already. It was the fastest after all!

market requested a larger engine to take advantage of the recently adopted International Sporting Code Appendix J limit of 1600 cc. The Twin Cam model was to be marketed primarily for the amateur racer, so the new class limit was an important consideration. In light of these arguments, the introduction, scheduled for October, was postponed and the cylinder bores

An early weaker crankshaft, troublesome piston, and layshaft are shown here.

were increased from 73.025 to 75.4 mm. The new displacement was 1588 cc, comfortably under the 1600 cc limit with room for one or two oversize bores. The increased bores necessitated the elimination of the water jackets between cylinders one and two and cylinders three and four. This was necessary in order to maintain the distance between bore centers allowing the machining of the blocks on the "B" series engine lines. The increased bore also created problems with the piston design and a redesign had to be done to tailor the piston clearance to the new bore. At last the Twin Cam model was ready for production. Announcement of the new model was made in July, 1958, five years after the development of the original test engine was started, and in September, 1958 production began.

Production of the Twin Cam was originally scheduled at 25 cars per week. The necessary special finishing of the engines combined with a predicted low demand for the model, dictated the low production rate. It had been quite a battle for John Thornley and the people at MG to get permission to go ahead with the Twin Cam project; and they must have viewed its introduction with a degree of triumph. Historically, the introduction of the Twin Cam marked the first production MG to use overhead cams since the PB model which was phased out in 1936.

In keeping with its problem riddled path to production, the introduction of the Twin Cam did not go as smoothly as MG would have liked. On July 14, 1958, four pre-production Twin Cam roadsters were assembled at the F.V.P.E. track at Chobham where they were made available to the motoring press to wring out on the twisty two mile course. As luck would have it, one car retired early with a broken generator bracket and some time later another Twin Cam was crashed! The engine had not been fully run in and consequently the performance suffered. One journalist complained that the engine felt reluctant to rev beyond 6,000 rpm and ran on "furiously" when switched off. The short straight prevented top speed testing. An indication of oil consumption problems with the pre-production models was evidenced by a team of MG mechanics checking the oil level of the cars every three laps. Probably in an attempt to prevent burned valves and pistons, the mixtures were set a bit rich. After such a long wait for the Twin Cam, British enthusiasts had to wait an additional seven months for quantity deliveries in Britain as the first seven month's production had been accounted for by

The long awaited Twin Cam MGA suffered a disappointing number of faults early in its production. By the time they were corrected its fate was sealed.

orders from the U.S. and Canada amounting to over one million dollars.

Just as the cries of despair over the use of the push-rod operated valves in the TA model of July, 1936 were raised, so also were cries of jubilation raised over the introduction of the Twin Cam model which boasted such refinements as double overhead cams and four wheel disc brakes. The ever important road test results by the major motoring magazines reflected this enthusiasm.

> The Motor. . . . *Those who contend that racing and record breaking no longer serve any useful purpose in developing production cars need look no further for an up-to-date example to prove them wrong. Of all the cars so far tested by* The Motor *only machines built specifically for sports car racing would keep pace with this 1600 cc touring two seater in a standing start match to speeds of 60, 70, or 80 mph.*[2]
>
> The Autocar. . . *In the road test of the 1-1/2 litre MGA coupe it was stated in summary that the car was capable of holding its own against more powerful vehicles; this applies even more markedly to the 1600 cc Twin Cam model. The extra performance is matched by the road-holding, steering and brakes, and this car maintains the MG tradition of good looks coupled with a very fine performance.*[3]
>
> Road and Track. . . *The new Twin Cam MG is a tremendous step forward for the firm. Designed primarily to regain prestige for the marque in production sports car racing, it should do just that. However this is a car for the genuine enthusiast and we think the push-rod type will be as popular as ever.*[4]
>
> Sports Car Quarterly. . . *There are no body changes to indicate that beneath the bonnet lurks enough power to give the Porsche Speedster a rough time on any race course.*[5]

Of the many changes which set the Twin Cam model apart from the MGA 1500 and later 1600, the engine is first in importance so let us examine the "heart" of the Twin Cam.

Basic machining was done at Longbridge Austin Works and finishing took place at the Morris Engine Works on a small line initially producing five engines a day. The cylinder head is aluminum alloy with chain driven double overhead camshafts operating symmetrically aligned single intake and exhaust valves set at an angle of 80° to each other. The camshafts are hollow and run in three white metal bearings each. The lobes are designed to give good mid-range torque with high peak power output. Three different cams were employed during the production run. The first design was used on only the first few pilot run cars and featured a 280° design. It was found that a 250° cam with 50° of overlap improved the acceleration over the 280° cam, so the 250° cam was introduced. Toward the end of the production run a hex nut was cast onto the front end of the camshaft to facilitate retarding the cam timing. A low instantaneous center and large nose radius are utilized for extended valve gear life.

This early Twin Cam may have been a test bed car. There are no "Twin Cam" insignias on the cowl. The hood prop was changed back to the right side during production. Later models routed the ignition wiring around the front of the cylinder head.

To give you an idea of what the development engineers had up their sleeves for future development of this engine, the intake cam was designed to drive an SU fuel injection pump at the rear end. Injection was to have been into the manifold to avoid modification of the cylinder head. Inlet valves are 1-19/32 inch in diameter and the exhaust valves are 1-7/16 inch in diameter. To increase exhaust valve life, KE 965 steel and stellited faces are employed. Intake valves are constructed from EN52 austenitic iron. Centrifugally cast austenitic iron valve seatings, which have a coefficient of expansion compatible with aluminum, are cast into the cylinder head and machined in place. The combustion chamber is hemispherically shaped with the sparkplug offset to allow maximum space for the valves. Champion designed the N4 sparkplug specifically for the Twin Cam engine.

The camshaft actuates the valves through what the factory terms "inverted buckets," made of brimol cast iron. These buckets were arrived at during experiments with the blown EX 181 engine. Early short skirt buckets running "barefoot" in the aluminum head occasionally stuck with disastrous results. Because of the pentroof piston design, the valves must be closed when the piston is at top dead center or a violent collision will occur between the valve and piston top. Beginning with engine number 1087 a long skirt bucket was introduced, but this merely served to accentuate the problem. Long time Twin Cam owner Reid Willis, who has owned his 1958 Twin

The left side of the twin cam engine showing the four branch exhaust system, front mounted distributor, radiator header tank which maintained the water level in the cylinder head and the dipstick at the extreme rear of the block.

The right side of the twin cam engine showing the finned aluminum oil pan and larger oval-shaped air cleaners.

I was negotiating a tight corner at what must have been 6,500 rpm when the inside rear wheel lifted and the engine over-revved toward 8,000 rpm. One of the buckets stuck and whamo, piston met valve and the latter was converted into an unguided missile! The valve came out of the head, broke the camshaft in two and put a rather substantial dent in the cam cover. When the engine was torn down, it was discovered that the piston and cylinder wall were unmarked. That's quite a testimony to the strength of the pistons. Needless to say, the head didn't fare quite as well, but MG came to the rescue with a new head shipped air freight and supplied free of charge. I guess they wanted to keep the British flag flying in Japanese racing circles!

The rather complex gear and chain cam drive. The chain tensioner is on the upper right and is adjusted through the oil filler cap!

Beginning with engine number 1587, sleeves were inserted into the head for the buckets to run it, thus eliminating the problem. Shims are used to adjust valve clearance. Double valve springs are used. In an effort to retain as many parts from the pushrod engine as possible, a gear was fitted to the nose of the crankshaft, which drove a gear fitted to the nose of the layshaft, which replaced the camshaft. The chain drive to the cams was driven by a sprocket fitted to the end of the layshaft. For strength, a duplex chain design was utilized. The layshaft also drove the distributor on the front, the Horburn-Eaton eccentric motor oil pump in the middle, and the tachometer drive in the rear.

A clever arrangement of securing the sprockets to the timing chain cover is used to allow removal of the cylinder head without upsetting the valve timing. Anticipating fine tuning and/or substitution of different camshafts, a vernier adjustment is provided for valve timing. Twin SU H 6 one and three-quarter inch carburetors are fitted on the right side of the engine while an extractor type exhaust manifold is located on the left side of the engine, providing full benefit of the cross-flow cylinder head. The carburetors are mounted at an angle of 22-1/2 degrees and utilize a shock mount for the float bowls in order to eliminate float needle vibration problems.

A balance pipe is employed in the design of the intake manifold which combines with a throttle linkage designed to open the rear throttle slightly ahead of the front throttle, providing a more progressive action of the dashpots when the accelerator is suddenly depressed. The porting within the cylinder head is exceptionally direct and smooth, aiding the flow of gasses from the carburetors to the exhaust manifold. The exhaust manifold incorporates separate pipes for each cylinder, with the number one and four pipes joining after a short distance and the number two and three pipes likewise. These two pipes are routed into a downpipe which carries the exhaust through a turn of 90°, and joins in a collector under the front floor board.

In response to an owner suggestion, an asbestos shield is fitted between the exhaust manifold and the engine block. The system is very similar to that employed on the present day MGB, and was in all likelihood its predecessor. Solid skirt, pentroof, and aluminum pistons giving 9.9:1 compression ratio are used. The solid skirt adds strength to the piston at the expense of quiet running and low oil consumption, brought on by increased piston to cylinder clearance. The usual practice is to employ a split-skirt design which compensates for the expansion allowing reduced piston to cylinder wall clearances.

The unusual pentroof design piston was laboriously arrived at during experiments with the EX 181 supercharged twin cam engine. The pentroof design gives more even combustion, reducing any tendency toward detonation. 8.3:1 compression ratio pistons were offered as a retrofit when fuel below 95 octane was to be used. Three compression rings, the top one chrome plated, and an oil control ring are employed. In an effort to reduce oil consumption and piston noise, three production modifications were subsequently introduced during the model run. The wrist pin is of the full floating type, providing additional strength. Connecting rods are beefier than the "B" series type and have webbed big-end caps for added stiffness. The crankshaft is made of forged

EN 22 steel, heat treated to 75 to 85 tons tensile strength, and runs in three lead-indium bearings slightly narrower than normal, as dictated by the thicker crank cheeks. The crankshaft weighs 32 lb and drives a lightweight steel flywheel. The sump has a capacity of seven quarts, nearly double that of the standard MGA 1500, and is constructed of aluminum alloy employing both internal and external fins to aid in cooling of the engine oil. Reflecting common racing practice, the sump has internal baffles to prevent oil from sloshing to one side during hard cornering or braking, which could uncover the oil pickup and result in a momentary loss of oil pressure.

Cooling of the engine is done in two parts, the cylinder head being cooled by water under pressure from the water pump while the block is cooled by thermosiphon action of the coolant. Due to the added height of the cylinder head, a

The underside of the Twin Cam showing the exhaust system, which closely resembles the MGB's, and the finned oil sump.

separate header tank is required to insure the water supply remains above the level of the head. This header tank is mounted alongside the left side of the engine above the exhaust manifold. The inlet and outlet pipes on the radiator are mounted on opposite sides from the standard MGA to accommodate the different cooling system. For the same reason, the heater is a mirror image of the standard MGA unit. As in the case of the Jaguar XK engines, the large oil capacity was a significant factor in engine cooling. In the case of the Twin Cam, the quantity of oil and the finned sump were sufficient to keep oil temperature low in all but the most grueling situations, therefore, an engine oil cooler was not standard equipment on the Twin Cam. An oil cooler was available as an accessory.

Weight of the completed engine with clutch, transmission and starter is 485 lb versus 403 lb for the MGA 1500. Starting with a basic engine in 1953 producing 60 bhp @ 4,600 rpm, the Twin Cam in finished form produced 108 bhp @ 6,700 rpm. Torque was rated at 104 ft/lb @ 4,500 rpm while valve crash (float) occured at 7,400 rpm on earlier engines and at 7,700 rpm on later engines (engine number 2251 onward). Horsepower with the 8.3:1 compression ratio pistons was 100 @ 6,700 rpm.

Chassis And Running Gear Development

The Twin Cam engine is, of course, the major change in this new model, though by no means the only change. Gazing into the engine compartment for the first time, one is struck by the massive cylinder head with its twin polished aluminum cam covers and the spark plugs neatly lined up like soldiers down the center of the head. The twin carburetors on the right side of the engine and the header tank on the left side nicely balance each other adding to the visual enjoyment.

The engine and transmission assembly ready for installation. The remote gearchange has not been mounted yet. The assembly weighs a hefty 485 lb.

Unfortunately, all this show and go is had at the price of engine accessibility. Any "Twinkie"* owner will tell you the skinned knuckles and hours of frustration endured in adjusting the generator belt tension, distributor settings or changing the oil filter. An indication of their inaccessibility is the inclusion of access panels incorporated in later models in the front inner fenders to allow access from the wheel wells to these components. Shortly after production started, holes were drilled in the front cross member to allow access to the front five oil pan bolts.

To accommodate the longer engine, the radiator has been moved slightly forward. Likewise the rack and pinion steering gear has been mounted further forward. Longer and stiffer steering arms, steering swivel pins with greater length between pivot centers, off-set tie rod ends, a slightly wider front track and Timken roller bearings on the front hubs are employed, resulting in a three foot increased turning diameter. Sturdier U-joint and axle shafts are employed to cope with the extra torque provided by the DOHC engine.

Dunlop center-lock disc wheels, a la the D-type Jaguar, are fitted with 5.90 x 15 Dunlop Road Speed tires. Disc wheels were chosen over the traditional wire wheels for their greater strength, reflecting the emphasis on performance in this model. The wheels are drilled for lightness and increased cooling of the disc brakes. Instead of a spined hub, four dowels are used to locate the wheel, eliminating the possibility of an overzealous pit crew member jamming a wheel on the splines. A similar design is used today on many formula one cars. Dunlop four wheel disc brakes with quick change pads are fitted as standard equipment. The pads are easily changed by undoing a single bolt which holds the retainer clip of the caliper, removing the clip and withdrawing the pad by hooking a wire through a hole drilled in the pad securing plate for that purpose. To reduce wear, the brake pads do not ride lightly against the disc when not in use, instead they are held slightly off the disc. This can result in some anxious moments when braking in the rain. On occasion there will be an unsettling pause between brake application and effect while the pads clear the disc of water. The brakes incorporated a stop to prevent pistons coming too far out or the pads being pushed through its guide.

Separate master cylinders for the clutch and brake systems are used and their greater separation on the bulkhead dictated different brake and clutch pedals from the MGA 1500. Stiffer springs and shocks are used to compensate for the slightly higher weight of the twin cam engine. A front anti-roll bar was available as an option on later models. The chassis is also specially braced to accommodate the extra torque and provide increased torsional rigidity.

*An affectionate nomer for the Twin Cam, originated in England.

1500 and Twin Cam Engine Comparison

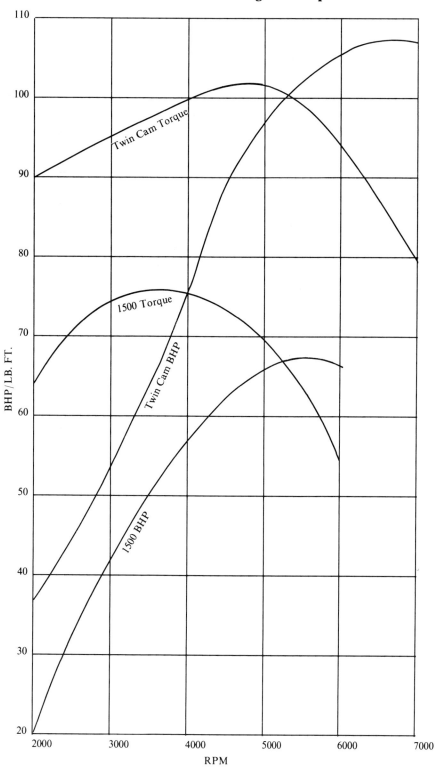

The substantial improvement in output offered by the Twin Cam is shown here, especially past 4000 rpm.

Body

    The interior sports a 7500 rpm tachometer, redlined at 7000 rpm and a vinyl covered instrument panel with chrome trim around the bottom edge and speaker grill, as in the coupe model and later in the 1600 Mk II. A

centigrade temperature gauge was fitted to export cars (other than North America) from chassis 713 onward. Twin Cam identification badges beneath the cowl vents and MG crest on the trunk lid complete the trim changes. To clear the slightly taller engine, the hood was given a higher crown. To save on production costs, this reshaped hood was used on all MGAs produced after the introduction of the Twin Cam. A three window roadster top greatly improved rearward vision. Accessories offered for the first time on an

The knock-off disc wheels closely resembled those on the D-type Jaguar. They quickly identified the car as a Twin Cam MGA.

A front disc brake from an MGA 1600 showing the quick change pad feature.

A rear disc showing the parking brake arrangement which is always troublesome on four wheel disc brake cars.

MGA included competition deluxe seats, cigar lighter and sun visors on the coupe. Telescopic steering wheel was standard equipment on export model Twin Cams.

Driving Impressions

Just what is it like to drive this hot rod from Abingdon? Climbing into the driver's seat one notices few changes from the 1500 model. The higher red line on the tachometer is the first indication that this model holds some surprises in the performance field. Most Twin Cam models come with the optional competition seats which provide additional lateral support and have a longer bottom cushion giving greater thigh support. The engine starts readily, settling down to a lumpy idle at 1,000 rpm. Taking the car up through the gears, the additional power makes itself felt, especially above 4,000 rpm, where the tach needle fairly rockets toward the 7,000 rpm red line in first and second gears.

A considerable increase in engine noise, mostly due to the valve train, is noticable on full throttle acceleration with an accompanying increase in exhaust noise over the 1500 engine. In a car designed for racing, this is not to be considered objectionable; however, high speed cruising in the 90 mph range can become tiring. In the Twin Cam, a cruising speed of 90 mph is not so impractical as one might imagine and the engine and the car feel very comfortable at this speed. At speeds above 90 mph the engine begins to feel and sound busy, although top speed is in the neighborhood of 113 mph. The engine eagerly pulls smoothly and strongly, with slight vibration periods at 2,500 and 5,500 rpm, right up to the red line. Repeated shifts at 7,000 rpm can be managed with no protesting from the engine and 6,500 rpm is easily held for long stretches.

The 9.9:1 compression ratio requires the use of 100 octane fuel to prevent knocking and running on. Oil consumption is approximately one quart per 250 miles, which while high for a street car is not all that much out of line in a racing car such as this. The four wheel disc brakes haul this runner down from 100 mph quickly and controllably, showing no signs of deterioration from the effects of heat and rain, except for an occasional delay in the rain. A smooth and progressive action assists the driver in utilizing maximum braking action regardless of surface conditions.

The gearbox retains the standard ratios of the 1500 with the attendant wide spacing between second and third gears. A close ratio box is available for those planning to use the car in competition, which greatly enhances the car's performance. Optional rear axle ratios are also offered as an alternative to the standard rear axle ratio of 4.3:1. With the close ratio gearbox and 4.55:1 rear end fitted, the car is better suited to short, medium speed tracks commonly found in amateur racing. Second gear top speed increases from 56 to 72 mph @ 7,000 rpm and a 40 mph corner leaves the driver in the fat part of the torque curve for good acceleration out of the corner. A comparison of the two combinations follows:

Maximum speeds in gears at 7,000 rpm

	4.3:1 axle Std gearbox	4.55:1 axle Close ratio gearbox
1st	34	48
2nd	56	72
3rd	90	92
4th	121 (theoretical)	117

The handling of the Twin Cam is little changed from that of the 1500, retaining the predictable, sure-footed grip with a tendency toward oversteer if the accelerator is not used judiciously. A road test published by *Road and Track* magazine in their November, 1958 issue is perhaps the most accurate

This 1500 bodied Twin Cam is identified by the vinyl covered dash with chrome edging and the tachometer redlined at 7000 rpm. This particular model is fitted with the optional competition deluxe seats.

The improved acceleration of the close-ratio gearbox equipped Twin Cam is nearly as great as the improvement of the standard Twin Cam over the 1500.

Acceleration Curve Comparison

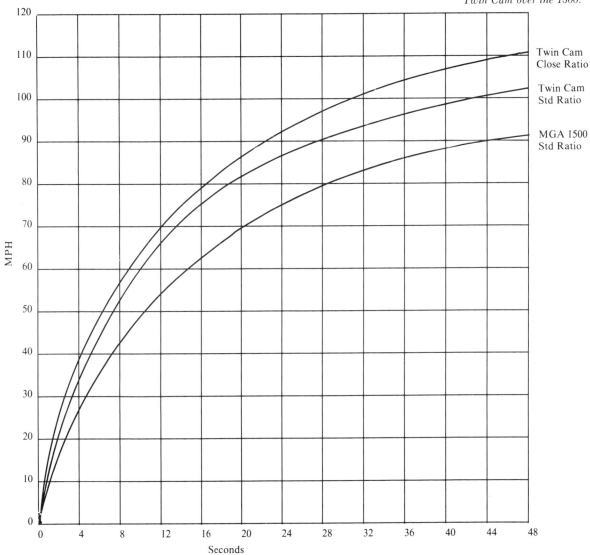

Twin Cam Close Ratio

Twin Cam Std Ratio

MGA 1500 Std Ratio

MPH

Seconds

representation of the performance of the Twin Cam model. For comparison, figures for the MGA 1500 and the Twin Cam equipped with the 4.55:1 axle and Le Mans close ratio gearbox are given.

	MGA 1500	Std Twin Cam	Twin Cam w/ 4.55:1 axle and CR box
0-30	4.6	2.7	---
0-40	6.8	4.8	---
0-50	10.2	7.3	---
0-60	14.5	9.9	9.1
0-70	19.9	13.8	---
0-80	28.0	18.1	16.2
0-90	42.5	27.0	---
0-100	------	41.0	30.0
1/4 mile	19.6	18.1	17.1
max. speed	95.1	113.0	117.5
fuel econ.	30 mpg	19.5 mpg	---

The Good Die Young

Despite an inordinately long gestation, the DOHC engine continued to defy sorting out. MG had purposely kept the production low in order to facilitate sorting out the engine. Many production modifications were implemented, a number of them attempting to resolve the excessive oil consumption and piston holing problems. In the midst of solving the piston problems, an unfortunate turn of fate occured. John Thornley describes the incident. "We were just running into our troubles with burned pistons which was the main difficulty when the man who was production director of BMC going round the engine factory at Coventry lighted upon the line where the Twin Cam engine was being built and said, 'What's this? How many of those are you doing? Twenty-five a week? Well you could easily do 75 couldn't you? All right, 75 it is!' That immediately meant that 50 Twin Cams a week went into the hands of bloody fools. The piston trouble overtook us and Harriman said, 'Cut the thing. There you have it. I told you you ought not to have a Twin Cam engine anyway.' "

This was not the sole reason for the Twin Cam's demise, but it did proliferate the engine's problems which were beginning to besmirch the model's and MG's reputation. This was particularly true in the U.S. where nearly half of the Twin Cam production went. The final fix which came at the end of the Twin Cam's life was a switch to 8.3:1 compression ratio pistons. While they did take the edge off the engine's performance, the horsepower penalty was only eight bhp. These pistons were originally designed to be used when fuel had an octane rating lower than 95. With the degradation, and in many instances, demise, of premium fuel, this modification might offer a solution to present day Twin Cam owners.

The Last Twin Cam

The Twin Cam had a very short life, being in production from September, 1958, when chassis number YD1/501 rolled off the line, until June 14, 1960, when the last Twin Cam, YD1/2611, a specially painted Woodland Green roadster, was delivered to its proud owner. A total of only 2,111 roadsters and coupes had been produced. That last Twin Cam roadster is still owned by its original purchaser, Mike Ellman-Brown, along with a covey of gorgeous MGs of various types.

As a J production racer, the Twin Cam was a successful car, carrying the MG name into winner circles all over the globe. As a street car, the Twin Cam was not so successful. Because of its high state of tune, the Twin Cam engine required more frequent and precise attention than its 1500 and 1600 brothers. Improperly adjusted ignition timing, valve timing, tappet clearance or wrong heat range plugs would soon result in the same catastrophy, burned or holed pistons. Given proper attention and meticulous adherence to tuning specifications, the Twin Cam engine would give as long a life as the push rod version; however, this was not very often the case and the car quickly gained a reputation for being unreliable. In marketing a car which was perhaps too good for many of its owners who were only looking for something with a little more performance, the Twin Cam sealed its fate before the first car left the line.

The last double overhead cam MG?

Specifications:

Introduced: 14 July 1958
Production dates: September 1958—14 June 1960
Total Production: 2,111 (roadster and coupe)
Chassis numbers: YD1/501—YD1/2611
Engine numbers:
Base price:
    Roadster—$3,345/£1,265 17s
    Coupe—$3,550/£1,357 7s
Engine:

Displacement	1588 cc (96.9 cu in.)
Bore	75.4 mm (2.97 in.)
Stroke	88.9 mm (3.50 in.)
Compression	9.9:1 (8.3:1)
Main bearings	3, lead-indium
BHP	108 (net) @ 6,700 rpm
	110 (max SAE) @ 6,750 rpm
	100 (net with 8.3:1 pistons) @ 6,700
Torque	105 lb ft @ 4,500 rpm
Red line	7,000 rpm

Transmission/rear axle: Same as MGA 1500 except as indicated below.
    MPH per 1000 rpm in top gear:
        17.3 w/ 4.3:1 axle
        16.8 w/ 4.55:1 axle
Chassis: Same as MGA 1500 except as indicated below.
    Wheels and tires: Dunlop center-lock steel disc type wheels with Dunlop 5.90 x 15 Road Speed tires.
    Dimensions:

Curb weight roadster	2185 lb
Curb weight coupe	2222 lb
Turning circle (between curbs):	
to right	32 ft 1 in.
to left	32 ft 6 in.

Production Modifications:

The following is a listing, in numerical order, of those modifications made to the MGA Twin Cam during the production run. The listing is divided into two parts, chassis and engine modifications. This represents the major modifications, but not all modifications.

Chassis Modifications

Chassis number 528 onward—Modified Engine Mounting: Commencing at Chassis number MGA 528, a packing plate (Part no. AHH5896), together with longer set screws (Part no. HZS0506), is fitted under the engine mounting on the left-hand side only.

This packing plate is introduced to give an increased clearance between the starting dog (on the crankshaft pulley) and the steering-rack housing.

The modification can be fitted to chassis prior to the one given above.

Chassis number 528 onward—Modified Air Cleaner: In the case of the first 28 cars it is possible for the elements in the air cleaners to move out of position and foul the carburetor inlet. The remedy is to spot-weld a piece of .031 in. thick steel strip, 1-3/4 in. long and with turned ends, to the air cleaner inner bracket as shown in the accompanying sketch. This modification was incorporated in later cars from chassis number 528 onward.

Chassis numbers 575, 613, 623, 633, 648, and 652 onward—Remote Radiator Pressure Valve: To prevent loss of coolant due to vibration of the valve in the filler cap, a 7 lb (3.175 kg.) remote radiator pressure valve is now fitted. Cars equipped with this are numbered as follows: Car numbers 575, 613, 623, 633, 648 and from 652 onwards.

To modify an existing radiator the following procedure must be carried out.

(1) Remove the existing filler neck from the header tank, rotate through 180° and replace.

(2) Fit the pressure valve (Part no. AHH5903), together with its bracket (Part no. AHH5906), to the inner face of the left-hand air duct.

(3) Fit the rubber connecting hose (Part no. AHH5905) from the filler neck to the valve, and the overflow pipe (Part no. AHH5907) from the valve to the draining point. The overflow pipe is retained in position at its lower end by a clip (Part no. PCR0607).

Chassis number 824 (Europe Less France), 1618 (France) and 2418 (Sweden) onward—Modified European Light Unit: Cars exported to Europe are now fitted with the new European-type headlamps. These lamp units are fitted with special bulbs and front lenses giving an asymmetrical beam to the right-hand or left-hand side according to the regulations prevailing in the country concerned.

Access to the bulb is gained in the same way as described in Section N. 16 (*The MG Series MGA (Twin Cam) Workshop Manual AKD 926A*). The bulb, however, is released from the reflector by withdrawing the three-pin socket and pinching the two ends of the wire retaining clip to clear the bulb flange.

When replacing the bulb, care must be taken to see that the rectangular pip on the bulb flange engages the slot in the reflector seating for the bulb.

Replace the spring clip with its coils resting in the base of the bulb flange and engaging in the two retaining lugs on the reflector seating.

Chassis number 2192 (Coupe) and 2193 (roadster) onward—Modified Bodies: Commencing at Chassis numbers 2192

(Coupe) and 2193 (roadster), modified bodies incorporating tail lamp plinths and front flashing indicator lamp mountings have been introduced to provide for the fitting of separate front and rear amber flashing direction indicators. The electrical relay is not used with this type of indicator.

Provision is also made for the fitting of sliding side screens to the standard body.

Additional body space has been made available in Coupe models by re-positioning the spare wheel mounting in the boot and reducing the size of the parcel shelf.

Chassis number 2275 onward—Anti-roll Bar Assembly: Commencing at Chassis number 2275 a modified front extension, modified spring pans and bottom wishbone assemblies, and an anti-roll bar assembly were introduced.

Cars prior to Chassis No. 2275 may be modified to permit the fitting of anti-roll bar equipment by fitting the following components in lieu of the existing ones.

AHH5924X	Front extension assembly
AHH5925Z	Spring pan assemblies
AHH5927Z	Bottom wishbone assembly-R.H.
AHH5929Z	Bottom wishbone assembly-L.H.

Andrex dampers and anti-roll bar equipment must not be used simultaneously.

Chassis number 2371 onward—Modified halfshafts: From chassis number 2371 onward an involute design half-shaft and differential with finer teeth were employed.

Later models—Modified wheel arches: Later models of both the Tourer and the Coupe are fitted with louvred detachable panels in the front wheel arches.

The modification is introduced primarily to assist in cooling and secondly to give access to the retaining bolt on the oil filter.

This modification cannot be incorporated on earlier models.

Engine Modifications

Engine number 272 onward—Modified Dynamo Pulley and Fan Belt: To increase the dynamo charging rate at any given engine speed a smaller dynamo pulley (Part no. AEH605) and a shorter fan belt (Part no. AEH621) were introduced at engine number 272. This modification raises the dynamo pulley/crankshaft pulley speed ratio to 1.2:1.

The old and new dynamo pulleys and fan belts are interchangeable in sets.

Engine number 313 and 315 onward—Modified Half-speed Shaft and Oil Pump Driving Spindle: In cases of excessive wear on the oil pump driving spindle and half-speed shaft skew gearing, a modified shaft (Part no. AEH619) and spindle (Part no. AEH620) may be fitted. The number of teeth on the oil pump driving spindle has been increased from 10 to 11 and on the half-speed shaft from 9 to 10.

The new components can be fitted on earlier engines provided that they are both fitted at the same time.

Engine numbers 446 thru 605—Modified Piston Rings: To improve oil consumption, twin-segment scraper rings (Part no. AEH615) were introduced at engine number 446. These rings are interchangeable with the micro-land scraper rings previously fitted.

Engine numbers 606 thru 2042, 2044 thru 2052 and engine number 2056—Modified Pistons and Rings: To overcome any tendency to piston noise, piston assemblies (Part no. AEH640) incorporating new top rings (Part no. AEH649) were fitted to engines listed above.

Engine number 657 onward—Modified Crankcase Beather Pipe:
A new crankcase breather pipe was introduced at engine number 657. The purpose of this modification is to overcome any possibility of oil leakage from the engine breather onto the exhaust system, thus causing fumes to enter the car. Fitting the modified breather pipe (Part no. AEH628) necessitates the use of a new clip (Part no. 1G1309) and a longer clutch bell housing bolt (Part no. HBZ0511) in substitution for the clip and bolt which previously secured the original breather pipe to the crankcase.

Fit the breather pipe to the vent pipe on the engine rear side cover, slide the clip over the end of the pipe, fasten the clip to the gearbox mounting plate with the longer bolt specified, and secure with the existing nut and spring washer.

Engine number 1087 onward—Modified Tappets: To increase the tappet contact area with the cylinder head and eliminate the possibility of tappet fracture the length of the tappets has been increased by .25 in. (.635 mm.) to 1.5 in. (38.1 mm.).

The new tappets (Part no. AEH651) may be fitted to earlier engines in complete sets of eight.

Engine number 1343 onward—Modified Connecting Rods: To improve balance and to strengthen big-ends a modified connecting rod with bosses at the small end for balancing purposes and heavier big-end bearing caps was introduced beginning with engine number 1343.

The new type are interchangeable with the earlier pattern in sets only.

When fitting a single connecting rod of the later pattern to engines after number 1343, no weighing is necessary.

Engine number 1587 onward—Modified Tappet Bores: Commencing at engine number 1587, tappet bushes have been fitted to the tappet bores in the cylinder head to reduce tappet wear to a minimum. Each bush is locked in the head with a screwed plug.

Engine numbers 2011, 2028, 2038, 2040, 2041, 2188, 2200 to 2206, 2209 to 2219, 2222 onward—New-Type Distributor: A new distributor (Part no. AEJ41), having a roller weight mechanism with a positive stop (to prevent over advance) and no vacuum advance mechanism, has been introduced. When this distributor is fitted, the vacuum advance pipe must be removed and the carburetor union blanked off with a blanking plug (Part no. AEH1289).

Engine number 2043, 2053-55, 2057 onward—Modified Piston Rings: Twin segment scraper rings fitted with expander rings (Part no. AEH672) were fitted on the above engines to improve oil consumption.

Miscellaneous Modifications

Modified Carburetor Damper Assemblies: To allow the carburetor pistons to lift more freely new hydraulic damper assemblies have been fitted in production. The damper pistons of the new assemblies have been shortened from .378 in. (9.596 mm) to .308 in. (7.823 mm).

The new hydraulic damper assemblies (Part no. AUC8114) are identified by the letter "O" stamped on the brass hexagon caps. They can be fitted, with advantage, to earlier carburetors in pairs. Alternatively, the original damper pistons may be modified by machining .070 in. (1.78 mm) off their lower faces.

Modified Timing Cover Gasket: To obviate complete dismantling of the timing gear each time a new timing cover gasket is fitted, a gasket that it partially cut to provide four sections has been produced under Part no. AEH377.

The gasket may be fitted in the same way as the previous gasket or alternatively any one or more of the four sections may be detached and used separately.

Chapter 4

The MGA 1600

So we analysed the mind of the MGA user and asked ourselves: 'What does he want?' This produced a simple answer: 'Even better performance.'[1]

John Thornley

MGA 1600—Safety Faster

After nearly four years of production, from September 1955 to June 1959, the MGA 1500 was in need of change to attract new customers among those already owning MGAs, as well as the first time sports car buyer. The displacement of the Twin Cam had been increased from 1489 to 1588 cc in order to take advantage of the International Sporting Code's Appendix J; and the decision to increase the standard engine to this new size was a logical step. In an interview with Kenneth Ullyett in *The MG Companion*, John Thornley describes the genesis of the 1600.

> *We were thinking in terms of giving the MGA a facelift, after all, the car had been in production from 1955 to 1959, and there comes a time when the designer is called in to give a car extended currency, no matter how successful is the basic conception. As the MGA doesn't wear out, anyway, it was necessary to consider a change even if only to interest the potential buyer going into the showroom! As nobody likes change merely for change's sake, our design team was set the problem of ascertaining what really could be an improvement.*
>
> *We played about with alternative fronts. But bearing in mind the MGA is an idealized design, conceived as an entity, it is hardly surprising that no matter what we did to the front, the result was less satisfactory, and usually less aerodynamic. We experienced the same not-unanticipated disappointment when we experimented with the back-end. Each of the alterations seemed to have a stuck-on look. It did not take long to realize that worth-while improvement was not to be had this way. So we analysed the mind of the MGA user and asked ourselves: 'What does he want?'*
>
> *This produced a simple answer: 'Even better performance.'[2]*

The result of the redesign was the MGA 1600 with six bhp more than the 1500 under the hood, disc brakes at the front and improved drum brakes at the rear. With a scant increase of 99 cc in displacement (6.7%), horsepower was up 10% and torque 17%. The increase in torque provided noticeably increased acceleration and the greater horsepower raised the top speed past the magic 100 mph barrier.

At speed down a narrow country lane the MGA 1600 is in its element putting the improved acceleration and braking to good use.

Road tester's opinions reflected favorably on the engine and braking changes.

Autosport... *The MGA 1600 is a fast sports car that may almost be described as luxurious. It is lively, flexible, and a pleasure to drive, responding admirably to the proper use of that delightful gear lever but being perfectly willing to cooperate if one is in a lazy mood. It is, in fact, as practical a mode of everyday transport as many more staid vehicles and its fade-free brakes, snappy acceleration and good road-holding are all important safety features.*[3]

Road and Track... *...this is the same old reliable sports car it always was. It is very easy to drive, the ride is remarkably good as sports cars go, the handling qualities are first class. The new brakes are terrific. We always go a little overboard on the subject of the MG, which is a first love type of machine. We still say this is the best all-around sports car for use in America, especially for the new enthusiast.*[4]

The Motor... *With its share of the imperfections from which no car ever altogether escapes, this remains a very attractive and versatile sporting two-seater. Sturdy, well furnished and probably built with more thorough care than most of its contemporaries, it travels fast and is enjoyable to drive or ride in, yet can also serve as a reliable and weather-proof form of everyday transportation.*[5]

Sports Cars Illustrated... *Beyond a shadow of a doubt, this is the best touring MG yet.*[6]

There were few differences in the engine compartment from the 1500. The master cylinder had an enlarged reservoir and the coil was moved from atop the generator to a bracket on the motor mount.

The 1600 power unit complete with transmission. This one has the remote gear-change fitted.

The 1600 engine and transmission from the right side. The lighter toned transmission housing is aluminum.

Engine

The engine increase noticeably improved engine flexibility which allowed top gear acceleration from 10-100 mph in top gear. Acceleration was most improved in the higher speed ranges. The price for this increased performance was a slightly harsher and noisier engine at full throttle and a slightly increased fuel consumption. Where the 1500 model felt rather busy at 70 mph, the 1600 had to be held back at this speed with plenty of power in reserve for passing. A comparison of 1500 and 1600 performance tests graphically illustrates these improvements.

	MGA 1500	MGA 1600	Twin Cam
0-30	4.6	4.2	2.7
0-40	6.8	6.4	4.8
0-50	10.2	9.8	7.3
0-60	14.5	13.3	9.9
0-70	19.9	19.0	13.8
0-80	28.0	26.5	18.1
0-90	42.5	36.4	27.0
1/4 mile	19.6	19.0	18.1
max. speed	98.1	103.0	113.0
fuel economy	30 mpg	28 mpg	19.5 mpg

Brakes

The improved brakes also received praise from road testers. Their action was described as slightly harder than the drum brakes of the 1500,

1500, 1600 and Twin Cam Engine Comparison

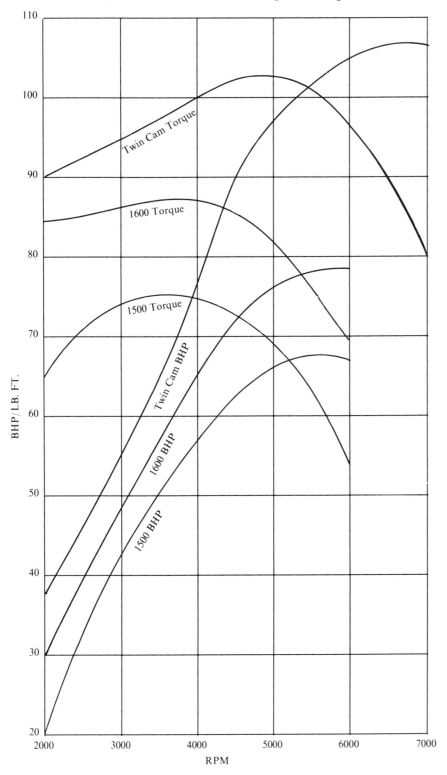

The power output of the 1600 engine is almost exactly between the 1500 and Twin Cam. Notice the flatter torque curve of the 1600 engine which improved low speed response.

especially in wet conditions. A slight amount of disc brake squeal was heard when very light braking was applied at low speeds, a common fault of disc brakes even today. The brakes of the 1500 received much praise for their adequacy and the disc/drum combination of the 1600 added a great reserve of stopping power to this already adequate system, easily coping with the increased speed potential of the engine.

Acceleration Curve Comparison

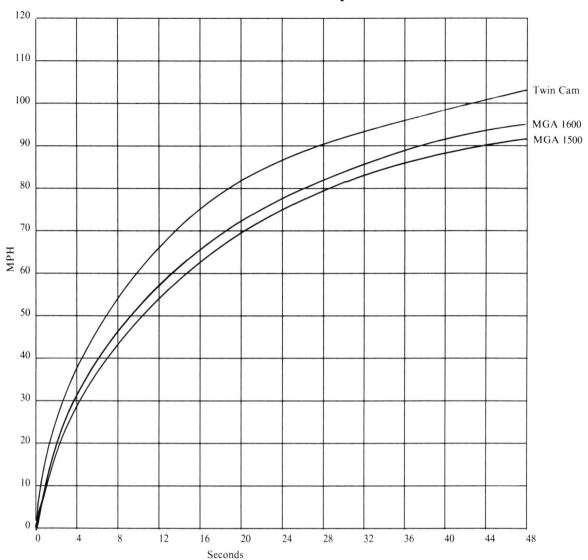

The performance of the 1600 was a significant improvement over the 1500 but a far cry from the Twin Cam.

The sliding plexiglass side curtains which were standard on the 1600 roadster were a welcome improvement, although the leading edge still had a tendency to curl under as this has!

Suspension

Changes in the engine and brakes were the most noticeable changes in the 1600; however, the engineers at Abingdon were very busy underneath the car as well. The slightly stiffer springs and valving of the front hydraulic shocks resulted in reduced dive on braking and less lean while cornering briskly. These changes made the car easier to drive fast while retaining the widely acclaimed handling characteristics of the 1500.

Body

Numerous detail body changes were incorporated in the 1600 model. The sliding side-curtains, available on the Twin Cam, were made standard on the 1600 model. Larger, flat lens parking lamps were the only changes to the front end styling while a small round turn signal lamp was added at the rear above the main tail-lamp of the 1500. These changes were in response to a US regulation requiring amber turn signals in front and seperate turn signals in back. The single wing nut used to secure the side curtains, a hold-over from the TC, was replaced by a simple round knurled knob. A third securing point for the top, in the middle of the windshield, solved the problem of the middle of the front top brace lifting at high speeds (over 90 mph). On the coupe, the spare tire location was shifted slightly and the parcel shelf trimmed back to allow greater storage room. The small parcel shelf was carpeted. The coil was moved from its former position atop the generator to a location on the right inner fender. 1600 badges were placed behind the cowl vents and below the MG crest on the trunk lid to identify this latest model from the Twin Cam and the 1500.

New offerings on the accessory list included a headlamp flasher switch, anti-roll bar, battery covers, close-ratio box power unit, and wheel discs. A considerable change in paint colors resulted in green being dropped, beige and grey added and different shades of blue and red being introduced. The interior also came in for some changes. Green and grey seats were dropped and beige added. The two-tone scheme of the 1500 coupe interior gave way to a more elegant monochromatic scheme.

The MG Car Company has adopted a philosophy through the years regarding the building of automobiles—"Satety Fast." John Thornley provides his interpretation of "Safety Fast." "I have always done my best to persuade people that if they want a motor car to go faster, the first thing they look at is its stability, the second is the ability to stop it and the third to increase its power. In that order." As much as any MG, the 1600 reflects this thinking with its improved suspension, disc brakes and increased power output.

As its production life was ending, the 1600 model was offered with an interesting option, four wheel disc brakes. On the face of it, this option looks intriguing, probably designed for the true enthusiast who is looking to wring the last ounce of performance out of his car. In actuality, this option involved building a 1600 body and drive train on a Twin Cam chassis! The Twin Cam had been phased out of production and there were these left over chassis and bits. Never one to leave such "goodies" to gather dust, MG decided to offer what was left to the public in the form of a four wheel disc brake option. Very few of the four wheel disc brake optioned 1600s were built. Perhaps the most famous were the coupes built for the 1961 and 1962 Sebring races. They made ideal competition vehicles because the 1588 cc engine was just inside the class limit and the advantages of the improved suspension and brakes were perfect for racing. By far and away the majority of the 1600 "Deluxes," as they were known, were produced in the form of 1600 Mk II Deluxes, and in deference to this fact, I will save further discussion of these interesting cars for that chapter.

In response to the changing lighting regulations, the 1600 had this redesigned front parking lamp. The upper portion was yellow for the turn signal and the lower was clear for the parking lamp.

The rear lamp came in for some changes as well. The regulations stipulated separate turn signals so a small round turn signal lamp was added atop the familiar rear lamp.

A clip was added to the top of the windscreen frame to prevent the top bow from lifting at high speed.

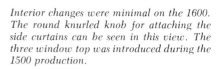

Interior changes were minimal on the 1600. The round knurled knob for attaching the side curtains can be seen in this view. The three window top was introduced during the 1500 production.

The coupe also came in for some minor improvements. By relocating the spare tire and trimming back the parcel shelf, a bit more room behind the seats was obtained for the "doggie seat."

Safety faster! The MGA 1600 poses on the soccer field behind the Abingdon plant.

Specifications:

Introduced: 31 July 1959
Production dates: May 1959—April 1961
Total Production: 31,501
Chassis numbers: G/HN 68,851—100,351
Engine numbers: 16GA
Base price:
    Roadster...$2,485—L940 7s 6d
    Coupe.....$2,706—L1,026 15s 10d
Engine:
    Displacement   1588 cc (96.9 cu. in.)
    Bore   75.4 mm (2.97 in.)

Stroke	88.9 mm (3.50 in.)
Compression	8.3:1
Main bearings	3, steel back white metal (babbit)
BHP	78 @ 5,500 rpm (79.5 @ 5,600 rpm)
Torque	87 ft/lb @ 3,800 rpm
Red line	5,800 rpm

Transmission/rear axle: Same as MGA 1500

Chassis: Same as MGA 1500, except as indicated below:

Weight...2,016 lb (curb wt)

Colors....Alamo Beige, Chariot Red, Iris Blue, Dove Grey, Old English White, and Black

Production Modifications:

The following is a listing, in numerical order, of those modifications made to the MGA 1600 during the production run. The listing is divided into two parts, chassis and gearbox modifications.

Chassis Modifications:

Chassis number 68,851 onward—Sliding sidescreens: From car number 68,851 aluminium deluxe sliding sidescreens are available as an optional extra on the MGA 1600.

Chassis number 78,106 (wire wheels) and 78,144 (disc wheels) onward—Improved Brake Pad: These improved brake pads are available in sets only. If the improved pads are fitted to earlier cars it is essential that both right and left hand brakes are equipped. The later type pads are colour coded red.

Gearbox Modifications:

During the 1600 production run three modifications to the gearbox were made to prevent automatic disengagement of third gear.

Chassis number 70,222 onward—Headlamps: From car number 70,222 Mk VIII headlamps with sealed beam units (Part no. BHA4144) were fitted to cars exported to the US.

Chassis number 72,040 onward—Headlamps: from car number 72,040, cars exported to Sweden have special headlamps with asymmetrical left dip (Part no. BMK391). These are interchangeable with earlier types in pairs only.

Engine Modifications:

Engine number 16GA6272 onward—Lucas C40/1 Dynamo: From engine number 16GA6272 a later type of dynamo with increased output, Lucas type C40/1, was introduced, complete with Lucas connectors, modified Lucas type RB106/2 control box, and a new type ignition coil bracket.

The modified control box must not be fitted with the earlier type dynamo.

Chapter 5

The MGA 1600 Mark II

The 100 mph MGA sports two-seater was first introduced in September 1955. With its engine now enlarged and stepped up in efficiency for the second time, it should more than keep pace in its latest Mark II form.[1]

The Motor

Save The Best For Last!

As 1961 drew around, MG was already planning the successor to the MGA; however, rapidly dwindling sales figures demanded something be done to bolster MG sales in the interim. BMC had plans to introduce a new 1622 cc engine in its line in late 1961 so it was natural that the new MG model would have this new engine. From a production standpoint this was a significant step forward because the 1600 cc engine had been unique to the MG line, which meant the tooling on the engine line had to be changed every time a batch of 1600 cc MG engines came along. From MG's standpoint, the engine change was a mixed blessing. It brought with it increased performance, but with the penalty of moving the car into the next higher class, 1600-2000 cc. The increase in performance was not as great as that achieved with the 1600 model, but it was a significant change and not just a facelift.

Road tester's comments reflected the now somewhat dated ride and weather protection of the Mark II, though the handling and performance still got high ratings.

> The Autocar... *In this latest MGA, which costs no more than the previous model, the engine modifications provide a little more performance, making this ample for most people's requirements but, more important, this is achieved in a more effortless manner. Basically, the MGA's traditional character, which has appealed to so many, is unchanged.[2]*
>
> Road and Track... *...the MG remains one of the most desireable sports cars on the market. It is big enough to avoid being called a toy, it is nice looking without being flashy, it steers and handles impeccably, it performs extremely well, and its reputation for durability and stamina is widely acclaimed by many thousands of satisfied owners. In our opinion, this is truly the 'universal' sports car.[3]*
>
> The Motor... *The 100 mph MGA sports two-seater was first introduced in September 1955. With its engine now enlarged and stepped up in efficiency for the second time, it should more than keep pace in its latest Mark II form with the general progress that has taken place since its inception.[4]*

Engine

The 34 cc increase in displacement from 1588 to 1622 was negligible; however, the internal changes to the new block were substantial. The cylinder head received considerable attention with improved gas flowing and higher compression. Intake and exhaust valve diameters were increased by 1/16 inch to 1.562 inches and 1.343 inches respectively while the intake and exhaust passageways were reshaped to aid air flow. The combustion chamber was reshaped and its volume increased from 38.2 to 42.5 cc. Quality of the valve steel was also improved. These changes resulted in increased combustion efficiency allowing an increase in compression ratio from 8.3:1 to 8.9:1. For markets where 100 octane fuel was not available, the old 8.3:1 ratio was available. The increase in compression ratio was achieved through the use of flat-top pistons as opposed to the dished pistons used in the 1500 and 1600 engines. The new pistons were solid skirt with four rings, three compression and one oil control ring. The top compression ring is chrome plated.

Moving down to the block itself some major changes are evident. The bore has been increased 1/32 inch to 3.0 inches while the stroke remained at

3.5 inches. The larger bore necessitated a new block casting with decreased size water passages between cylinders. To stand up to the increased torque and horsepower, the crank came in for some detail modifications. Crank web sections were increased at the expense of main bearing widths. The front and rear mains were reduced by 0.125 inches and the middle bearing by 0.0625 inches. Extensive testing was done to insure the decrease would not have an adverse effect on bearing life. Stiffer connecting rods were fitted and wrist pin diameter was increased from 0.69 to 0.75 inches. To make all these new parts spin more effectively, a new distributor, Lucas model DM2 with roller centrifugal weights, was fitted. All these improvements increased the torque by 12% over the 1600 model from 87 lb/ft @ 3,800 rpm to 97.5 lb/ft @ 4,000 rpm. Horsepower increased by 13% from 79.5 @ 5,600 rpm to 90 @ 5,500 rpm.

Incidentally, MG measured its horsepower without engine fan, but with gearbox, air cleaners and test stand exhaust system fitted. Using the American SAE system, horsepower was 95 @ 5,000 rpm. The increased horsepower and torque combined with the higher rear axle ratio combined to give a significantly improved performance while fuel consumption remained about the same for normal day-to-day driving. On open road motoring, the mileage showed some improvement as a result of the longer "legs." As shown by the chart, 0-50 time is improved by a full half second and 0-70 by a full second. Looking back over six years of development, the Mark II

1500, 1600 MkII and Twin Cam Engine Comparison

The 1600 Mk II offered a torque curve that matched that of the Twin Cam at 3000 rpm but was not as flat as that of the 1600. The horsepower curve also matched that of the Twin Cam from about 2800-3800 rpm.

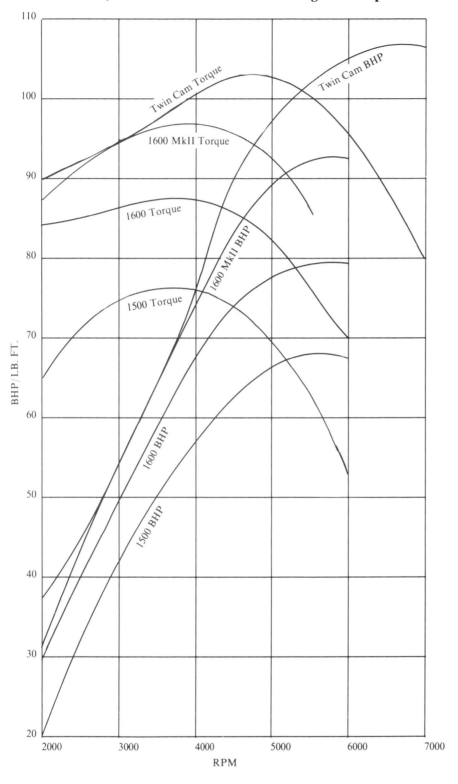

improved on the 1500's 0-60 time by 1.7 seconds and decreased the 0-80 time by 2.6 seconds.

	MGA 1500	MGA 1600	MGA 1600 Mk II
0-30	4.6	4.2	4.0
0-40	6.8	6.4	6.0
0-50	10.2	9.8	9.3
0-60	14.5	13.3	12.8

Acceleration Curve Comparison

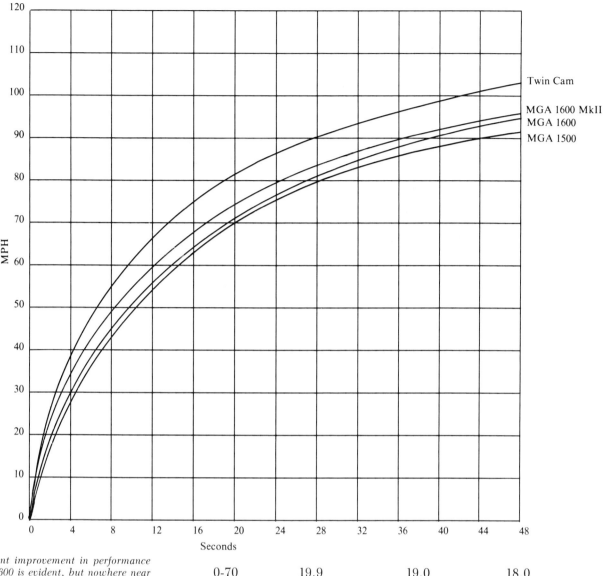

Seconds

A significant improvement in performance over the 1600 is evident, but nowhere near that offered by the Twin Cam despite similar engine output in the mid-range.

0-70	19.9	19.0	18.0
0-80	28.0	26.5	25.4
0-90	42.5	36.4	36.0
1/4 mile	19.6	19.0	18.7
max. speed	98.1	103.0	105
fuel economy	30 mpg	28 mpg	28 mpg

The new engine exhibited a harsher, more mechanical sound than its predecessors, probably a reflection of the higher compression ratio. Above 5,000 rpm the engine was a bit rough. Following in the footsteps of its forerunners, the Mark II was quick to start and warm up. It showed excellent flexibility even with the taller rear gearing, pulling smoothly from 20 mph in top gear. This offers quite a contrast with today's temperamental machines! Another less desirable characteristic carried forward was an annoying tendency to run-on after being switched off.

Gearbox And Rear Axle

Moving aft a bit, the clutch received a better balancing and the flywheel was lightened by eight pounds. To handle the increased torque, the external webbing of the gearbox case was increased in depth while the internals were unchanged. With the taller rear axle ratio of 4.1:1, the overall ratios were 14.92, 9.08, 5.63 and 4.10:1. Speeds through the gears at 6,000 rpm were:

First	29	mph
Second	48	mph
Third	79	mph
Fourth	107.4	mph

As a result of the new engine and rear axle, the cruising speed, as determined by one automotive magazine, increased from an actual 77 mph in the 1600 to 84 mph in the 1600 Mk II.

The distinctive Mk II grill is a financially painful item to replace.

The rear lamp came in for another government regulated change. This time the Mini provided a suitable substitute. Many felt this tail lamp treatment was more esthetically pleasing than the previous versions.

Body

Telling a Mark II from a 1600 MGA is relatively easy due to the revised grill and lighting. The former was a styling change, the latter was dictated by changing regulations. MG had no styling department, so the most likely explanation for the revised grill was a desire to make the model stand out among all the other MGAs on the road. The design was probably conceived by the MG "styling club" consisting of John Thornley, George Harriman, etc. Tail lamp changes were dictated by revised lighting regulations from various countries. The Mini had a tail lamp which complied with the regulations and would also fit the MGA, so it was incorporated into the MGA 1600 Mark II. The scuttle (the area between the windscreen and dash) was covered in a matt waterproof plastic material called Nuvon which was helpful in reducing reflection in the windshield at night. The same covering was also applied to the dash. Improving the safety aspect, anchors were fit-

The 1600 Mk II interior incorporated a vinyl covered scuttle to reduce glare. The dash on the roadster was also covered as on earlier coupes and the Twin Cam roadster.

ted for attachment of seat belts, though seat belts were not offered as an option. The dimmer switch was relocated in a somewhat more convenient position, though it still drew criticism from testers. Completing the list of changes, "1600 Mk II" badges were affixed beside the cowl vents and on the trunk lid.

During its production run, two important changes were incorporated. Beginning with chassis number 102,737, engine oil coolers were fitted as standard equipment to models destined for export. From chassis number 103,192 onward Dunlop "Gold Seal" nylon tires were installed on all cars except those for West Germany.

In what has to be the most extensive (and expensive) accessory ever offered on an MGA, the four wheel disc brake option was made available on the Mark II, as it was previously on the 1600. This option involved no less than 190 separate part changes from the standard Mark II. When boiled down to its essentials it involved building a Mark II on a Twin Cam chassis. The chassis were left over from the Twin Cam production which had been cut short and were complete in every regard to Twin Cam specification right down to the different brake and clutch pedals! About the only thing beside the engine that is missing are the access holes in the front cross member and access panels in the inner fenders. This option has been variously refered to as the "Deluxe" model, "1600 Mk IIb," or "Competition" model. The factory recognizes no special model designation for this version of the MGA.

Rob MacKenzie has had the pleasure of owning both a 1600 and a 1600 Mk II Deluxe. Here he is shown giving his Mk II Deluxe a rest after one of his many long distance treks to attend club gatherings. Rob lives in London, Ontario, Canada.

"Deluxe," "1600 Mk IIb," "Competition," or whatever, the 1600 Mark II with the disc brake option represents for some the MGA design taken to its highest level of refinement, offering superb braking, sure-footed handling, impressive performance and reliable motoring. A combination of the best from the Twin Cam and Mark II. The cost of the four wheel disc brake option was just under $500, and offered excellent value for the would be club racer. The close-ratio gearbox, 4.55 rear axle, anti-sway bar, and competition seats were not included with the "Deluxe" option; however, they were often ordered with the four wheel disc brake option. *Sports Car Graphic* did a test of a 1600 Mk II equipped with the four wheel disc brake option, close-ratio box and 4.55 rear axle in their May 1962 issue. They provide this interpretation.

The distinctive combination of a Mk II grill and knock off disc wheels announces this is a Mk II Deluxe.

May 16, 1962 and the 100,000th MGA rolls off the assembly line, six years to the day after a 1500 model marked the 100,000th MG to leave the factory.

What the MG people have here, then, is a car that a novice can use in stock form for driver's schools and practice sessions in complete safety, and still have a car that is perfectly suitable for the street. For the man with a competition license, it is a car on which all the heavy conversion work has already been done, leaving only super-tuning or allowable engine modifications to be done. In short, the MG Competition is a race basis rather than a race car per se. While more expensive than the standard version, it provides a means by which the purchaser can end up with a competitive car at considerably less cost then that of converting the standard MG-A and bringing it up to a similar state of preparation. For those interested in Class F Production competition, this latest offering from Abingdon is well worth the price of admission.[5]

The MGA's creator, Syd Enever, stands proudly next to the 100,000th MGA. The car was painted a special gold color and an insignia proclaiming "100,000" was attached below the "1600 Mk II" badge.

The exact number of 1600 and 1600 Mk II models equipped with the four wheel disc brake option will forever remain a mystery, as the production records do not permit identification of this version. An educated guess would be 400-500 cars, based on the relative scarcity of cars and the total production of 2,111 Twin Cams combined with a probable order for 2,500 Twin Cam chassis parts.

And so we come to the end of the line, but not before the 100,000th MGA was completed on 16 May 1962. Symbolically, the car was an export roadster model painted gold, with gold painted wire wheels, white wall tires and a cream interior. At the time of its replacement by the MGB, 101,081 MGAs had been shipped from the factory to the far corners of the world. Some left the factory in crates, "knocked down" as they called them, for assembly at their overseas destinations such as Australia and South Africa.

Reflecting the pride built into every MG, each MGA was road tested prior to final inspection. Three courses were available. A normal course for testing production models the first time. A longer course for rechecking models which had been sent back for a fix or to determine suspected production problems. The third course was used for testing and running in competition models.

MGAs left the factory and travelled to their new owners several different ways. These are being loaded onto rail cars.

Stacked six high, these MGAs are being prepared for shipment to North America. Tops were removed for compactness and headlamps were removed to prevent breakage..

A few models were dispatched as "knocked down" cars for assembly overseas in such countries as South Africa and Australia. This method provided a tax break for consumers and jobs abroad for those performing the final assembly.

Others were partly stripped down and stacked one atop another to be shipped overseas to North American customers who gobbled up 82% of all MGAs produced. The MGA had the largest production run of any sports car up to the time of its demise. Syd Enever's brainchild, bred on the track at Le Mans and the Salt Flats at Bonneville, had done everything it was designed to do, and more. The MG Car Company, Ltd. had grown from a modest manufacturer of sports cars destined for a small group of domestic customers to a vigorous, internationally successful company whose product enjoyed a dedicated world-wide clientele. The timing of the MGA had been fortunate, coinciding with the car boom of the late fifties and early sixties, during which time the British car industry proudly rose to the top of the sports car market, helped to a large degree by the popularity of the MGA.

Some cars were driven to their final destination. Whatever the means of shipment, they all had to undergo a final inspection, as these are, prior to passing out the gate.

Making its own contribution to MG history, the 100,000th MGA poses text to Old Number One.

Having sent 101,081 MGAs out into the world to provide pleasant memories for their owners, production of the MGA drew to a close in June 1962. The MGA had launched MG into the world market in a big way and firmly established the marque as the most popular sports car ever.

Having gone through all the MGA models, which is the best? The delightfully simple 1500 roadster? The elegant coupe? Perhaps the dazzling performance of the Twin Cam? How about a 1600 Mk II with the disc brake option? The choice is up to you, but the important thing is you *do* have the choice. Thanks MG!

Specifications:

Introduced:
Production dates: April 1961—June 1962
Total production: 8,719
Chassis numbers: G/IIN2 100,352 – 109,070
Engine numbers: 16GC
Price:
      Roadster—$2,485—L940 7s 6d
      Coupe—$2,706—L1,026 15s 10d
Engine:

Displacement	1622 cc (99.5 cu in.)
Bore	76.2 mm (3.0 in.)
Stroke	89 mm (3.5 in.)
Compression	8.9:1
Main bearings	3, steel backed white metal
BHP	90 @ 5,500 rpm
Torque	97 lb ft @ 4,000 rpm

Transmission/rear axle: Same as MGA 1500 except as indicated below.
      Overall gear ratios:

4th	4.1:1
3rd	5.633:1
2nd	9.077:1
1st	14.924:1
Reverse	19.516:1

      Rear axle ratio: 4.1:1
      MPH per 1,000 rpm in top gear: 18.3
Chassis: Same as MGA 1500 except as noted below:
      Colors:
            Exterior: Chariot Red, Iris Blue, Alamo Beige, Dove Grey, Old
                English White, Black
            Interior: Red, Beige, Black

Production Modifications:

The following is a listing, in numerical order, of those modifications made to the MGA 1600 Mk II during the production run. The listing is divided into two parts, chassis and engine modifications.

Chassis Modifications:

Chassis number 100,352 onward—Seat belts: The body of the car incorporates anchorage points to facilitate the fitting of BMC seat belts (Part no. AHH6122) to the driver's seat and to the passenger's seat. The fitting of the belts to the car should be carried out by an Authorized MG Distributor or Dealer.

    The anchorage points are located one on each frame side-member, one on each side of the tunnel, and one each under the left-hand and right-hand sides, respectively, of the tonneau panel (tourer) and rear wheel arch (coupe). The seat belt is made up of a long and a short belt, each of which is adjustable. When in use the two belts are connected by a quick-release buckle.

    NOTE: For cars made prior to chassis number 100,352, i.e. MGA 1500 and Twin Cam, a seat belt kit is available complete with anchorage fittings under Part no. AHH6141 (R.H.) and AHH6193 (L.H.) for roadster cars and Part no. AHH6175 (R.H.) and AHH6194 (L.H.) for Coupe cars. The description and fitting instructions are as detailed above, with the exception of the upper end of the long belt, which is fitted to the rear wheel arch instead of the tonneau panel on Coupe cars only.

Chassis numbers 102,589 (disc wheels) and 102,929 (wire wheels) onward—Disc Brake Dust Covers: Disc brake covers which reduce inner pad wear have been fitted. The covers may be fitted in sets to earlier cars.

Chassis number 102,737 onward—Oil cooler kits: Oil cooler kits are fitted as standard equipment to all export cars from car number 102,737 and are available as an optional extra for Home Trade cars. All bodies are now drilled to accept the oil cooler and its associated equipment.

The kits are available under Part no. 8G2282 for standard cars and Part no. 8G2325 for cars fitted with disc brakes all around.

The oil capacity of the cooler is approximately 3/4 pint (0.42 litre) and this quantity must be added to the sump when the cooler is fitted.

Chassis number 103,192 onward—Gold Seal nylon and Road Speed tires: Gold Seal nylon tires for Home and Export (except West Germany) were introduced at Chassis number 103,192. Gold Seal (white wall) and Road Speed (white wall) tires are available as optional extras. Standard Road Speed nylon tires are fitted to cars exported to West Germany.

The tire pressure recommendations for these tires are as follows:

Dunlop Gold Seal nylon tires
> For all normal use, including motorways, etc., up to 100 mph. (161 kph):

Front	21 lb/sq in. (1.47 kh/cm²)
Rear	24 lb/sq in. (1.68 kh/cm²)

> Where maximum or near-maximum performance is required:

Front	24 lb/sq in. (1.68 kg/cm²)
Rear	27 lb/sq in. (1.9 kg/cm²)

Dunlop Road Speed RS 5 tires
> When the car is fitted with Dunlop Road Speed RS 5 tires as an optional extra (recommended when the car is used predominantly at very high speeds):
> Normal use:

Front	17 lb/sq in. (1.1 kg/cm²)
Rear	20 lb/sq in. (1.4 kg/cm²)

> When maximum or near-maximum speeds are sustained for lengthy periods or for competition use:

Front	24 lb/sq in. (1.68 kg/cm²)
Rear	27 lb/sq in. (1.9 kg/cm²)

Chassis numbers 103,261 (disc wheels) and 103,834 (wire wheels) onward—Modified caliper units: A modified disc brake caliper dust seal and retainer was introduced.

The new seal is 'U'-shaped in cross-section and is retained in the counterbore of the caliper by a retainer having an 'L'-shaped cross-section. The seal is carried within the retainer flange and abuts the face of the caliper counterbore.

Chassis number 103,857 onward—Commencing at Chassis number 103,857, Mk X sealed-beam light units are fitted to all cars exported to the USA.

Engine Modifications:

Engine numbers 16GC/U/H101 and 16GC/U/L101 onward—A modfied Type DM2 distributor incorporating a rolling weight centrifugal advance mechanism superceding the standard toggle type was introduced.

The rolling weight mechanism consists of a shaft and action plate with two action cams and two spring pillars riveted to the plate. Two rolling weights, each located by a boss on the under side of the cam foot, roll around the action plate cams and thus alter the position of the contact breaker cam relative to the distributor driving shaft when the distributor is rotating within the speed limits of centrifugal operation.

The rate of advance is controlled by springs anchored between the pillars on the action plate and two pillars on the cam foot, which strikes one of the spring pillars when maximum advance has been reached.

The modified distributor is interchangeable with the previous model.

Chapter 6

Competition

The use of the cars in racing has the advantage that the calendar is superimposed on you and you have to get things done by a certain date.

John Thornley

Safety Fastest!

The MGA had a history richly steeped in competition. What is more remarkable is the great variety of competitions in which the MGA competed successfully. Racing around the grueling tracks of Le Mans and Sebring, pounding along exhausting rally routes in Europe and screaming across the blistering salts at Bonneville, the MGA left its legacy in record books in nearly every corner of the globe. These successes did much to further the reputation of MG and boost MGA sales to all time record levels. Many have asked the question, "Why go racing anyway?" For MG, racing was far too expensive an endeavor to indulge in without the promise of tangible benefits. One of the benefits which frequently springs to mind is to prove components for production use. This was a minor consideration for MG as explained by John Thornley, "In terms of straight forward proving of the vehicle, the chassis, the engine, what you will, except possibly body shape, you can do the whole thing so much better under controlled test conditions than you can in a race." To put it quite bluntly, MG used competition to sell cars. MG's philosophy on promoting competition efforts was to compete to prove the car first, and then build on that image rather than ballyhoo a competition effort prior to the event. A conservative approach which could save a lot of red faces the day after the night before.

MG had been out of factory sponsored racing since 1935, when the reorganization of the company coupled with economic pressures forced their withdrawal from competition. Shortly after another reorganization, the creation of BMC, and in the euphoria which followed World War II, MG was back in racing once again. In January, 1954, Sir Leonard Lord announced that BMC would begin a factory sponsored competition program later that year. On 1 December, 1954, the Competitions Department, with Marcus Chambers as its head, was organized with its offices appropriately housed at the MG works.

The MGA, with its rugged chassis, was well suited to endurance races, but its cramped cockpit and cantankerous twin cam engine made it a poor choice for rallying. The sophisticated twin cam unit could be put to good use on the salt in flat out runs, measured in seconds rather than hours, where sheer power was more important than reliability. For these reasons, and in

the interest of simplicity, this chapter will focus on three major competition thrusts of the MGA; the Bonneville Salt Flats, Le Mans, and Sebring.

The Salts

When speaking of the Bonneville Salt Flats and MG, one must mention George Eyston, for he was instrumental in getting the two together. George Eyston had a long association with MG record breaking, beginning with the first MG record breaker, EX 120 in 1931 and ending with the last MG record breaker, EX 181 in 1959. George Eyston, or the Captain as he was known, was appointed a director with Castrol Oil Company in 1945 and subsequently was given a position in the U.S. From his vantage point in the states and his past association with MG record breakers, the Captain was in a natural position to organize MG attempts at Bonneville. His frequent trips to the nearby town of Wendover, Utah, made him a familiar figure in this small town.

Competing in a car which must travel nearly 6,000 miles to get to the start point presents some onerous organizational problems. Eyston's attention to detail and excellent organization abilities were a major part of the success of the MG efforts at Bonneville.

The Salts—EX 179

Eyston was somewhat miffed at MG for selling EX 135 in 1935 and had little to do with them until 1953. Eighteen years had lapsed since the sale of EX 135. MG sales in the U.S. were dwindling, and with an enthusiast like John Thornley at the helm of MG, the Captain decided to let by-gones be by-gones and approach MG with an idea he had. With Eyston's background in record breaking and the importance of the post war market in the states, it was natural that he would propose that MG come to America, to the Bonneville Salt Flats, to engage in a record assault in order to give MG sales a much needed boost. In the ensuing conversation with John Thornley it was agreed that such a record attempt would be a good idea. The brass at BMC agreed; however, they wanted the record car to resemble a production model as much as possible. EX 175 (HMO 6), which had been turned down for production earlier in the year, was brought out and fitted with an under-tray, spats, passenger tonneau, and perspex bubble windscreen. The end result closely resembled the production MGA which was yet to come; however, it was not aerodynamically efficient enough to get the job done. At this point it was determined that a streamliner along the lines of EX 135 would be needed to do the job rather than a cleaned up production model. EX 135 would have been a logical choice; however, when EX 135's owner, Goldie Gardner, sold the car back to MG in 1952, he stipulated that the car was not to be used for racing. Additionally, EX 135 was based on older production components, not really in keeping with the spirit of the project.

At this point, it was clear that a new record car would be constructed using as many production parts as possible. The shape of EX 135 was known to be quite good and so it was used as a basis to design the new record breaker, designated EX 179. The body was shortened approximately one foot, and provision was made for two passengers, in keeping with the original mandate from BMC; otherwise, EX 179 was "very much a Dutch copy of EX 135." The body was constructed by Midland Sheet Metal at Nuneaton, using 18 gauge sheet aluminum. The body was supported by 5/8 inch diameter 16 gauge tubes to which the body panels were attached using 7% magnesium alloy countersunk rivets. The complete upper body was removable. The car was completely undertrayed using 14 gauge aluminum panels. Midland Sheet Metal was later to do the EX 181, EX 186 and MGA coupe tops for MG.

Strong and lightweight, this structure formed the skeleton to which the body panels of EX 179 were attached.

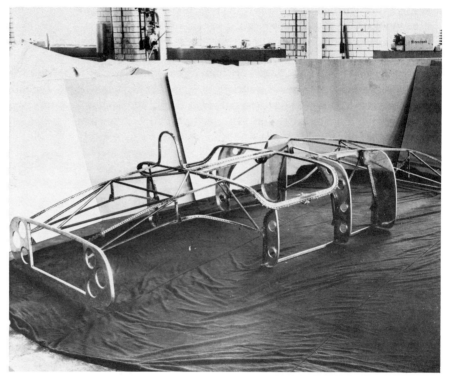

The body design was carefully thought out. At the front there were three air inlets, the center inlet provided cool air for the combined engine water and oil radiators. The left inlet provided air for the driver's compartment which could be adjusted by means of a cable control. The right inlet provided cool air for the carburetor intakes. The air outlet for the radiators was located just forward of the engine compartment, which was sealed off from the radiators. The engine compartment was likewise sealed off from the passenger compartment. Exhaust pipes exited through the engine cover to minimize heat build-up in the engine compartment. With the undertray, air flow in the engine compartment was minimal and cooling was a big consideration in view of the long distance records and the summer heat of Bonneville. A perspex bubble was closely fitted around the driver's head and air outlets were incorporated into the head fairing to assist in drawing air through the driver's compartment. The driver's windscreen and head fairing were designed to be mounted on either side of the passenger compartment in anticipation of the twin cam engine being used on later attempts. Interestingly, this British car was left hand drive in deference to the right hand exhaust of the XPAG engine. The body was attached to the chassis at 14 points with quick release fasteners for easy removal to aid accessibility for

repairs. Wind tunnel tests showed the new body design was a significant improvement over the EX 135 shape.

This efficient body was attached to the spare EX 175 chassis which had been lying about the Experimental Shop. To offset the weight of the rather heavy chassis, chassis members were heavily drilled. The center section was braced top and bottom to compensate for the weight of the large 30 gallon fuel tank mounted where the passenger seat would have been. The tank was filled via two quick release filler caps and emptied using two SU fuel pumps mounted behind the dash. A radiator header tank was mounted behind the dash on the left side where it would be above the water level in the cylinder head. This placement was necessitated by the low placement of the water radiator at the front of the car.

The resemblance between the EX 179's frame and that of the production MGA is apparent here. The EX 179 wheelbase was one inch longer and the chassis was drilled for lightness and reinforced at key points. Notice the oversize fuel tank next to the driver and the oil and water reservoirs on the firewall. These were needed for the long distance records attempted.

A rather ingenious method was used to maintain the oil level in the engine sump. A 2-1/2 gallon tank was mounted next to the water header tank behind the dash on the right hand side. This tank was connected to the sump where an arrangement similar to a toilet flushing mechanism was employed to keep the oil level topped up. The engine oil and water radiators were combined in a single phosphor-bronze aircraft type radiator mounted on a tubular extension of the frame. This extension would also allow sufficient room for a supercharger to be mounted forward of the engine. Independent front suspension was similar to that used in the TD/TF and later the MGA, with slightly stiffer springs and Andrex shock absorbers fitted in addition to the Armstrong hydraulic units. The friction type Andrex units imparted a better feel of the road in the shallow turns of the ten mile circle where suspension travel was not sufficient to fully engage the Armstrong units. This arrangement had already been used on the TD Mk II. EX 179 was the first record breaker from MG to employ independent front suspension. The rear suspension also employed the Andrex units in addition to the Armstrong shocks. Rear springs were also wrapped for additional stiffness. Steering was via a TD/TF/MGA rack and pinion design employing a steering wheel with a peculiar shape, having the bottom portion flattened. This was done to allow the driver optimum leg room due to the lowered position of the steering wheel. Turns were to be very shallow so this would not prove to be a handicap in maneuvering. The steering wheel design was very similar to that employed on the MGA. The driver's seat was also very similar to that later seen on the production MGA, the chief difference being that the seat-back angle was greater to lower the driver's head, thus allowing a lower silhouette. Early photographs of the car show four wheel drum brakes were fitted; however, it appears likely that the front brakes were later removed in an effort to reduce unsprung weight at the front. Lockheed drum brakes similar to those on the TF were used on the rear. TF wheels were employed and fitted with Dunlop racing tires. The tread on the tires was buffed down to reduce centrifugal forces tearing the tread off at high speed. Tread wear was no problem on the salt as the surface remained cool and was not abrasive to the rubber. Instruments included a tachometer driven from the front of the camshaft, oil temperature gauge, water temperature gauge, oil pressure gauge, battery master switch, starter button, mixture control and ignition switch. A super light weight single 12 volt aircraft battery was mounted behind the driver's seat. Total all up weight with 30 gallons of fuel and driver was 2,198 pounds, about the same as the production MGA. Weight was distributed 55% front and 45% rear. Overall dimensions were:

EX 179 dimensions

Length	15 feet 8-7/8 in.
Width	5 feet 3-1/2 in.
Height (w/o canopy)	32-5/16 in.
Height (w/ canopy)	40-5/8 in.
Wheelbase	95 in.
Front track	48 in.
Rear track	48-1/2 in.
Frontal area	11.8 sq ft

Instruments included, from left to right, water temperature, 8,000 rpm tachometer, oil temperature and oil pressure. Notice the fuel shutoff valves at the end of the instrument panel and the sharply angled shift lever.

The engine for EX 179 was based on the TF 1500 XPEG engine. The XPEG engine was derived from the 1250 XPAG engine which powered the TC, TD, and early TF. This engine had shown some impressive power outputs in the hands of private owners; and Goldie Gardner's exploits with the XPAG engine in EX 135 in 1951 and 1952 led the way for this production engine to be used in the latest record breaker. The XPAG engine was sometimes enlarged to 1466 cc by the rather unusual technique of boring out the cylinders into the water passages and then sleeving the bores down to 72 mm. Demands for higher power output from the Americans and improved casting techniques prompted the birth of the XPEG engine which had the 72 mm bores without resorting to sleeving. This new 1466 cc engine was to have been introduced at the time of the record attempt; however, slow sales of the 1250 cc engined TF made it necessary to delay the introduction of the 1500 cc TF, thereby losing some of the publicity impact of the record attempt.

There were two XPEG engines built for the record attempt, a long distance engine and a sprint engine. A backup engine, lying somewhere between the two in power output, was also built. This spare engine was "accidentally" left behind and fell into the hands of Ken Miles who used the engine in his successful MG special known as the "Shingle."

The long distance engine produced 81 bhp @ 5,500 rpm which is a rather healthy jump up from the 57 bhp @ 5,500 rpm from the standard engine. Displacement was 1466 cc, with a bore of 72 mm and a stroke of 90 mm. Compression ratio was raised to 10.7:1 with the help of light alloy, competition, solid skirt pistons. Torque was a substantial 90.2 lb. ft. @ 3,500 rpm. It was originally thought supercharging would be necessary; however, the engines responded so well to tuning that the idea was given up even on the sprint engine.

The long distance engine used dual 1-3/4 inch SU carburetors. Water jackets were eliminated between the adjacent bores of paired cylinders. For strength, the connecting rods were beefed up. A somewhat higher output camshaft was used to regulate the flow of premium grade fuel which had methanol added for its cooling effect. The cylinder head was carefully modified to increase the gas flow and lapped to the block to eliminate the head gasket in the interest of reliability. The aluminum sump carried six quarts of oil. To provide the lowest possible hood line, the valve cover was reversed to place the oil filler cap at the rear, but this was later changed again with the filler cap mounted on its own filler pipe behind the valve cover.

The sprint engine produced 97.5 horsepower at 6,500 rpm and was to be used on the shorter record attempts where performance was favored over endurance. Domed pistons were employed to raise the compression ratio still further to 11.8:1. Carburetion was via two enormous 2-3/16 inch SUs and the camshaft had a radical specification previously designed for use in Gardner's EX 135. Modifications previously mentioned for the long distance engine were also employed. Although the engine had no fan, a fan belt was used to drive the generator and water pump. In the event of failure, a spare fan belt was attached just forward of the engine.

Transmission was standard TF with Borg and Beck competition dry single plate clutch. Care was taken to reduce centrifugal forces on the clutch mechanism. Ratios were 3.5:1 in first, 2.07:1 in second, 1.385:1 in third and 1:1 in top.

The rear axle was an MG built affair using a VA nosepiece and a specially fabricated axle casing to accommodate the large 2.88:1 ring gear. Straight cut gears were used because of their ease of construction and reliability. Ratios available were 2.88:1, 3.125:1, 3.33:1, giving 26, 24 and 22.5 mph in top per 1,000 rpm respectively. The rear axle, and the other drive train components, ran in still air due to the full undertray. To assist in the cooling, a small radiator was attached to the rear of the differential casing in such a way that the axle oil would be flung from the teeth into the radiator and drain back into the axle case. The radiator was mounted horizontally to take advantage of the up and down movement of the axle which would provide the air flow through the radiator core. Prior to its dispatch, EX 179 was run on the Comparator, a device for measuring relative performance, to insure its performance was up to specification. It was. Additionally, a test session was held at the M.I.R.A. test track.

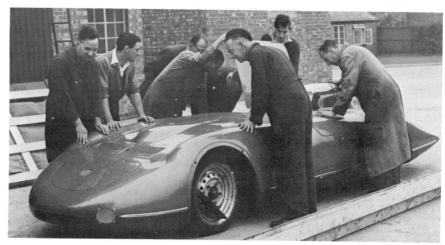

EX 179 is readied for shipment to America. Syd Enever, the car's designer, peers into the engine compartment with Alec Hounslow while other members of the Competition Department stand by to roll it into the shipping crate. Note the flange attached to the left front wheel.

The entire process from the time of George Eyston's suggestion that MG ought to consider going to the salts until the team's arrival at Bonneville took place in a little less than one year. MG's trip to the Bonneville Salt Flats and the logistics involved in such a move are certainly imposing. Fortunately, both MG and the Captain were old hands at record breaking, and Eyston's location in the States undoubtedly helped. EX 179, complete with spare engines, parts, etc. was crated in a wooden shipping container built by Morris Industry Export and shipped across the Atlantic. Upon arriving in America, EX 179 was loaded onto a railroad flat car for the overland journey to Wendover, Utah, which was seven miles west of the salts and home for the MG crew during the speed record attempts. As the mechanics, timekeepers, and crewmen arrived, one person was strangely missing. Syd Enever, who was largely responsible for the design of EX 179, was not with the team. While EX 179 was on its way to the flats, BMC had given the belated go ahead on the MGA project, and Syd was staying behind to make it a production reality. When EX 179 arrived at Wendover, it had to be off-loaded by hand and put onto a transporter which took it to a make-shift work area beside the Western Cafe. Whenever EX 179 needed to be taken to the salt flats, there was only one way to get it onto the transporter, by hand.

The team arrived about ten days prior to the record attempt and used the intervening period to get the car and drivers sorted out. Practice was held in the early morning hours in the cool of the day, and again in the heat of the day. These runs were used to get fuel consumption figures, oil and water temperatures and establish other temperature sensitive variables. The course was laid out in a ten mile circle, about three miles in diameter. A pit area was built at the start-finish line and three posts were set up around the track to signal the pits if something went wrong. The curvature of the earth meant EX 179 was out of sight from the pits during most of its run. The US Air Force at nearby Wendover Air Base pitched in with volunteers to man the posts. The drivers were given signals only at the pit area. The car was not equipped with a speedometer, so the drivers were told to drive at a certain rpm. They would drive three hour shifts after which the fuel tank would be topped up, the car checked, drivers changed and sent back out. The driving chores were much less strenuous than at Le Mans, aside from the incessant heat beating down through the perspex bubble. The biggest problem was keeping track of where you were on the circuit! There were no landmarks to guide by, just the black oil stripe in the salt.

At last the preparations were complete and the drivers, George Eyston and Ken Miles, were ready to begin their driving chores. The team felt confident of their chances and began the run on 17 August, 1954, at first light, around 5 am. The car ran like a clock, consistently lapping at around 125 mph for the entire twelve hours. When EX 179 was at last given a well deserved rest, no fewer than seven International and 28 American Class F records, including 12 hours at 120.74 mph, had fallen. The previous records for 1,000 kilometers and beyond had been nearly doubled. When George Eyston stepped out of the cockpit of EX 179 after the 12 hour run, it marked the end of his great career of record breaking with MG, spanning 23 years. George Eyston was 57, and it was fitting that he should end his career smashing international and American records driving an MG which he had inspired. Two days later, on the 20th, Ken Miles took EX 179 out with the sprint engine and a different rear axle ratio, and made an attempt on the flying 10 mile records. The runs netted MG the international and American flying 10 mile records with an amazing speed of 153.69 mph.

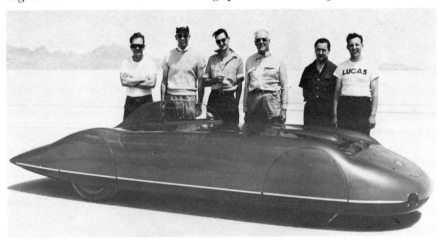

Beaming with the success of their efforts, the MG crew poses with the record breaking EX 179 after the 1954 record runs. From right to left, Henry Stone, Alec Hounslow, G.E.T. Eyston and Ken Miles.

This may have been the last record attempt as a driver for the Captain, but he would be back again at the salt with EX 179 two years later as team manager.

The following year the 12 hour record was broken by an Osca (in October 1955) with a speed of 132.1 mph. The challenge had been laid and MG would respond. This time they had a twin overhead cam engine up their sleeve. Once again, EX 179 was readied for an assault on the Class F records. The basic body shape was already proven, the only changes necessary were to switch the driver's positon to the right side as the engine exhaust exited on the left side. The chassis was virtually unchanged except for slightly stiffer front springs and the fitting of wire wheels in place of the TF disc wheels. Once again two engines were prepared. The long distance engine was a surprisingly stock prototype twin cam unit. Displacement was 1489 cc and compression ratio 9.3:1, which produced around 100 bhp @ 5,300 rpm. The sprint engine produced a healthy 120 bhp. It was decided to first go after the long distance records from 50 km up to twelve hours, which were held by the Osca between 143 and 132. A final attempt would be made on the 10 mile record with the sprint engine. The 200 mile record was judged too high to be attempted within the long distance records, and so it would be attempted separately with the long distance engine.

Once again EX 179 was crated up and shipped to Wendover. The same arrangements regarding the 10 mile track, pit area, signaling posts, etc. were made as in 1954. Preparations and practice were along the same lines as 1954, and all was ready on the fateful day. EX 179 started out running well, but at nearly the half-way mark, the right rear wheel bearing seized

The Twin Cam engine in the chassis. Wire wheels were used on this car in lieu of the previous disc wheels. The mechanic is holding an electrical cable in his right hand used for starting the engine.

after 5-1/4 hours. The reason was lubricant starvation due to the centrifugal force exerted around the 10 mile circle. The problem was soon fixed and the car began its run again at dawn on Wednesday the 15th of August, 1956. Lapping consistently, EX 179 took every record from 250 miles to 12 hours, exceeding its previous run in 1954 by over 20 mph in establishing a new record of 141.86 mph for the 12 hours. The run presented little difficulty, except for one portion on the back side where the salt had become a little mushy and tended to make the back end twitch a bit.

The next target was the 200 mile record which stood at 143.5 mph. The tire people from Dunlop were consulted on the effect of such a high sustained speed on the tires. After some thought the verdict was delivered; the tires would last 200 miles at the planned speed, but no further. With these thoughts echoing in their ears, the crew set out after the 200 mile record on Friday, 17 August. As the speed of the car asserted itself at 50 km, record after record fell up to the 200 mile mark. The car was allowed to continue in hope of breaking more records, but the Dunlop man had the last say, and the tires threw a tread shortly after the 200 mile mark had passed. It was at this point that the posts spaced along the course on the back side came in handy, fixing the position of the car so the car and driver could be quickly recovered.

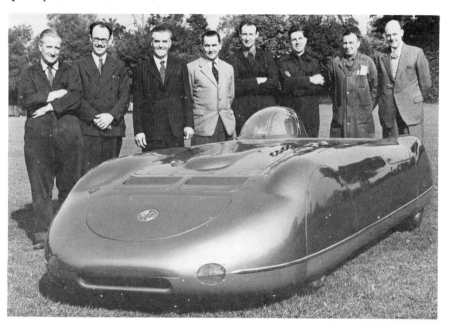

The men responsible for the design and construction of EX 179 stand behind their creation. From left to right starting second from left, Terry Mitchell—chassis and suspension design, Syd Enever—Chief Designer and Alec Hounslow—Foreman Competition Department.

The tire was replaced and the 120 bhp sprint engine installed for a flat out attempt on the 10 mile record which stood at 160.45 mph. The first run was made at an incredible 177 mph and the average for two runs established the new record at 170.15 mph.

The long journey to the salts had certainly been worthwhile for MG. They captured 16 International and 46 American Class F records from the 10 mile flying start at 170.15 mph to the 12 hours at 141.86 mph. This was the last part EX 179 would play in the history of the MGA, but not its last use in MG record taking. In 1957, EX 179 would return to the salts with a tiny 948 cc Austin engine setting new records in that class. EX 179 now resides in the Motor Museum at Donnington after a long and illustrious career.

The Salts—EX 181

Flushed with the success of EX 179 in capturing the long distance records from 10 miles to 12 hours in International Class F, MG decided on a bold new project to take the remaining records from 1 kilometer to 10 kilometers. These records were set by Goldie Gardner in EX 135 at speeds between 182 and 204 mph. The magnitude of such an attempt was enormous as explained by John Thornley, General Manager of MG at the time, "The EX 181 project was a matter of world wide significance in that it was an achievement almost the same category as the world land speed record—the fastest ever out of 1-1/2 litres." It became clear from the outset that this would require an all new record car design. EX 179, even with the twin cam engine, was only capable of 177 mph, far short of the goal of four miles per minute, 240 mph. To attain such a speed with EX 179 would have taken around 295 bhp, a figure no one felt possible from the then unsupercharged twin cam engine. Using another engine was ruled out in the interest of establishing an MG 1-1/2 litre record. And so it was that Syd Enever was put in charge of creating the fastest 1-1/2 litre car in the world, surely the greatest challenge of his career.

Ken Miles on the left and Johnny Lockett on the right were the drivers on the 1956 attempts. Under the guidance of George Eyston they piloted the record breaker to 16 International and 46 American records.

It had been the usual practice at MG to design a record breaker from an existing chassis and then design a body shape as smoothly as possible around it. EX 181 was no ordinary record breaker, and Syd Enever was given a free hand in its design. He began by designing the body shape which would be the chief factor in attaining such speeds. The flattened torpedo shape or inverted airfoil was chosen as the ideal from which to develop the body. Six different wooden models were built and tested in the nearby Armstrong-Whitworth windtunnel. The final shape closely resembled a flattened raindrop, being wide at the front and tapering toward the rear. In view of its shape, it was quickly dubbed "The Roaring Raindrop." The only substantial protrusion was the perspex windscreen bubble for the driver which incorporated a head fairing running the full length of the body. In choosing this unusual layout, Enever borrowed from Reid Railton's experience in designing land speed record cars which featured a wider track at the front and placed the driver at the front of the vehicle with the engine amidships. Railton used this concept successfully on John Cobb's 1938 Railton Special establishing a land speed record which endured from 1938-63. The design finally arrived at provided a 30% improvement in wind resistence over EX 179, aided by a 10% smaller frontal area. Taking into account rolling resistance, the new body shape would require 20% less power than EX 179 to reach a given speed.

Having established a general body shape, the next step was to fit the major components in a workable position. To increase weight on the rear driven wheels and keep the mass of the engine near the "fat" center of the raindrop, a mid-engine arrangement was chosen with the driver seated in a steeply reclining position ahead of the engine. The track would be decidedly crabbed with the front considerably wider than the rear. The design of the chassis which would tie all these components together was given to Terry

Mitchell of the MG Design Office. Terry was a great believer in tubular chassis members and so fittingly he chose two 3-1/2 inch diameter 14 gauge mild-steel tubes for the chassis rails. The tubes were fairly simple in design, having about only four bends in their length, and Terry gave little thought to the complexity of their fabrication when he sent the order off to the chassis builders. Some time passed, and the chassis tubes still hadn't arrived, so Terry went up to the chassis builders to see what the problem was. I'll let Terry tell the story.

> *The foreman said, 'We've got a bit of problem. We can't seem to find a pair within more than 3/8 of an inch.' I said, 'What, those tubes have to be within a few thousandths!' He took me out to his shop and there was a wall; piled up against it was, in those days, over £1,000 worth of tubes, about 125 or 126. Out of all those, they couldn't get a pair within tolerance. In the end, we had to pick out the two that were nearest to a pair and nearest to the drawing and when we got them back down here (Abingdon) Harold Wiggins set them up on a table and put some heat on here and there and got them within about five thousandths.*

At the front of the chassis rails was an MGA front suspension which was narrowed by the removal of 5-1/2 inches from the center section. A standard MGA rack and pinion steering gear was employed, the only difference being a light alloy case in place of the heavier steel one. Moving back along the frame, 2-1/2 inch diameter 16 gauge steel tubing was used to form the cross members. The rear axle was a De Dion type, which was Terry's favorite form of rear suspension, incorporating a spiral bevel gear arrangement in a light alloy casing. There was no differential, as only straight line runs were contemplated, and drive to both rear wheels was important in getting all the power onto the salt. Two axle ratios were provided. The 1.94:1 ratio unit which was actually used in the record runs, provided 36.2 mph per 1,000 rpm in direct, and an alternative 1.825:1 ratio provided 38.6 mph. The axle was suspended by quarter elliptic leaf springs with radius arms located below. The rear axle roll center was 14 inches, providing good resistance to rolling the vehicle. Spring travel, front and rear, was only three inches. Overall, the frame was very short utilizing a light extension in front to

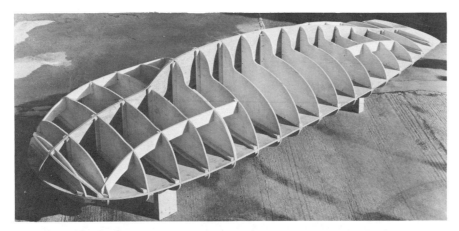

This plywood form was used to shape the panels for EX 181 which were hand-formed over it.

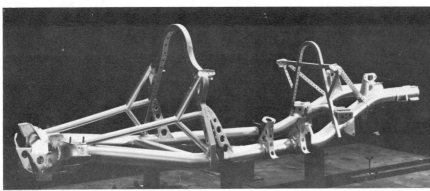

The beautifully simple frame designed by Terry Mitchell consisted of two main tubes to which the cross-members and supports were fitted. It proved to be more difficult to construct than expected!

The narrow rear axle employed a single center-mounted disc brake and two lever action shock absorbers. The single rear disc brake was to cause some anxious moments. Because of its marginal efficiency it was not to be used at speeds above 100 mph.

mount the brake, clutch, and throttle pedals while the tail was a frameless stressed-skin affair. Front and rear bulkheads were built from square section tubing, liberally drilled for lightness. These bulkheads were amply braced to the frame rails and to each other by an ingenious method whereby the brace between them could be unbolted for engine removal.

Turning now to the engine, we find the twin overhead cam design first seen in the Dundrod Tourist Trophy race and later in the 1956 EX 179 runs at Bonneville. The most noticable external difference is the huge Shorrock supercharger which is nearly as large as the twin cam engine. Initial calculations indicated a power output of 240 bhp would be necessary to achieve a speed of 240 mph. Engine designer Jimmy Thompson of Morris Engines Branch wisely decided the only way to go was with a large displacement supercharger to boost the horsepower up to the desired level from the 110

EX 179 and EX 181 Drag Comparison

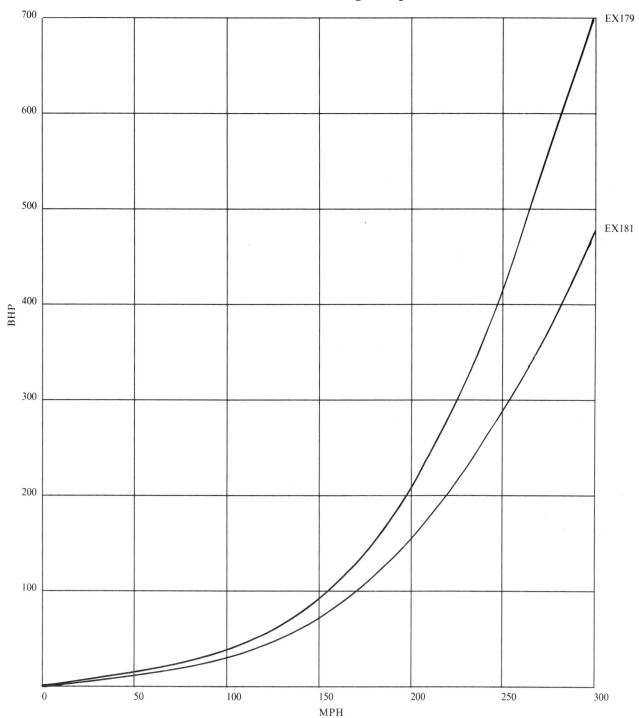

The target speed of 250 mph would have required around 400 bhp, more than was thought possible from the 1500 c.c. Twin Cam engine, if the EX 179 vehicle were used. EX 181 was the resultant answer to reduce drag.

bhp obtained from the stock twin cam unit. The supercharger had been designed by Chris Shorrock for a commercial diesel engine, providing 15 psi boost for the 10 litre engine at 4,500 rpm. It was calculated this would produce 30 psi into a 1-1/2 litre engine at 7,000 rmp. Apparently this was pretty good figuring, because the actual boost was 32 psi at 7,000 rpm. The supercharger went together straight from the drawing board and performed faultlessly without modification. Drawing five litres of air each revolution through two 2-3/16 inch SU carburetors, the supercharger rammed 61 gallons of methanol laced fuel into the engine every hour for a very un-MG like four mpg! The supercharger was driven by a set of spur gears from the front of the crankshaft. These gears could be changed to provide a 0.9, 1.0, or 1.1:1 ratio to vary the boost. The extra boost pressure would impose

The end of the quarter elliptic rear spring can be seen in this view. Notice the enclosed wheel box with cut-outs to allow for suspension travel.

"The" Twin Cam engine! With a power output around 300 bhp called for, a supercharger was a must. The enormous, beautifully finned blower attached to the EX 181 engine performed admirably. The drive for a proposed fuel injection pump is visible at the rear of the intake cam cover.

The left hand side of the EX 181 engine reveals the additional webbing added to the block to help contain all those horses. The Riley gearbox is clearly shown at the right. A magneto-type ignition provided the hot spark needed at high speed. Notice the shallow sump.

EX 181 Horsepower and Torque Curves

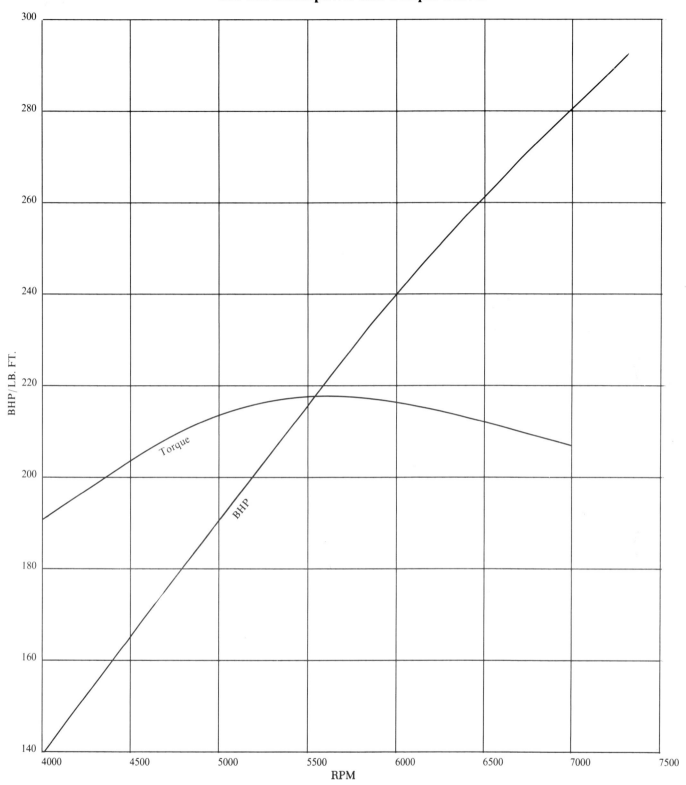

The EX 181 engine delivered a surprising flat torque curve while the supercharger helped the horsepower rise proportionally to engine speed.

awesome loads on the basic twin cam engine which employed only slightly modified "B" series engine parts. To contain the stresses about to be imposed upon it, the block was stiffened. The crankshaft was formed using EN 40 steel of 60-70 ton tensile strength, additionally strengthened by nitriding. Main bearing diameter was increased from two inches to 2-3/8 inches and crankpins were similarly increased from 1-7/8 inches to 2-1/16 inches. All major components were X-rayed prior to assembly and two crankshafts were rejected before a suitable one was obtained. The completed crankshaft weighed 50 pounds versus 32 pounds for the standard twin cam crank. Connecting rods retained the floating wrist pin design, but were greatly strengthened. As is the usual practice when supercharging, the compression ratio was reduced from 9.9:1 to 6.82:1. The design of the pistons proved to be a tricky process for research engineer Eddie Maher, who was in charge of supervising the construction of the engine. Originally, a domed piston was used in the hemispherical combustion chamber; however, the design proved difficult to control. In the words of Eddie Maher, "The flame travel seemed rather long and it was in the habit of going off bang." After a long series of experiments, aided by the piston firms of Hepworth and Grandage, a pent-roof design was arrived at. This design was later used in the production Twin Cams, with some modifications to the rings during the production cycle. In deference to the higher combustion temperatures imposed by the supercharger, the pistons had a heavier crown to resist melting. The heavier crown was made possible by eliminating one of the piston rings, reducing the number to three. Larger valves were fitted, with the exhaust valves sodium

Discussing the unique tire design are from left to right (foreground) Stirling Moss, Syd Enever and John Thornley. The tire is totally devoid of any tread and in fact looks more like an inner tube than a tire!

The air outlet for the engine oil radiators can be seen here. The design of the vital cooling air inlets and exits was an important consideration in a vehicle designed to travel at such high speed. The pressurized fuel tank can be seen beneath the fishtail shaped exhaust pipes. Note the air pressure gauge on the fuel tank.

filled to assist in cooling, as is the practice in some high performance cars today, such as the Alfa Romeo. The cams were designed with a 70° overlap.

A problem with scuffing of the chrome plated cam lobes was experienced during bench testing. Elimination of the chrome plating on the cam solved this problem.

Speaking of the tappets, these little devils have had a colorful history in the story of the Twin Cam engine. Originally tappets were of the same type employed in the Wolsclcy 4/50 and Alfa Romeo engines, that is discs screwed into the ends of the valve stems. After a period of running, the threaded shank had a habit of cracking at the base. To eliminate this problem, the "inverted bucket" was employed, fitting over the valve spring and moving like a miniature piston between the valve stem and cam lobe. This was the origin of the tappets used on the production Twin Cam engine which needed some modification to operate reliably in the hands of Twin Cam owners.

To eliminate any possibility of head gasket trouble (a very real concern with a supercharger providing 32 pounds of boost) the water passages between the cylinder head and block were blocked with sealing rings placed atop the bores, and the head and block were lapped together to provide a tight seal. The same procedure had been used by Alec Hounslow in preparation of the EX 179 record breaker in 1954. Stiffening webs were formed in the engine block and crankcase to help contain the forces within trying to get out. A Lucas racing magneto supplied spark to spin all these exotic parts. Displacing 1489 cc with a bore of 73.025 mm and a stroke of 89 mm, the engine used in the record attempt produced 290 bhp @ 7,300 rpm while the backup engine produced a thumping 300 bhp @ 7,300 rpm.

Power was transmitted via a 7-3/4 inch Borg and Beck three plate clutch which was activated hydraulically. The gearbox was a Riley 1-1/2 litre close-ratio four speed unit which was based on the TC box. Reverse gear was removed and a remote control gearchange was fitted with the shift lever on the driver's left. A diminutive six inch long driveshaft transmitted power to the rear axle.

To aid in cooling the combustion chambers, the fuel is methanol based. An unusual method is employed to deliver the fuel from the small 7.9 gallon fuel tank to the carburetors. The fuel tank is pressurized from a separate air tank which is held at 80 psi. Air from the tank is fed to the fuel tank through a pressure regulator which insures a constant 5 psi is forcing the fuel out of the tank. This system offers many advantages. There is no electrical fuel pump to fail, pressure is constant despite widely varing demands from the carburetors, and fuel flow is even in contrast to the spurting characteristic of electrical or mechanical fuel pumps.

One of the most technologically challenging tasks in building a record breaker is the design of the tires. At the speeds MG was shooting for with EX 181, most constructors used large diameter tires to reduce the rotational speed of the tire and thus lessen the centrifugal forces which try to tear the tire off the rim. In a car the size of EX 181, the use of large diameter tires would have meant bulges in the body shape to clear the tires, something to be avoided at all costs. At the urging of Reid Railton, George Eyston specified tires mounted on standard MGA disc wheels with an overall diameter of only 24 inches. The Dunlop people worked on the tire problem long and hard and finally arrived with the solution. The tires were as smooth as a baby's behind with a "tread" thickness of only one millimeter. They were inflated to 60-65 psi. Despite their rather fragile construction and high inflation pressure, the tires had to survive some pretty tough treatment. In transfering 300 horsepower onto the salt to produce forward motion, they were subjected to a thrust of approximately 340 pounds. At the projected speed of 250 mph, the tires would be spinning at 3,500 rpm, which meant the wheels and tires had to be very carefully balanced. At speed, the tire was drawn into an eliptical shape by centrifugal force and actually ran on the tip of the ellipse.

Having established the basic body shape and the major components

Nearing completion, the unpainted body shell is in position while two Competition Department mechanics are busy fitting the internals. The "MG" insignia was placed on the body for the benefit of the photographer!

One of two quick release fasteners which allowed the nose to tilt forward for driver ingress/egress.

The tiny brake fluid resevoir is perched on a bulk-head above the air pressure tank which was used to pressurize the fuel tank.

necessary to push it through the air at 250 mph, the tedious process of refining the design began. Air within the engine compartment was stagnant while the carburetor intake was provided with positive pressure. The exhaust system utilized four individual dual pipes, the ends of which were

A small instrument panel was fitted to the engine compartment to monitor the car's vital signs while the mechanics were warming it up. The gauges, from left to right: rear axle temperature, supercharger pressure and engine oil temperature. Two fuel shut-off valves are located just to the right.

The radiator header tank looks a bit like an octopus with arms reaching to the various cooling system components!

formed into a fishtail shape and fitted flush with the body to provide some local boundary layer control of the airstream over the body. The individual exhaust pipes were cut to a specified length to maximize the extractor effect. The positioning of the radiator inlet and outlet ports required special care so as not to interfere with the airflow over the car. Twin intakes at the front of the car provided cooling air via ducts to the twin aluminum aircraft type radiators mounted in the engine compartment. Exit ports for the radiators were designed so as to contribute to the local boundary layer control. Total drag from the cooling system was calculated at 14 pounds at 250 mph. Fairings were bolted in front and back of the wheels to smooth the airflow around them. The wheels ran in separate boxes to minimize pumping losses. The body was built by Midland Sheet Metal, the same company that built EX 179. The lightweight body was fabricated from 18 gauge Hiduminium 33 aluminum alloy formed over aluminum alloy bulkheads with some supplemental square steel tube framing. The body was welded and rivetted to the chassis. Detachable panels, secured with Dzus fasteners, included the front hinged nose, which included the driver's windscreen and provided access to the driver's seat, and the engine compartment cover with head fairing and four panels, allowing wheel removal. One of the most unusual features of the car was the single Girling disc brake mounted inboard on the rear axle. To cool this brake, a trap door was built into the head fairing which opened when the brake pedal was first depressed, directing cool air onto the brake disc via an air duct. The brake was a marginal performer and the drivers had explicit instructions not to use the brake above 100 mph. Once the trap door was opened, there was no way to close it without stopping the car and manually resetting it. The drag effect of the trap door was no where near that of the infamous Mercedes "air brake" used in the tragic 1955 Le Mans race; however, if the driver accidentally touched the brake pedal during a run, the drag would preclude attaining full speed.

In this form, EX 181 had a frontal area of 10.99 square feet, and a drag factor of 0.000292, approximately one-tenth that of a standard car of that time. In practical terms, this meant EX 181 needed only 29 bhp to reach 100 mph.

In late May 1957, John Thornley unveiled EX 181 to the motoring press. Its unpainted gleaming alloy body was the subject of close scrutiny and Syd Enever, standing by like a proud father, was available to answer questions. At this point the engine was not available for inspection and a mock-up was used in its stead. Stirling Moss was chosen to drive the car at the salt flats and he also stopped by for the introduction. At his suggestion, a fire protection system was fitted to the car by the Graviner Co., who had considerable experience in aircraft fire control systems. The system they installed consisted of a detector cord wrapped around the engine and fuel tank which activated a warning light in the cockpit which flashed if a fire broke out. A button in the center of the small instrument panel fired the chlorobromo-methane fire extinguishers in the engine compartment.

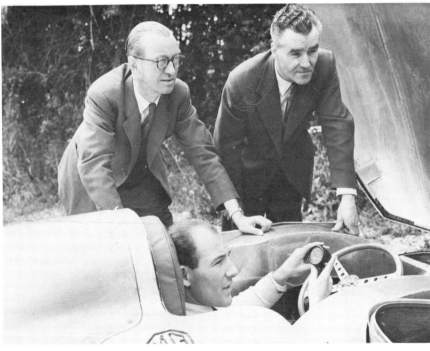

Three key players in the EX 181 story gather at its introduction. From left to right, John Thornley, Director and General Manager MG Car Company, Stirling Moss, driver and Syd Enever, Chief Designer for the MG Car Company. Moss is holding a tachometer.

Originally EX 181 was to be painted metallic blue; however, in the end result it was a light metallic green. In a last minute decision, George Eyston, the team manager, decided to incorporate a vertical tail into the aft protion of the body to improve lateral stability. The mid-engine placement gave EX 181 excellent lateral stability to begin with. Its location minimized the polar moment of inertia about the center of the vehicle, providing quicker reaction to steering inputs and a reduced tendency toward tail wagging. Additionally, the body was mounted in a slightly nose-down attitude to provide downforce on the steering wheel and minimize aerodynamic drag, not to mention keeping the car from flying!

Initial testing of the car was done at nearby Brize-Norton airbase with the permission and assistance of the base commander. The first run down the

Prior to the test runs at Brize-Norton Air Base, Alec Hounslow, who supervised the car's construction, enjoys a rare moment at the controls of EX 181. The rest of the crew seem to be holding on to make sure he doesn't drive off! The tilt steering wheel is in its rearward position. Notice the front wheel boxes with their peculiar shape to allow the wheels to turn. Gathered around Alec are, from left to right, J. Thompson, chief engineer of Morris Engines Branch responsible for the engine design, J. Goffin and Eddie Maher, Assistant Chief and Chief Experimental engineers of the Engines Branch, who developed and tested the engine, Syd Enever, designer, G. Iley, MG Assistant General Manager, John Thornley, General Manager of MG and Terry Mitchell, responsible for the suspension details and chassis design.

At speed on the second run. The cockpit is such a tight fit, Tom Haig was unable to wear a helmet!

runway was not photographed, just in case something was amiss. During the course of testing, a four engined Constellation, which had been flying all the way from the Azores, entered the traffic pattern for landing. EX 181 was ready for another run, but politely, the men from MG held back to wait for the plane to land. Much to their amazement, the base commander ordered the "Connie" to circle until the run was completed!

At last everything was ready for the long journey to Utah. 1957 was a banner year for MG on the salt, taking both EX 181 and its predecessor, EX 179, now sporting a 1,000 cc Sprite engine. The plan for EX 181 was to assault the flying kilometer and mile records in the International Class F (1500 cc). The goal was to achieve 240 mph or four miles per minute. Stirling Moss, who was in his peak at the time, was chosen to drive the car in the record attempt for the logical reason that he would bring the project maximum publicity. Stirling was engaged in a rigorous racing schedule, so plans were made to fly him from the Swedish Grand Prix to Utah in time to make the run. The salt was booked for the period 10th-24th August and EX 181 was sent on its way along with EX 179. Syd Enever would accompany the car this time along with George Eyston, who headed the entire team and John Thornley, MG Director. After asking Moss to drive, John Thornley began to consider the impact on the effort if Moss should be unable to drive. After some deliberation, it was felt prudent to have a backup driver so Phil Hill was asked to drive as Moss' backup. Phil was coming into his prime at that time and the American connection was unquestionably a consideration in the selection of this likeable Californian.

EX 179 was scheduled to make her record runs first at the flats which she did in fine fashion, finishing on the 17th.

EX 181 sustained some minor body damage to the tail during shipping, but this was quickly put straight and early on Sunday the 18th she was ready to run. Stirling Moss was running in a race at Pescara, Italy that weekend

EX 181 returned to the Salt Flats in 1959, this time without the tail fin which was determined to be ineffective. Phil Hill's patience pays off on this record run in which he piloted EX 181 to a new class record of 254 mph, the fastest MG ever.

and was not due at the flats until Tuesday. George Eyston, with his usual meticulous attention to detail and excellent organizing ability, had everything ready for the run. Backup driver Phil Hill was there, but Stirling Moss was not. The Captain believed in the saying, "Don't put off until tomorrow what you can do today." He called John Thornley and asked him if they couldn't go ahead with the run since everything was ready. Moss could run the car later in the week as planned. Thornley agreed and so it was early Sunday morning that EX 181 was rolled out and prepared for the trial run.

EX 181 was fitted with a tow bar and attached to, appropriately enough, an MGA driven by Australian Bill Pringle. With Alec Hounslow, who supervised the car's construction, in the driver's seat, EX 181 was tow started at around 8:45 am. The twin cam 290 bhp engine was warmed up and a set of hard plugs put in. Early Sunday morning in the middle of the Bonneville Salt Flats is not a good place to find an extra hand or two to help out with a record run, so at least one journalist was pressed into service to help man the phones along the five mile course. With the nose of EX 181 tipped forward, Phil Hill gingerly took that first long step into the cockpit. Entry is anything but graceful, requiring the driver to stand by one of the front wheels, place one foot on the seat and swing himself over to the seat. At this point you are standing on the seat and simply slide down into it. This maneuver is made somewhat easier by the steering wheel which tilts forward. Once in the seat, the Blumel woodrim steering wheel is pulled back into the driver's lap. The driver finds himself in a rather strange position with his feet on the pedals in front of the front axle. In fact, the front suspension passes just behind the driver's knees and is padded for comfort. The nose is lowered into position providing a snug fit around the driver's helmeted head. This is certainly no place for anyone over 5 ft 10 in.! Sitting up ahead of the engine was a strange position in 1957, although in today's race car the mid-engine arrangement is accepted as normal. Stirling Moss, for one, was not particularly fond of the unusual driving position. One advantage was the excellent visibility accorded the driver. Additionally, the windscreen was not likely to be obscured by a catastrophe in the engine compartment which could spray hot oil onto the windscreen in a front engine design.

Observing a modest rev limit, Phil took EX 181 northward along the five mile course on a warmup run. He pronounced the car fit, commenting on its excellent stability and somewhat heavy steering at slow speeds. New tires were fitted and EX 181 was ready for her first high speed pass. For Phil, this would be the entrance to a new domain of speed. His fastest previous drive was 181 mph at Le Mans in 1955 driving a Ferrari 121 LM. Hopefully he would be moving up from three miles a minute to four miles a minute! With orders to run at 6,500 rpm (and a column of smoke from a crashed jet aircraft marking his heading), Phil started off on his first high speed run. Accelerating swiftly and strongly through the gears, Hill shifted into second at

60 mph, third at 100 mph and fourth at 160 mph. While accelerating through the 200 mph barrier, he approached the speed traps which he flashed through at around 240 mph.

Pleased with the successful run, Phil began to slow down. What happened next was not so pleasant. Phil tells the story, "When I got up to over 200 mph with this amazing thing—1-1/2 litre, mid-engined—I took my foot off to slow down and the cockpit, with the deceleration forces, filled with the fumes from that nitro-glycerine-methanol-liquid dynamite-special fuel. I took two breaths and thought this was it. Then I could scarcely breathe and waited for the car to slow down. Of course it took forever with its perfect streamline form."[1]

The MG mechanics quickly got to work and a slit was made in the radiator air intake duct to blow more fresh air on the driver's face. Tires and plugs were checked. Well within the regulation hour EX 181 made its return trip toward the north, which hopefully would establish a new record in International Class F. If all went according to plan, this record would be broken on Wednesday by Stirling Moss. The car was push started in second gear, and as it accelerated away it was misfiring rather badly. Luckily, the engine cleared in time to achieve 6,600 rpm through the traps and establish a new record. Taking no chances, Phil quickly shut off the engine and slipped the gearbox into neutral employing the single disc brake at the rear to come to a secure stop.

Having insured the record for MG, a clamp was put on releasing the information to the press. The publicity was geared for Moss, and he would be the one to take the official record. Now the team would wait his return. Later that Sunday afternoon rumbling thunder was heard in the distance bringing one question to the forefront in everyone's mind, "Would it rain and wash out Moss' try at the record?" The rains did come and the salt flats were flooded as so often happens at Bonneville, turning the once hard, nearly ideal surface into mush. Moss arrived on Tuesday, but the scheduled run on Wednesday was not to be, due to the condition of the salt. Thankfully, the track began to dry out ever so slowly, starting in the middle and working its way toward the start and finish points as the precious hours ticked away. With the rental of the salt, hiring the time keepers, observers, setting up the timing apparatus, etc., record runs are an expensive business and MG only had the salt until Saturday the 24th. Almost literally at the eleventh hour, Eyston and Moss confered on the condition of the track late Friday afternoon and decided to have a go at it. The track wasn't completely dry yet; however, they were concerned more rains were on the way. Moss' first run went smoothly, marginally faster than Hill's previous average. On the return trip, which was run at dusk, Moss flashed through the traps setting five new International Class F records. Concentrating on getting the record and possibly due to the failing light, Moss went past his braking point and had to apply the brake early. This, combined with the loss of second gear to assist in the braking, burned out the brake and he was forced to finish out his ride far down the course in the rough salt. EX 181, with Moss driving, had established new records for the one kilometer at 245.64 mph, one mile at 245.11 mph, five kilometer at 243.08 mph, five miles at 235.69 mph and ten kilometers at 224.70 mph, smashing the previous records set by EX 135 by over 40 mph.

How did Phil Hill feel about playing second fiddle to Stirling Moss? Hill and Moss were both professionals, and understood the reasons behind the way the runs were orchestrated, though Phil did have some tongue-in-cheek comments to make. "When we came to the salt, I'm not sure I got the best of the bargain because Moss was to drive as well. Somehow or other, when they were playing with the car—and there were quite a few problems—it was always me who went out first to see how things were."[2] Well, as they say, "All's well that ends well.", and Phil got the last record in EX 181 two years later.

It was decided to run EX 181 again at Bonneville in 1959. This time MG would resort to one of its old tricks and bore out the spare 1489 cc engine ever so slightly to 1506 cc in order to compete in the next higher classification, International Class E. It was hoped the goal of the previous attempt, 250 mph, could be attained now that the salt was in better shape and the engine slightly enlarged.

There was no drastic change in the design; however, there was one significant and externally noticeable difference between the two attempts. The tail which was added just prior to the 1957 runs based on the design of Sir Malcom Campbell's land speed record car, was removed. Wind tunnel tests showed the tail was ineffective because it didn't extend high enough to get into the airstream where it could have a stabilizing effect. Removal of the tail improved the drag factor by 7%, which further improved the team's chances at breaking the 250 mph barrier. The only other substantial change was to switch to wire wheels. This time Hill was chosen to be the primary driver. MG felt they owed it to him after the 1957 runs. At this point in his racing career, Phil was driving for the Ferrari team and was ranked as a top driver. Only two years later he would become the first American to win the World Driver's Championship in 1961, driving for Ferrari. Phil was interested in driving again for MG, perhaps remembering that he got his start in racing driving MGs after World War II. Because of his committments to Ferrari, John Thornley wrote a letter to the Commendatore himself, Enzo Ferrari, requesting permission for Phil to drive on the salts in September, while Ferrari was between the Grand Prix of Italy on 13 September and the Grand Prix of Morocco in October. Permission was quickly and graciously granted and the necessary men and equipment were sent off to the salts once again for what was to be the last MG record breaking attempts, probably for all time.

The salt conditions were not much improved over the attempts by Moss in 1957, and the beginning and finishing points were still soggy. This would mean considerable wheelspin while accelerating toward the magic 250 mph figure. Because of the limitations imposed by the wheelspin, it was decided not to run the old 1489 cc Class F engine and only incrementally increase the old records set in 1957. It was felt more advantageous to attack the Class E records with the 1506 cc engine.

Hill was suffering from the flu at the time of the record attempt, but he was a professional and determined to get those records which he had worked so hard for in 1957. Eyston, an old hand at record breaking on salt and wet sand beaches, inspected the course and advised Phil, "Take if from me Phil, it's all right." With that pronouncement, Hill was off with a vengence, wheels spinning and the car skidding about on the initial wet portion of the course. When the return run was completed and the results computed, Hill was the proud co-owner with MG of six International Class E records, including the flying kilometer at 254.91 mph and mile at 254.53 mph, both being in excess of the target of 250 mph.

The records set by EX 181 in 1957 and 1959 still stand unbeaten, an enduring testimony to the far-sighted engineering skill and innovative design by Syd Enever and his team who worked so hard to make this last MG record breaker the best of the line. MG had started record breaking on December 30, 1930, with EX 120 covering 50 miles at a speed of 86 mph. George Eyston was the man at the wheel then and it was only appropriate that he was present as the last MG record breaker smashed international records travelling nearly three times the speed of EX 120.

EX 181 was not going to sit out the rest of her days gathering dust in some museum. Since the record runs, EX 181 has been exhibited in Australia and the United States. The latter trip, in 1979, was in commemoration of the 20th anniversary of the record run at Bonneville which finally broke the 250 mph barrier.

In preparation for the year long tour of the U.S., which was to include most major cities, EX 181 was completely restored by the apprentices in the MG works in Abingdon. Upon completion of the work, EX 181 was taken to the nearby Abingdon airport where an entourage of MG personalities such as John Thornley, Syd Enever, and George Eyston were to review a pass by the record breaker down the runway. A camera crew was going to be there to film the event for posterity, moving slightly ahead of the car down the runway and allowng it to pass them as it was being filmed. Tommy Haig, who had been the test driver for EX 181 at the initial runs at Brize-Norton airbase was present, but it was decided to let Jimmy Cox, the head MG apprentice, have the honor of driving EX 181. He was instructed to run at a certain rpm until he was past the camera truck and then brake to a stop. This was all well and good; however, no one took into account the fact that the truck was moving down the runway at 50 mph. The end result was Jimmy Cox missed his braking point, just as Stirling Moss had missed his in EX 181. The results, unfortunately, were much worse for young Jimmy Cox. Finding himself motoring at an alarming rate with scarcely a quarter of the runway left and no hope of stopping with the brake, Jimmy applied whatever lock he could to avoid the trees at the end of the runway, and rolled the car over. Needless to say, EX 181 was a complete wreck, but miraculously the old MG slogan of "Safety Fast" held true and Jimmy was not seriously injured. The departure date for the US tour was fast approaching and a furious rebuilding of EX 181 was undertaken. Thanks to a herculean effort on the part of the apprentices, EX 181 sailed off to America only three weeks behind schedule!

Le Mans

If there is one sports car race which is the embodiment of endurance racing, it is the 24 Hours of Le Mans. From four p.m. on Saturday afternoon, starting ironically with a foot race to the cars, every imaginable shape and type of automobile is pitted against each other in pursuit of a myriad of awards. Round and round the tortuous course they travel, accelerating to top speed down the Mulsanne straight, testing the brakes to the limit on every turn, punishing the gearbox and clutch with countless shifts and hanging on to every last ounce of traction in a delicate ballet known as the four wheel drift, the teams engaged in a tightrope walk between reliability and performance. This drama is repeated every four minutes or so with the passing of each lap for twenty-four long hours.

At Le Mans, time, that almost imperceptible transference from daylight to dusk to dark to dawn to daylight once again, presents its own challenge for man and machine. As daylight fades into dusk and finally darkness, the driver's depth perception and visual acuity change, requiring constant adjustments on the part of the driver to his own senses. As for the machine, the added demand on the electrical system from the requisite illuminating devices has spelled death for more than one team who might have made it through a race run solely in daylight. As the night wears on, fatigue begins to set in for driver, machine, and crew. Running a race, any race, is a precision operation where seemingly minor errors in performance or judgement can mean defeat for the team. At Le Mans, this level must be sustained despite fatigue, darkness, and numbing repetition. As morning approaches, another factor may enter the equation, fog. It is the one weather condition which brings together the elements of chance, fear, and courage in an ever changing blanket of uncertainty. Man has devised machinery to combat fog in the form of improved lighting, but machinery alone cannot defeat the fog. It is up to the driver call forth his best abilities in beating the element of chance, tempering his fear with sound judgement, and calling on his courage to defeat this elusive element.

As morning arrives, the temperatures which have been dropping since the race began, begin to rise. It is June, and the temperature can rise very high indeed before the end of the race at four o'clock Sunday afternoon. The cars have been running around eighteen hours, and every fluid, every scrap of metal and rubber, and of course the driver, is hot. As the air temperature rises, the cars' and drivers' cooling systems fight to maintain their delicate thermal equilibrium. It is at this point that so many cars have dropped out, having completed three-fourths of the race only to succumb to the unrelenting rise in temperature of some critical component which causes its failure.

To win any race you first must finish, but really finishing the 24 hours of Le Mans is winning. Winning against mechanical failure, winning against fatigue, winning against the weather, and winning with Lady Luck! It was into this cauldron of mechanical and physical torture that MG chose to forge and temper the MGA.

Le Mans 1955

John Thornley's enthusiasm for using competition events to publicize MGs was the inspiration for the MG team effort at Le Mans in 1955. The introduction of the MGA was to be in June 1955, and John thought it would be a most fitting way to introduce the MGA to the world, coinciding as it did with the planned introduction date. Le Mans was a race of world wide reputation offering a natural stage upon which to debut MG's first truly world car. BMC had been out of competition since 1935 when a team of six women drivers competed at Le Mans. The decision to re-enter competition was made late in 1954, and the BMC Competition Department opened its doors on 1 December 1954 with Marcus Chambers as Competitions Manager. The 1955 Le Mans race would be one of the first undertakings by the new department. It was decided to enter a team of three cars, plus a practice car.

Ken Wharton prepares to take EX 182 out for tests at Silverstone. Marcus Chambers, fifth from left, was BMC Competitions Manager from 1954 until 1961. Alec Hounslow, extreme left, was responsible for the cars construction. John Thornley, shaking hands second from left, was responsible for the concept of the Le Mans effort.

As the months passed, problems with the body die tooling made it obvious that the assembly line would not be running in time for production cars to be entered in the race. The decision was made to go ahead with their entry, but change from production to prototype class. Permission was granted by the organizers and additional development was initiated to take advantage of the new classification without making the cars overly different from the production models. Six sets of aluminum body panels were stamped on the body dies, twice the requisite amount, to insure a proper fit with the prototype bodies. Aluminum has a different "memory" than steel and as a result the panels would require extensive hand finishing. Because the panels were pressed on body dies which were not yet finalized, many of the panels are not compatible with production MGAs. Alec Hounslow was put in charge of preparing the cars, a task he was well suited for, having prepared C-types, J-4s, and K-3s for races over twenty years before. While Alec was preparing the cars, others were busy lining up drivers, timekeepers, pit crew, mechanics, lodging, and all the other details which need tending to make the effort a success. A large van was obtained and modified by Appleyard of Leeds for use by the team. Its gasoline engine was replaced by a diesel engine and the interior was fitted with a kitchen, bunks for sleeping, space for storing spares and a small mechanical work area. One interesting feature incorporated in the van was a set of ramps which could be pulled out from under the body of the van to serve as a service rack for working on the underside of the cars.

Preparation of the cars went very smoothly and they were completed about one month prior to the race. MG took one of the cars to Silverstone for performance testing. The car was outfitted with engine, gearbox, and rear axle temperature gauges to monitor the effect of the undertray. It was a cool rainy day in May when Ken Wharton took EX 182 out for its first trial on the track. Performance tests indicated a sustained lap speed of 85 mph, with a maximum lap speed of 94 mph theoretically possible. These estimates were amazingly accurate, as car number 41 averaged 86.76 mph and turned in a fastest lap of 93.729 mph.

Syd Enever, left, and Alec Hounslow, right, discuss a braking problem. Notice the scoops on the brake drum held by the gentleman in the foreground. They were there to evacuate water and air from the drum.

Alec Hounslow, white lab coat, with his young work force. He shared with them his past experience in building MG race cars and they responded with enthusiasm and dedication to "get it right."

One modification to come from the testing was the addition of an air intake between the radiator grill and the parking lamp which passed cool air back to the driver's compartment via a duct. Excessive heat in the driver's compartment was a continual problem with the MGA, and since these cars were undertrayed, the problem was compounded. This air duct for the driver was used on many racing MGAs afterward, although the placement of the intake often varied. An additional modification, also related to heat dissipation, was a result of the test session. The drum brakes just were not up to the job demanded by the rigors of Le Mans, so additional cooling was provided. About five holes were drilled in the brake backing plates and covered with gauze to keep unwanted debris out. The drums themselves were drilled with about eight holes to evacuate the air taken in from the backing plates. To keep water from getting into the drums, small scoops were fabricated from sheet metal to cover the holes. These modifications were made to the other cars as well, and at last the team of three race cars and one practice car stood ready. It was heart warming the way Alec Hounslow had taken up right where he left off some twenty years before and had done an absolutely magnificent job in instructing and supervising his group of young mechanics in preparing the cars. These young workers had learned their lessons well from one of the best and were fully capable of carrying on the proud reputation of MG on the tracks of the world. MG had always been noted for the thorough and fastidious preparation of their racing entries.

A few weeks before the race, the practice car was sent down to Le Mans to sort out axle ratios, gearbox ratios and tires. It was not possible to run a complete lap as the tunnel at Tetre Rouge was still under construction at the time; however, it was felt that sufficient data had been collected to confidently establish the gearing and tires. A close ratio box with the 3.7:1 rear axle coupled with 6.00 x 15 rear tires seemed to be an ideal combination.

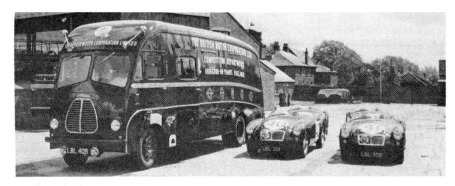

The Le Mans team stands ready to make the trek to the race.

Car number 64, driven by Lund and Waeffler, leads a TR under the Dunlop Bridge.

The race entry from MG included two firm starters, cars 40 and 41, with the third car, number 64, listed sixth on the reserve list. Based on past experience, it was reasonably certain the reserve car would also race. The team goal was to finish the race with all three cars at an average speed of just under 80 mph, which would qualify the team for the Biennial Cup the following year. A lap speed of 85 mph was deemed ideal to attain this goal without punishing the cars.

At last all stood ready. MG had decided to drive the team cars to the race in yet another indication of the production aspect of this entry. Certainly this must be one of the few prototype sports car entries since World War II to be driven to the 24 Hours of Le Mans. The plan was for the team to converge on Le Mans the Monday before the race, allowing nearly a full week to prepare the cars, drivers, and crews for the race on Saturday afternoon. The main party would leave together, with some of the others coming from various points in England and Europe.

The drivers for the team were Dick Jacobs of "Heavenly Twins" fame and Joe Flynn, a convivial Irishman, driving car number 40 (later changed to number 42). Ken Miles from California, who broke into sports car racing driving MGs and co-drove EX 179 with George Eyston in 1954, was paired with Johnny Lockett in car number 41. Miles and Lockett would find themselves driving together again the following year in the Bonneville Salt Flats with EX 179 fitted out with the prototype Twin Cam engine. Car number 64, the back up car, was driven by Ted Lund and Hans Waeffler from Switzerland, who joined the team at Le Mans coming directly from Zurich. Ted would be back again racing an MG at Le Mans in 1959, 1960, and 1961. The team manager was Sammy Davis, characterized by John Thornley as "guide, philosopher and friend." Marcus Chambers, BMC Competitions Manager, was in charge of the overall operation. John and Joanne Thornley provided the liaison with management, and likewise with BMC in England. Several BMC engineers were along to insure the technical side was properly tended to. Chief among them was Sydney Enever, the man most responsible for the MGA's design. Russell Lowry and his wife were along to serve as interpreters. They were to insure that no misinformation concerning MG flowed from the public address system to the track, and to keep Marcus Chambers apprised of race developments as announced. By good fortune, Lowry composed an excellent report on the 1955 race immediately after his return and this report is reprinted in John Thornley's book *Maintaining the Breed*.

Mechanics on the MG team were top notch. Chief among them were Alec Hounslow, who had been in charge of preparing the team car, Dicky Green and Reg Jackson. Two of the MG mechanics, Henry Stone and Tommy Wellman, were left behind at Abingdon to help move the newly formed Competition Department to its new location within the factory. The indominatable George Eyston was around to help as needed, lending an air of confidence and encouragement to the team. He arranged for the team to stay at Chateau Chene de Coeur, a somewhat aged structure, but nonetheless well suited for the purpose.

Those departing from England met at the Burlington Hotel in Folkestone on Sunday evening, the 5th of June, to receive last minute instructions in preparation for the departure on Monday morning. Monday morning saw the team off in good spirits, and high hopes of what lay ahead. The crossing was made on the Lord Warden, sailing from Dover to Boulogne, arriving in France around noon. Following a long lunch, the team was somewhat pressed for time to make Le Mans by dinner time. En route, the team ran into a bad thunderstorm which strewed their path with branches and reduced visibility to zero. Luckily, the only casualty was a hole in one sidescreen. The Chateau was made in time, and the weary team made its way to a nearby restaurant, Les Rosiers, for dinner. Les Rosiers was to be the scene for many subsequent MG team dinners, not only through the coming week, but in later MG competitions at Le Mans in 1959, 1960, and 1961.

Tuesday morning, the team inspected their new home at the Chateau. Its spacious quarters were able to house the entire team of thirty-six and the stables provided parking for the racing cars and the transporter as well. A bulletin board in the hall showed team assignments, tasks to be completed with an arrow pointing to the latest item and goodwill messages all over. One message particularly bolstered spirits. It was from the Vice-Chairman of BMC. The main order of business on Tuesday was the scrutineering of cars and crews. This infamous event, called the *Pesage*, has been the scene of many heated exchanges between inscrutable inspectors and over enthusiastic teams. For MG, the *Pesage* was a credit to their thorough preparation under the watchful eye of Alec Hounslow. The cars, gleaming in their British Racing Green colors, drew many favorable comments from those in attendance. An indication of the preparation of the team was evidenced by their appearance exactly on time with the cars lined up in perfect formation accompanied by their mechanics clad in matching green overalls. This initial impression was to spawn comments all through the week on how well the team looked on this their first appearance at Le Mans in twenty years. The only fixing the cars needed was to square off the tail pipe ends instead of the diagonal cut made initially. This was done to comply with dust-raising restrictions. The drivers' physicals went without hitch.

Tuesday afternoon was spent in intensive pit-stop training using the spacious courtyard of the Chateau to good advantage. The pit crew's performance was somewhat lax at first, but with coaching, the men realized how important their teamwork and individual competence were, and the crew quickly gained the proficiency necessary.

Wednesday, the 8th, saw the remainder of the team arrive. Dr. Michael King and his brother together with their wives arrived in, pardon the sin, a pair of TR 2s! They were to help out in the pits with the scoring. The timekeeper, Stan Nicholls, flew in from England bringing along some last minute spares. Sammy Davis took the drivers on a tour of the circuit in anticipation of the evening's first practice.

That evening the crew arrived at the designated pit area and found the accommodations cramped, having only a double pit area for the three MGs and an Austin Healey which accompanied the team. The cars went well in practice that evening, starting out lapping in the 60 mph range, rising gradually into the target 80 mph range. After darkness set in, the lights were adjusted. The only anxious moment of the evening was when Johnny Lockett threw a fan belt and boiled the water out of his radiator. The Mercedes' controversial airbrake was the main topic of discussion. Prophetically, Moss' Mercedes ran into the back of another car in this first practice, putting the victim out of the race. This drop out gave MG 64 a place on the reserve list.

Thursday saw Dicky Green laboring over the Lockett car. The head was pulled and found to be unscathed by the previous evening's mishap. The engine was reassembled by noon, and that evening the car was taken back out onto the circuit for practice, to make sure all was well. Number 41 was the only MG to practice, the remainder of the team staying back to rest up for the ordeal which lay ahead. The Lund/Waeffler car, number 64, moved up to first on the reserve list with the retirement of the Arnolt. The Arnolt was a total wreck and thus dropped out of the competition which fortunately allowed MG to take over their pit, which was adjacent to their own. Dr. King, from the MG team, provided the Arnolt driver with medical attention. This was regrettably not the last time his professional services would be required at Le Mans.

Friday brought good news for the MG team. Car number 64 was now officially a starter in the race. The controversy over the Mercedes airbrake raged on, but Mercedes was unyielding. Sammy Davis and Marcus

Chambers conducted a "Le Mans start" practice in front of the Chateau in the last phase of preparation for the race on Saturday. Confident that the cars and crews were prepared, the team retired early Friday night in hopes of recharging for the long ordeal which lay ahead. Despite the need to sleep, there was much tossing and turning that night.

Saturday dawned clear and bright and all hands were busy preparing to move the team to the track. By ten o'clock all was ready and the team set off, following a photo session with the transporter and team cars on the terrace of the Chateau. The MG camp was soon established, though there still were too many people even with the take-over of the Arnolt pit. As a solution, a white line was painted parallel to the pit wall behind which anyone not directly concerned with the cars was to retire upon the sounding of a whistle. There were lots of things to be done which thankfully helped pass the time. The spares and equipment were all checked by race officials and found in order. Droves of journalists and photographers were coming by, talking and taking pictures. The general impression was that the cars were well received, even though they certainly weren't the most exciting cars present.

As the clock ticked off the last few seconds before four o'clock, silence settled over the crowd and the tension was so thick you could cut it with a knife. Lund, Lockett, and Jacobs stood poised to sprint to their appointed charges. At last they were off, not with a mighty roar, but rather with the soft patter of rushing feet. As the drivers reached their cars, the cacophony of accelerating cars quickly grew to deafening proportions. Lund, Lockett and Jacobs were away without a hitch in the mad scramble for position; however, some were not so lucky. The great Fangio leaped into his car and promptly put his foot through the steering wheel spokes causing himself no end of embarrassment and delay as he untangled his foot! The MGs began lapping around 5 minutes 30 seconds, no doubt being caught up in the early fast pace which saw record after record fall. The object of the race was to finish and qualify for the Biennial Cup the following year at a set average speed. An overall win at Le Mans was not part of the strategy! Something had to be done to insure the race strategy was followed. John Thornley, a very interested spectator at the time, tells what happened, "It became apparent by about the end of lap six that Dickie (Jacobs) was going quite a bit faster than he need do, and this could have an adverse effect on his long term chances. So after some debate, we decided to slow him down. We had an understanding that if we put out the slow sign, that meant cut 100 or 200 rpm. Dick took the signal, acknowledged it, got round again once more, but the next time going into White House, he'd been accustomed at going in at say 5,600 rpm in third and he went in at 5,400 rpm, and the drift left him in the wrong position to get out of the corner and so he dropped it. It was as easy as that."

On lap 28, Jacobs flipped his car (number 42) off the road where it burst into flames, seriously injuring Jacobs and destroying the car. His accident occurred almost simultaneously with the Pierre Levegh/Mercedes crash which took place just before the pits as the first change of drivers was beginning. The Macklin Healey which had accompanied the MG team to Le Mans was pulling into the pits when the Mercedes driven by Levegh climbed up the rear of the Healey, sending the Mercedes on a sickening flight into the crowd of spectators. Russell Lowry tells what the scene was like from the pits, ". . . just as the first relief of drivers came due, tragedy struck. A bang, a gasping shriek from the crowd, the commentator's voice rising in a frenzy. A huge billow of black smoke. People running. From our pit, calm instructions to mobilize fire extinguishers. And keep out of the way. Sammy Davis is not easily rattled. Although the crash was only 150 yards or so away, none of us knew the magnitude of the disaster. Frankly, we didn't believe all we heard as shocked onlookers came away, some seeking first aid duly rendered by Dr. King."[3]

Reports concerning Jacobs were conflicting, and in the confusion of the moment and relative isolation of the pits, Jacobs' wife was bravely enduring the uncertainty. Still, the cars continued to run like clockwork in a race which had seemingly become detached from the reality of the crash. The MG crews were in good spirits, encouraged by the running of the cars which were lapping consistently at 5 minutes 37 seconds. They were not told about Jacobs' fate; however, Lund had seen Jacobs being treated by the side of the road. Ken Miles and Ted Lund put in the fastest time for MG at 5 minutes 22 seconds, or 93.729 mph. The fastest speed through the flying kilometer on the Mulsanne was 117.39 mph, which the drivers reported they could hold with "a whiff of throttle" once speed was attained. Jacobs condition was finally ascertained when he was located in the hospital at Coulaines and the news was rather alarming. At 2 a.m. the Mercedes team withdrew from the event and the remainder of the cars continued the endless grind through the night. John Thornley, who was grievously concerned over Dick Jacobs' fate, recalls that mournful night. "God, I remember being vaguely asleep under the tree about four o'clock on that Sunday morning and there was one extremely noisy Aston Martin and I could hear it all the way around the 13 km of Le Mans. They turned off all the squeeze box music and all the gala atmosphere normally associated with Le Mans was gone and it was a dreary round, round, round."

Russell Lowry, still in the pits, was soldiering on with the others as the endless jobs associated with the maintenance of the team went on. As night gave way to day, the weather continued the dreary mood as recalled by Lowry. "With dawn it rained. At first absent-mindedly and then with increasing, vicious intensity. Oddly enough, and this is confirmed by others, one had little impression that daylight did return. The aftertaste of that Sunday is of a dismal half-light."[4] At 5 a.m., the drivers changed and Ted Lund took over from Hans Waeffler. Perhaps he was trying to make up for lost time as the number 64 car was five laps behind Lockett and Miles in number 41, but on lap 175 at nine o'clock, he overcooked it at Arnage resulting in a damaged left front fender. Twenty years after the event, Lund described what happened to Jonathan Wood. "During the night a D-type Jaguar tried to pass me at Arnage and slid right into the sandbank and remained there for the rest of the race. Then later, toward the morning, I tried to do the very same (trying to pass a Triumph TR 2), at the same corner. Needless to say I shot into the back of the D-type in the same sandbank. I could have cried on the spot. . .to think through lack of concentration and probably tiredness after 12 to 14 hours of racing, I had done the very thing I should have been aware of."[5] Lund managed to limp back to the pits where the damage consisted of a bent frame, damaged left front fender and headlamp. The front suspension underwent some rather major realignment, being 1-1/4 inches out of track! Fortunately the car was able to continue under the hand of Hans Waeffler after only a six minute pit stop.

As the rain subsided and the sun shone brighter, so did the spirits of the MG team. The end of the twenty-four hours was approaching and the cars were running as easily as at the start. The only mechanical adjustment at this point being a minor brake adjustment. They would easily complete the entire race on one set of tires and brakes. At the cars began closing on the requisite number of laps to qualify, Lund came in at 2 p.m., complaining that something was not quite right with the steering. A check indicated all was well and he returned to the race. At last the magic number of laps was completed and the cars had only to finish the race. In anticipation of the finish, crews are cleaned up and the pits made ready to welcome the finishers. Russell Lowry describes the finish. "The police bring down their barricades. The eminences begin to assemble. The pit counters fill with our own people. Even the galley is deserted. The chequered flag comes out, and Ted Lund in No. 64 is actually the first car to receive it. After an interval comes 41.

Car number 64, still showing signs of the accident at Arnage, leads the parade of MGs back home to Abingdon. The fourth team car, severely damaged in the Jacob's crash, was left behind.

Cheers, flowers, champagne, claps on the back. A mad scramble between photographers and the French police. Carefully phrased speeches—for this is a tragedy as well as a celebration. We cling to 248 laps at 86.17 mph and 230 laps at 81.97 mph."[6] Following the celebration in the pits, the crew assembled all the gear and headed back to the Chateau. The team party was held at the by now familiar Les Rosiers restaurant. The evening started off boisterously enough; however, the previous thirty-six hours took its toll, as the revelers droppd off to a well earned sleep.

Concern over Dick Jacobs' condition continued, though seeing him remained a problem with all the confusion following the race where so many had been injured. Communications with the outside world were difficult at best and a lack of information in England was made still worse by misinformation concerning Jacobs' fate. The Monday *Evening Standard* carried a story which stated in effect that Jacobs was dead. Jacobs lay in the French hospital for nearly a week in very serious condition. Dr. King became quite concerned over his condition and contacted the Nuffield Chairman and the Nuffield organization doctor, Dr. White, in an attempt to summon assistance. Dr. White was able to raise an emergency team who all had valid passports and they flew to Le Mans in a chartered plane. After a "blazing row" with the French hospital authorities, Jacobs was flown back to England to Oxford where the top thoracic specialist cared for him. Following his transfer, Jacobs made a speedy recovery, much to everyone's great relief.

The 1955 race was a tragedy for those persons involved in the accident, but it was also a tragedy for motorsport. Much serious soul-searching was done following the race, in the same manner as that following the ill-fated Paris-Madrid race of 1903. In a memorandum to BMC management, Marcus Chambers, BMC's Competitions Manager, provides an insight into the thinking of the time.

As a result of the accident, the form of next year's race is most likely to be changed and there is no reason why we should not take steps through the R.A.C. and other channels to see that the race is run on lines to suit us and other British manufacturers. If we look back at the early years of this race, it will be remembered that it was for standard production models to which minor modifications were permitted. This category still remains in the race, but the introduction of the prototype has almost eliminated the Standard Production Sports Car and it is at present impossible to win the race or a class except with a prototype. In the opinion of the Competitions Manager, prototypes should be excluded, but bodies which conform to the F.I.A. rules should be permitted together with permitted modification to the chassis. I think the race would regain some of its past value and one off jobs such as the Nardi would make way for some serious entries and permit the return of the private entries which have by now been almost eliminated. Concerning the accident itself, no doubt the competent authority will make a pronouncement in due course, but whilst it is to be deplored, it should be realized that it was brought about by a chain of circumstances which might never occur again in a life time. Morris racing will still go on for the same reason that ships still cross the Atlantic although the Titanic is no more.

Le Mans 1956

MG was planning on entering the Le Mans race in 1956 in hopes of capturing the Biennial Cup which required a team effort two years running. For 1956 MG had something pretty special in mind. A series of around a dozen highly developed MGAs utilizing twin cam engines and a sleek body, not unlike that of the Mercedes 300 SL roadster of the time, were to be constructed for a select group of racers to spread the name of MG around the racetracks of the world, the premiere of which was to be the 24 Hours of Le Mans. This latest MG project was given the designation EX 186, and work on it was started right after the 1955 Le Mans race. The specification for this car would make the mouth of any MG enthusiast drool with anticipation. A standard MGA chassis was used fitted with a coil sprung DeDion rear axle, designed by Terry Mitchell. Four wheel Dunlop disc brakes using the Twin Cam style light alloy knock-off disc wheels were employed for stopping power. The motivation for this machine came from a Twin Cam engine which displaced 1489 cc. An engine oil cooler was provided. A standard MGA transmission was also employed with close-ratio gears. The body design was the work of Syd Enever and was refined in the wind tunnel at Armstrong-Whitworth. The two passenger design featured covered headlamps, side exhaust and a headrest fairing. A 21 gallon fuel tank with quick release filler cap was fitted into the tail. The interior sported complete instrumentation with fuel, water temperature and oil temperature gauges, an oil pressure gauge, a tachometer and an ammeter. MGA coupe style seats were employed. Interestingly, the coupe introduction was still over a year away. The body was built by Midland Sheet Metal, the same constructors of the record breakers, EX 179 and 181.

The wind tunnel model is exceptionally well done. Notice the detailed driver. The side exhaust was a nice touch and functional as well. It saved weight, blended in well with the aerodynamics of the body and didn't heat up the underside of the car. This last item would be important if the car were fully undertrayed, which it probably would have been. The tail lights were standard MGA.

This rare photo of EX 186 shows some differences from the wind tunnel model. The windscreen was increased to full width and the passenger side door has been added. The wheels are Twin Cam style but are made of light alloy instead of steel. The four wheel disc brakes were later used on the Twin Cam production models.

Unfortunately, the Tourist Trophy race which was held in September 1955 was marred by tragedy and BMC decided to withdraw from factory participation in sports car racing, cutting short the plans for EX 186. EX 186 stayed around the MG shops until sometime in late 1959 when it was shipped off in a great rush along with many spares to an unknown destination in America.

So it was that one of the most interesting MGAs was still-born in its bid to capture the Biennial Cup and hopefully many other trophies. There was to be no 1956 Le Mans for MG. Nor a 1957 or 1958 Le Mans.

Le Mans—1959

1959 saw a new dimension in MG participation at Le Mans. The Northwest Centre of the MG Car Club contacted John Thornley and asked the factory's cooperation in preparing a car for the 1959 Le Mans race. John agreed and preparation began. Ted Lund and Colin Escott were chosen as drivers. Ted had driven on the 1955 Le Mans team and had long standing ties with MG. His father had gone to school with Cecil Kimber and Ted got his start in racing driving a supercharged MG PB in 1947.

It was decided to compete in the 2 litre class with a Twin Cam roadster against the TR-3s. On this first outing, with some factory help but by no means full factory participation, the goal of the team was to finish second or third in class.

Starting with a Twin Cam roadster, Henry Stone, who was a factory mechanic working in the Experimental Department at the time, began to work the car into a competitor. Top speed of the car was projected to be in the 130 mph range. At speeds above 100 mph, an undertray is desirable to minimize air drag under the body, so the car received a complete undertray. A short competition windscreen was fitted to help ease the air over the top surfaces. The twin overhead camshaft engine was fitted with larger carburetors, different cams and tuned exhaust manifold. Power output was estimated at 120 bhp, not much more than a stock Twin Cam engine. Obviously the emphasis was on reliability rather than all out performance in the newly developed engine design. A close-ratio gearbox transferred the power to a 3.9:1 rear axle. A fresh air intake for the carburetors was provided between the radiator grill and the right front fender. The carburetor air was vented through an oval outlet in the right front fender. For long distance racing, a 20 gallon fuel tank with quick release filler cap was fitted in the trunk. The car was finished in Ash Green with a British Racing Green flash on the side.

To test the reliability of the Twin Cam engine over a 24 hour grind like Le Mans, the engine was put into another Twin Cam body and taken to the Motor Industry Research Association track at Lindley. Tom Haig, who had long been a test driver for MG, and Henry Stone, the mechanic in charge of the project, subjected the engine and drivetrain to a simulated run at Le Mans. They would run two laps flat out and then bring the car down through the gears to 20 mph and then accelerate away again. It was hoped this would simulate the top speed, braking and shifting aspects of Le Mans. On the 20th hour of the test the clutch failed. The centrifugal force had been so great at the high engine speeds generated by the Twin Cam engine that the clutch springs had given out. The clutch was replaced with a Hauseman diaphragm clutch similar to that used in the Porsche. The car was again tested with no problems, except for tire wear due to the steep banking. Prior to final assembly of the engine, the RAC checked all engine parts for compliance with the rules and stamped all critical parts such as the crank, pistons and cams.

The Northwest Centre was busy assembling a crew for the car. Certainly nothing like the 36-person entourage which accompanied the 1955 team was necessary, but there were a myriad of details to be tended to. Major Arnold Pownall was given the task of organizing the team, playing the role Marcus Chambers played in 1955. The King brothers were along again to help with the pits and signaling. Altogether about fifteen people accompanied the cars and drivers to Le Mans. The car was transported to Le Mans on a trailer towed with a Land Rover, arriving four days prior to the race. A Morris van on loan from the Northwest Centre carried the spare engine and other spares. The team stayed at the Chateau Chene de Coeur again and quickly got down to business.

The MG Car Club Northwest Centre team looks on apprehensively as an inspector examines the underside of SRX 210. The entry was rejected on a technicality which was soon remedied. Notice the headlamp screens to protect against flying rocks and debris. For scrutineering the car had to be completely roadworthy, and include weather protection. In order to support the top, two posts were attached to the sides of the cut-down competition windscreen.

The first order of business was to practice with the pit crew so that the loosely organized group of enthusiasts from the Northwest Centre could perform like the professionals they would be competing against. A pit counter was set up at the Chateau where practice was conducted.

The scrutineering on Tuesday had a small hitch for the team. The engine number plate indicated the spare engine installed in the car was not the engine listed as starting on the entry form, so the team was told to change the engine and come back the next day. That seemed like a lot of trouble for the mechanics involved, so the engine switch was performed using a time honored trick. The engine number plates were switched! The first day of practice showed the rear axle ratio of 3.9:1 was too "tall" so this was changed to 4.1:1 that night. The 4.1:1 axle would allow the car to get around the hairpin at the end of Mulsanne without shifting into the unsynchronized first gear. The pit crew was beginning to fall into place as Henry Stone tells it. "It started off with the Northwest Centre as sort of a holiday. Then when they realized on the first day of practice that the car was beginning to go well and that if we would just keep it in one bit we got a good chance, then they were all quite serious and they all took a vast interest."

Unfortunately, that first day of practice was marred when Colin Escott hit a sandbank at Mulsanne corner, damaging the front bodywork. Also during the testing, the transmission overheated and boiled gearbox oil, which in turn blew out the gearbox filler plug resulting in considerable oil loss. The gearbox was also plagued with a propensity to jump out of gear. Tommy Wellman, from the Competitions Department, and Henry Stone spent a long night working on the car. The front end damage was beaten out against a sand bag on the stable floor at the Chateau and the repaired panels repainted. The gearbox was also replaced and the rear axle ratio changed from 3.9:1 to 4.1:1. All in all, quite a night for the two hard working mechanics! Incidentally, they were both on two weeks vacation to attend the non-factory effort.

Back for more practice, the gearbox worked beautifully and the new rear axle ratio allowed second gear to be used through the Mulsanne corner while a top speed of 136 mph at 7,500 rpm was attained down the Mulsanne straight. 132 mph at 7,200 rpm could be held with partial throttle. Pit signals were worked out using a telephone line from the pit area to the signaling crew at Mulsanne corner. The car would be slowed to around 20 mph going through the corner and the driver would have a brief opportunity to read any signals passed to him. The signal to come in for fuel was given one lap in advance and this was about the only pit originated command, the rest being generated by the driver. Fuel consumption was determined by running six laps flat out during the heat of the day and another six during the cool of the night to determine accurately the fuel consumption during daytime and night time running. Fuel consumption was around 12-14 mpg. Having computed fuel consumption, fueling the car was done on a timed basis, utilizing a stop watch. Colin Escott had a problem with his back and to accommodate the different anatomies of Escott and Lund, different seat cushions were used. Colin's was red and Ted's was green, being switched when the drivers were changed. After a somewhat rocky start, the team was at last ready for the race on Saturday.

The trip to the track was not without its own incident, however. Henry Stone tells the story. "As the premier mechanic, I exercised the car down to the race circuit on race day. The first time we went over with the open car I had the reserve driver with me and we were going down Mulsanne, getting really carried away and I didn't realize how fast the hairpin was coming up. So then having seen the hairpin coming up, we realized that there was no

Four p.m. and the race is on! The MG entry is closest to the camera.

way I was going to get round there so we had to take the escape road. With Gendarmes and everyone else waving their bloody arms and things, we went down the escape road and turned it round. We rejoined the circuit proper and I said 'That ain't bad for a bloody mechanic is it, captain?' "

Fortunately, Henry did get the car back to the pits without further incident and the race began smoothly with Lund taking the first turn at the wheel. The car was running strongly and moving up in the placing. The only incident was a faulty carburetor gasket on the rear carburetor which resulted in a burned plug. The malady was quickly repaired and the car continued to move up in the standings. The night passed without further incident and dawn came with only a little mist to hamper progress. A thorough check of the car at the halfway point indicated all was well and the tires and brakes were judged able to last the entire race without replacement. At the scheduled pit stops every three hours, the fuel tank was filled, the engine oil checked and the gearbox oil checked. Anyone who has owned an MGA and had to check the gearbox oil knows what a difficult job that is. Imagine doing it under the pressure of a race in a car which is very hot from running at top speed and the gearbox is running just below the boiling point. Henry Stone was given this unenviable task because of his agility and short stature.

Around ten o'clock Sunday morning the Triumph crew protested that the MG was following the TR 3s too closely. Shortly after the complaint was lodged, the MG was lying eighth overall and had a good chance to move up to seventh because the Aston Martin in front of it was beginning to fade. With such success within sight after 18 hours of racing, disaster struck from a most unexpected quarter. Screaming down the Mulsanne straight at around 136 mph, a huge Alsatian dog wandered onto the course, directly into the path of the oncoming MG. The resulting impact severely damaged the front bodywork of the MG, although it was able to continue on the course. Colin Escott was driving at the time and he could not detect anything amiss with the steering so he continued. As he passed the pits, Henry Stone was the first to realize the car was damaged, he describes his reaction. "We were lying about eighth at the time and Colin Escott came by the pits and I said to Arnold Pownall who was the Chef d'equipe, 'By golly he's bloody hit something.' 'Where,' he said, 'I didn't see anything.' 'Get the bastard in. Get on to Mulsanne and get him in!'"

Henry thought Ecott had hit the back of the TR 3 which had been complaining shortly before that he was following too closely. The car was signaled in and the damage assessed. Because the car was fully undertrayed, the only cooling for the engine oil, water, and the transmission was through the front air intake. The impact of the dog had bent the front sheet metal up in such a manner that the air intake was partially blocked, which caused the

Henry Stone comes to Escott's aid on the run as Colin returns with gearbox troubles.

engine water, oil, and the transmission to overheat. At the point he came in, the engine was starting to cook and the gearbox was one step ahead of it. The gearbox oil was already running right on the limit and the blockage of air caused the oil to boil, blowing the plug out of the box along with most of the gearbox oil. After a frantic five minute session of vigorous bodywork, the car was sent back out in a desperate attempt to finish the race. Escott completed one and a half more laps and the gearbox locked up in third. After cooling off a little, Escott managed to get the car back to the pits where the anxious crew was awaiting more bad news. Ministering to the gearbox with some vigorous rowing on the shift lever, Henry got the gearbox working in second and fourth. With an admonishment not to select third gear again, Colin went back out in a last ditch effort to complete the race. All went as well as could be expected for a short time, when in the heat of battle, Colin forgot about third gear and inadvertently selected it, or at least tried to select it and the box promptly locked up, bringing the car to a screeching halt at Arnage for the last time. Colin walked back to the pits. By that time, the team was a virtual hostage in the pits and they were obliged to stay and watch the rest of the race which was only hours away. Henry Stone reflects on the mood at the time. "Everybody was pretty disappointed. All right, mechanical failure is mechanical failure, that's fair enough. Things go wrong. But to hit a blooming dog, it's crazy. You haven't hit another motorcar, you haven't left the circuit. You're going on your own sweet and proper way and across the road comes the largest Alsatian in France!"

The team spent the night at the Chateau and a very discouraged bunch of enthusiasts headed home on Monday. Since the car belonged to MG, arrangements were made to ship the car back by train. At that point there was no plan for a team the next year.

For 1960 the team returned with a new entry. This time a fastback coupe was used to increase the top speed and decrease driver fatigue. The large driving lamps were supplied by Ted Lund's father.

Le Mans—1960

The decision to run another team at Le Mans in 1960 came quite late in the year and resulted in much last minute work. It was decided to go with a coupe style body to take advantage of the latest rules change which required a full height windscreen. Don Hayter, who came to MG from Aston Martin and is now in charge of the Design Office, drew the lines for the coupe which featured coupe doors and top for the initial form. To cut down on wind resistance, the roof line was lowered about 1-1/2 inches and a fastback line extended to the tail. To accommodate the gas tank filler cap a huge "dust bin" was formed around the filler neck. The all aluminum body was built under the direction of Eric Carter by Bodies Branch. All windows were constructed from plexiglass except for the windshield. The rear quarter windows were sealed with windshield rubber seal and the open end was finished off with a piece of slat taken from the front grill! The scoop on the hood was designed to evacuate the air from the engine compartment. The finished body, painted in the same metallic green as EX 181, was delivered to MG a scant 2-1/2 months prior to the race and there upon started a period of intense activity.

Henry Stone was again put in charge of preparing the car. He attacked his charge with a vengence, lightening it wherever possible. He even drilled holes in the window cranks. It was said around the shop, "Don't leave your spanner about because Henry will drill a hole in it!" The air intake design of the previous year was retained; however, it was decided to try and incorporate a closed carburetor air box in an effort to get a ramming effect down the carburetor throats. When the air box was closed off, it resulted in throttle lag when opening the throttle. Investigation showed the high pressure air was blowing the fuel back down the jets when the throttle was closed which resulted in the throttle lag. A solution to the problem would have been to run pipes from the float bowls into the air box to equalize the pressure; however, it was decided to revert to the system used the previous year. A full undertray was again employed with some minor changes to improve cooling. The engine oil sump was allowed to protrude through the undertray and was sealed with gasket material commonly used in boilers for its heat resistance. No wind tunnel testing was done on the new body style. There was no time for that.

As before, Twin Cam four wheel disc brakes were used with knock-off disc wheels. 5.50 x 15 tires were fitted on the front and 6.00 x 15 on the rear to improve handling and help carry the extra weight of the larger fuel tank. The engine, from the year before, was bored out to 1762 cc and fitted with dual 40 DCOE Weber carburetors. A front anti-sway bar was added to improve the handling and the rear shock valving was slightly adjusted. A spare tire which only fitted the front tire size was stowed behind the seat.

There was only one seat which had an improved design to help hold the driver in position. The same cushion arrangement from the year before was employed as Lund and Escott would be sharing the driving chores again. A larger rev counter was incorporated along with an engine oil temperature and transmission oil temperature gauge. The interior was flock-sprayed for appearance sake, otherwise it was gutted. A bottle filled with lemonade was fitted on the passenger's side with a tube running to the driver.

To keep the front shocks filled, a small Coloron wood dye tin filled with shock absorber fluid was connected by tubes to the shock absorber filler plugs. An engine oil cooler was hung under the front splash apron. Ted Lund's father was in the business of selling driving lamps known as "Lund Lamps." A pair of these were neatly faired into the front. Protective covers were fitted over the lenses. Identification lamps were fitted on the roof (blue) and on the fender (white and red). A luminous patch was affixed on the left rear of the car to tell overtaking cars what speed category the car was in. SRX 210, as the car was registered, carried a blue patch which signaled a two litre class entry. There was no time for testing before the departure for Le Mans, although the basic design had been successfully campaigned the year before.

Once again the Northwest Centre was the organization responsible for the entry and most of the crew from the previous year came along again, headed by Major Arnold Pownall. The car was transported by Bill Hogg accompanied by Henry Stone in a transporter. All went smoothly until Bordeaux where the proper paperwork for Hogg to drive the transporter was not in order. Ironically, Hogg owned the transporter. It was Sunday, and there was no place open to contact his offices in England, so the pair had to stay in Bordeaux until Monday. After some delay, the transporter with SRX

210, Henry and Bill arrived at Le Mans square on Monday, where the rest of the team anxiously awaited them.

The team was once again headquartered in the Chateau Chene de Coeur and with most of the same people on the team as the year before, little time was wasted in settling in. Monday evening and Tuesday were spent preparing the crew for the various tasks to which they were assigned and some last minute preparation of the car.

On Wednesday scrutineering was held. The car passed with flying colors and was duly registered in the two litre prototype class; however, the drivers were not so lucky. Colin Escott made it through the physical all right, but Ted Lund failed the blood pressure test. Perhaps Ted had been enjoying the local "flavor" a bit too much Tuesday night! Ted returned the next day and passed the physical. Day practice was to be held on Thursday and was to be a busy day for all hands.

On Thursday fuel consumption figures were worked out and the gear ratios double checked. Drivers instructions were to hold to 7,000 rpm in the indirect gears and 7,200 in top. The actual top speed was 142 mph at 7,500 rpm. Henry was worried about the spark plugs lasting the race. A conference was held with the Champion representative, and it was agreed to test the plugs on a hard lap run in the heat of the day and another in the cool of the night and then take a reading from them. This was done and the plugs were given the okay. During the first day of practice, Ted heard an unusual noise coming from under the rear of the car. Fearing a problem with the differential, he brought the car in for Henry Stone to have a look at it. Henry couldn't tell anything was the matter so he crawled into the passenger's side, with no safety equipment whatever, faced the rear of the car while crouched on all fours listening for the sound while Ted drove round the track. The noise was the undertray vibrating against the underside of the car, and was easily cured back in the pits. Meanwhile Henry got two laps around Le Mans at racing speeds to his credit.

During pit practice, three sets of tires were prepared. One set marked with green paint was to be used for general purpose road conditions, tires marked with white were for dry roads and yellow marking indicated rain tires. In changing the tires, it was discovered that the lever type jack interfered with the muffler, so Henry had to go out and attempt to have a piece fabricated and welded onto the rear chassis. Needless to say, his French, punctuated by frequent and rapid arm movement, was pressed into service and the job successfully done. Interestingly, a stock exhaust system was retained and inclosed within the confines of the undertray.

Despite all the activity, or perhaps because of it, practice was fairly short. The team was satisfied with their preparations; and to prevent any accident with the car, it was locked up and the team took a well earned rest in preparation for Saturday's event.

Colin and Ted shared driving chores once again and the car was off and running without incident, lapping the course with encouraging regularity. Following the night running, a rainstorm came up in the early morning hours and continued until around ten o'clock. During the storm, one wiper blade, naturally the one in front of the driver, jumped its gear and began wiping the bonnet instead of the windshield! The misguided wiper was soon fixed and the car resumed its pace. At one point the rain came down rather furiously and Ted lost sight of the track for a second giving him quite a moment. This was later followed by a near miss with a Corvette. It will be remembered that the fuel was added using a timed method. At one point in the race, the car was brought in and filled. The subsequent calculation showed only two pints of fuel were left in the tank when it came in! Consumption was 12-1/2 mpg.

With one hour left in the race, the car was brought in for a final check. Le Mans rules state that all equipment must be functioning at the end of the race, so this was a precautionary pit stop. Everything seemed to be in order as the checklist was run off until the "Lund Lamps" were tried. One of them refused to light sending the mechanics into a flurry of activity. Fortunately, the problem was minor. A loose connection was quickly fixed and the car was off for the final hour with Ted Lund at the helm. Having had a bit of a scare, the mechanics swore next year there would be no "Lund Lamps" to worry them!

As SRX 210 neared the finish line, Ted noticed John Dalton's Austin Healey Sprite coming beside him down the last straight. In a display of Abingdon comraderie, Ted eased up so that the two Abingdon cars crossed the finish line together. The MG had won the two litre class, finishing 13th overall. In its victory in the two litre class, it averaged 91.12 mph, posting a fastest lap of 99.46 mph and beating all the Triumphs, an AC-Bristol and an Osca in the process. The performance of the MG would have been sufficient to garner an outright win in the 1950 Le Mans race.

Following the victory in the pits, the team headed for the by now familiar Cafe Les Rossier for a well earned celebration. Exuberant over their victory, the team decided to come back the next year, running the same basic car. The car was driven from the race course to a nearby home where it was subsequently loaded on the transporter and brought back home to Abingdon. Ted Lund picked the car up at the factory and drove it home without so much as a sparkplug change!

Le Mans—1961

For 1961 the Northwest Centre Team decided to retain the basic concept employed the year before with some minor modifications. The nose of the car was modified to improve penetration and help hold the front end down. The traditional MGA grill was removed and the air intake smoothed over. The front fenders were also cut back about 4-1/2 inches. A small lip was bolted over the top half of the opening to insure the air went into the opening instead of over the bonnet. The lip was removable so that if it were unnecessary, it could be removed for the race. Parts could be removed after scrutineering, but not added. As it turned out, the lip was not needed and the car ran without it in the race. The engine was switched again, returning to the original engine from 1959. The 40 DCOE Weber carburetors were replaced by a still larger pair of 45 DCOE Webers. Power output was 128 bhp @ 5,400 rpm, sufficient to propel the car to 55 mph in first, 87 mph in second, 112 mph in third and 140 mph in fourth at 7,000 rpm. The mechanics got their way, and the "Lund Lamps" were dropped. Given the luxury of time to prepare the car, the mechanics drilled and wired every nut they could find in the interest of reliability. Even the windscreen wipers were drilled and wired. Dunlop reinforced hoses, dual coils and other backup systems were incorporated to stack the odds against any unexpected problems.

For 1961 SRX 210 was back again, this time minus the Lund Lamps and sporting a new "nose job."

Colin Escott was not available to drive in 1961, so a young South African named Bob Olthoff was asked to drive with Ted Lund. Bob also drove for MG as a reserve driver at Sebring in 1961 and as a primary driver on the 1962 Sebring team. The team set off for Le Mans with the goal of once again winning the two litre class.

The Chateau Chene de Coeur was again the home away from home for the intrepid team which was once again sponsored and crewed by the Northwest Centre. This year scrutineering went without a hitch and practice was likewise without incident.

Ted led off the driving chores and was lapping at speeds around 100 mph. He soon became the first MG driver to lap Le Mans at over 100 mph, clocking a lap at 101.66 mph. Ted had been out for around two hours and Bob Olthoff was getting ready to take over. Bob was understandably anxious to have a go at Le Mans, and reportedly he had already tried his helmet on at least three times when disaster struck. Henry Stone tells what happened to Ted.

> After about two hours I heard over the PA system that his number had come to rest at Mulsanne and I thought, golly what the hell is gone wrong with this thing now. We'd got everything duplicated we could so that it would be easy to switch over. And the next thing they said over the PA system was that the driver had abandoned the car. We thought, well it must be something serious. Ted eventually arrived and I said, 'What the hell went wrong, Ted?' and he said, 'I always have my left foot hovering near the clutch and I was going down Mulsanne and it was going like a rocket and there was a God almighty bang and I kicked the clutch out and coasted onto the grass and a con-rod bolt had let go. There was a big shaft of daylight in the side of the engine.' That's expensive. If it had only done that in practice, we'd have put the spare engine in it.

With the car out of the race and nearly twenty-two hours left until the finish, the crew was held hostage in the pits. Fortunately, a group of spectators who had boxes over the pits befriended them and they spent the rest of the race in relative comfort.

So ended the MGA campaigns at Le Mans. The goals had been modest, the results surprisingly good. The cars had been exciting, the races varied and interesting, but most of all they presented a story of human endeavor against the vagaries of long distance racing.

Sebring

The 12 Hours of Sebring counted toward the Worlds Sports Car Manufacturers Championship, and as such, it attracted many of the world's finest cars and drivers. Sebring was an unusual location for an event of this stature. Located in south central Florida, in the heart of the citrus growing area, the weather was usually warm for the race, which was held around the middle of March. Sebring is a tiny town which swelled to enormous proportions on race week, attracting race fans from all over the U.S., many anxious to get a head start on summer. The course itself was unusual in that a portion of the airfield, which used to base B-17 bombers, was used for part of the course. The Track iself was marked off with traffic cones in some places, occasionally causing the drivers problems in identifying the edges of the "road," picking up or tipping over cones along their route. The course was quite bumpy in places and the turns were infamous for their lack of camber, taking a toll on suspensions and drivers' concentration through the twelve hour race. The race itself is run on Saturday, beginning at ten o'clock in the morning and running until ten o'clock that night. Certainly not as grueling as the 24 Hours of Le Mans, but very demanding in its own right.

At the time of the MGA's running, 1956—62, the race at Sebring was

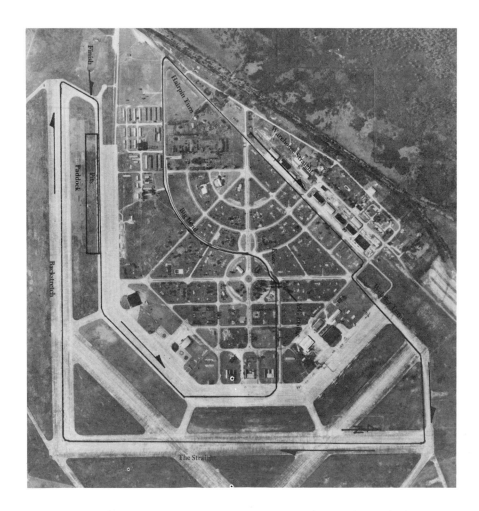

Finish
Hairpin Turn
Warehouse Straight
Paddock
Pits
Big Bend
Backstretch
The Straight

The racecourse at Sebring is laid out on an airfield as shown here. The field was still in use at the time and most of the accommodations had to be erected each year. The MG bridge was erected just before the esses, a favorite spot for photographers. The airfield offered the spectators a lot of room to wander around the course, however accommodations were a long drive from the course.

very much a small town American affair, with the towns people, and the Automobile Racing Club of Florida (organizer and sponsor of the event) acting as enthusiastic hosts. The Sports Car Club of America (SCCA) was the sanctioning body that licensed ARCF to hold the event annually. Great care went into making sure things ran smoothly race week, despite the isolated location and lack of lodging nearby.

The MGA's campaigns at Sebring can be divided into two periods. The first period was 1956 and 1957 when a team of three cars was run each year. The cars were given some backing from Hambro Automotive, but they were prepared and entered by three dealerships in New York, Washington, and Pennsylvania, with the urging of a dedicated group of SCCA racers. The MG factory made some parts available to the teams, but these were in every sense of the word private entries. The three cars were entered as a team under the sponsorship of Hambro Automotive, MG distributor for North America.

There was no MGA team at Sebring in 1958, though Austin Healeys did run that year. From 1959—62 the MG factory, with the cooperation of Hambro Automotive, ran teams at Sebring along with a sister team from Austin Healey. The main purpose of these entries was to publicize the MG and Austin Healey in the U.S. and Canada. The drivers were carefully chosen to represent a good geographical mixture, lending a regional flavor to the teams. The cars themselves were prepared at the MG factory Competitions Department and shipped over to the States. Following the races, the cars were sold at discounted prices to the dealerships or individuals interested, for continued racing in North America—thus continuing to spread the reputation of MG.

Sebring 1956

The 1956 Sebring 12 Hours saw a team of three MGAs entered only six

months after sales of the MGA began. Indeed, the 1956 Sebring race was the first major competition appearance for the MGA in North America. Car number 49 was prepared in New York by Inskip Motors and driven by Dave Ash and Gus Ehrman. Car number 50 was prepared in Washington by Manhatten Auto and driven by Bill Kinchloe and Steve Spitler. Car number 51 was prepared in Warren, Pennsylvania and driven by Fred Allen and Johnny Van Driel. The cars were raced in the sports 1100-1500 cc class against some pretty stiff competition, namely the Porsche 550 Spyder.

The cars were little changed from stock. The most obvious external differences being the Brooklands style windscreens and the auxillary driving lamps up front. The cars were individually prepared so they were somewhat different in their individual specification; however, a basic plan was followed. The emphasis was on reliability, understandably so with the newness of the model and the length of the race. Redundancy of components such as dual fuel pumps and dual coils were employed. An oil pressure light to draw the driver's attention was added to the already comprehensive instrumentation. Safety items included hood safety straps, seat belts, fire extinguishers and first aid kits. Spare parts were taped to the chassis. The engines were carefully disassembled, inspected, brought exactly into tolerance and reassembled with an eye to reliability. Exhaust systems ran straight through. The cars were trucked down to the race.

Arriving at Sebring, the smell of oranges and the snarl of high strung racing engines punctuated the air, heralding the start of the racing season for many racers. All the big teams were there; Maserati with Jean Behra and Piero Taruffi, Ferrari with the great Juan Manuel Fangio, Mike Hawthorn was piloting the Jaguar while Aston Martin boasted such names as Peter Collins and Stirling Moss.

Scrutineering on Wednesday went by without a hitch. The first day of practice went well with Gus Ehrman turning the fastest time of the day for MG with a 4:28 lap. The plan was for the MGAs to lap at 4:35 to 4:40. To put this into perspective, Stirling Moss was lapping at 3:32 in the Aston Martin, which he confided wasn't fast enough to win. The second day of practice was used to bed in the tires and brakes and put a last minute tune on the engines. A short practice lowered the times down to 4:24.

Race day was bright and sunny. The teams were at the track early and by 8:30 the fuel tanks were drained and refilled with the requisite AMOCO blend and sealed. The drivers' meeting over, there was nothing to do but await the Le Mans style start. Ash, Spitler and Allen talked about how to best avoid the crush at the start. They all agreed the best way was to simply be among the first away at the start! The drivers were on their marks and the countdown began its downward spiral from 20. At last they were off in a mass of smoke and noise. The MGs all got off cleanly, with Ash in the lead. The others quickly caught up and the three cars lapped together around 4:37, right on schedule. By the second refueling, car number 50 had its throttle linkage come adrift which cost it a lap to have it fixed. By late afternoon, the brakes on car number 49 were beginning to fail, requiring four pumps to get adequate pedal. Would they last another six hours of hard running with five hard braking points each lap? By early evening car number 49 was ahead of number 50 by one lap and ahead of number 51 by three laps when misfortune struck, and car number 51 spun off the track into a sandbank. Fortunately, the driver and car were not damaged and the driver managed to dig the car out and continue the race, having lost 33 minutes. By this time, the brakes on number 49 were on the rivets and number 50 was now running in the same lap. Just after darkness fell, the Portago-Kimberly Ferrari withdrew leaving the MG entry the only team left intact for the team prize. At this point things were looking good for the team; and with only 20 minutes left to race, the cars were called in and drivers told to nurse the cars around at a 5:00 pace and finish abreast. This was in fact the way the team finished, three abreast, taking the team prize and finishing 4th, 5th, and 6th in class behind the three Porsche Spyders. A 65.433 mph average speed was posted by cars 49 and 50.

The race results were as shown below:

Car	Drivers	Laps	Class Position	Overall Position
49	Ash/Ehrman	151	5	20
50	Kinchloe/Spitler	151	4	19
51	Allen/Van Driel	139	6	22

Sebring 1957

For 1957, the same sponsors and dealerships got together and entered a team of three MGA roadsters which were visually similar to the previous year's entries, but were in fact different cars. They were prepared in much the same manner as 1956, remaining largely stock with attention to reliability. The goal was another team prize, and perhaps a better class finish. Carrying the same numbers as the previous year, the team ran like clockwork and captured the team prize for the second year in a row with all three cars crossing the finish line abreast. Well, almost abreast. You know how hard it is to keep a competitor in check. Well, it seems car number 50, driven by Steve Spitler, lunged ahead at the last possible moment and nosed out car number 51 for the class win. The MGAs had a great year in 1957, taking the team prize with all three cars finishing the race and taking first and second in class. Car number 50, driven by Bill Kinchloe and Steve Spitler won the class and were followed in second place by Dave Ash and Gus Ehrman in car number 51.

Sebring 1959

1959 marked the return of the MG factory to long distance racing. A team of three Twin Cam coupes plus one practice car were prepared under the watchful eye of Douggie Watts, the Competition Departmet foreman. The specification for the cars was reasonably close to stock. A locked differential, auxilliary lights and requisite safety equipment were of course carried.

The BMC team at Sebring that year consisted of the MGAs and a team of three Austin Healey Sprites. A total of fourteen Canadian and American amateur drivers were selected along with a team of fifteen Canadian mechanics. John Thornley was along to supervise the entire operation while Marcus Chambers, Competitions Department Manager, was charged with coordination between the Austin Healey and MGA factions. Douggie Watts was in charge of the MGA pit crew. With such a diverse group, the management aspect of the race may have been more difficult than the race itself! Geoffrey Healey, Douggie Watts and Marcus Chambers were to leave

Sign posted on the pit door in 1959 just about covered it all!

NOTICE

ABSOLUTELY OFF LIMITS FOR

PRESIDENTS
VICE PRESIDENTS
CHAIRMEN
MANAGING DIRECTORS
DIRECTORS
SALES MANAGERS
and
OTHER V. I. P. s.

also

DRAGSTERS
SPORTS CAR ENTHUSIASTS
CALIFORNIAN HOT RODDERS
KINGS OF SPEED
HERO RACING DRIVERS
RACING MECHANICS
HOT OCTANE OPERATORS
LIVING DOLLS
and
OTHER TALKATIVE HUMANS

AUTHORISED PERSONNEL INCLUDE FOLLOWING

CHIEF TIME KEEPER
MG AND A. H. SPOTTERS
CHART KEEPERS
TEAM MANAGERS
MG AND A. H. GENERAL MANAGER AND DIRECTOR
B. M. C. TEAM MANAGER

together with Stan Nicholls on a Britannic night flight from London to New York. Stan was the chief timekeeper at the 1955 Le Mans race and likewise he was the chief timekeeper on this occasion; however, there may have been some second thoughts about his selection as the flight was held up due to his late arrival! In all fairness, it should be noted that the airline tickets erroneously listed the departure time as 2359 instead of 2300. Strong headwinds were encountered and the flight was forced to land in Iceland to refuel. Arriving in New York, Marcus luggage was late and after what seemed like an interminable delay, the group was on its way to Florida on what turned out to be a bumpy, uncomfortable ride. Arriving 45 minutes late in Tampa, the tired group must have thought this was not their day. Jack Flaherty met them at the airport in a brand new Magnette, the first any of them had seen. Perhaps letting the crew in on what was going to transpire in the coming days, the distributor cap cracked and they just made it to Sebring. . . to the wrong hotel!

After such a rocky start, Marcus was buoyed by the enthusiasm of the spectators, officials and drivers, as he wrote in the May 1959 issue of *Safety Fast*. "Never have I felt under such an obligation to do the right thing by the officials; their charm is compelling, and one's pit marshalls immediately identify with the fortunes of the cars that they are supervising." Unfortunately the weather didn't hold up and the spring showers which came along washed out practice for one session. During the practice which was

Members of the MG team await an inspector during a pause in the rain. The cars were fitted with optional Lucas driving lamps.

They're off! In a cloud of smoke number 28 on the right and number 29 on the left leave the start line. Twelve hours later they were to finish in the same order, second and third in class.

For 1960 BMC mounted a team of three MGA Twin Cam roadsters and three Austin Healey 3000s shown here with the MGAs on the left.

run, the Twin Cams gave twice as much trouble as the Sprites. A 5,000 rpm rev limit was imposed on the drivers and a tell tale was employed to check for compliance. The three race entries were driven by a group of seven drivers. Number 28 was driven by Gus Ehrman, a veteran of the 1956 and 1957 Sebring races, and Ray Saidel. Jim Parkinson and John Dalton drove number 29. Car number 30 was piloted by Ray Pickering, Jack Flaherty and Sherm Decker as reserve driver. Driver selection was done with a thought toward regional distribution and dealer volume, guidelines which didn't sit well with Sherm Decker who was turning laps significantly faster than the others, and yet was relegated to being a reserve driver.

Frequent pit stops for fuel were a necessary part of long distance racing; and Gus Ehrman and Hal Wallace had been working on a plan which they hoped would cut down the refueling time. A pressurized fuel container was devised which fed the fuel into the tank at one gallon per second. Unfortunately, the device was not fully developed and many gallons of fuel found their way onto the pit floor. At the last moment, the fix was found and the fueling operation went smoothly and quickly during the race.

The old nemisis of MGAs, heat in the passenger compartment. reared its ugly head in the Florida sun. In an effort to get more air into the

With British license plates still in place, the Twin Cam coupes were very stock in appearance but underneath the typically thorough MG preparation had been followed. Notice the quick release gas filler cap.

Lucas Le Mans high power headlamps were fitted to ease the night driving chores.

passenger compartment, holes were drilled in the toe-board behind the pedals to direct fresh air onto the drive's feet.

Race day brought clear weather with it, and the team was in place and ready to go by 8:30. The starting drivers were Ray Saidel, John Dalton and Ray Pickering. The Twin Cams were away in good shape. The race plan was to hold the Twin Cams back and see how the race developed. Unfortunately, it began to rain with a vengence about the same time the increase speed signal was given. The track was treacherously slippery and this greatly reduced the speed. Car number 28 had a run-in with a straw bale, but was able to continue. Car number 29 had its starter motor go out, and that cost them an hour long pit stop. It was after dark by now, and the rain was still coming down. The Porsches were pulling away from the MGs and the decision was made to have Sherm Decker come in to drive number 30 and try to make up some time on the Porsches. Sherm was disgruntled at this time and the prospect of finally getting to drive one of the cars in the dark, in a rainstorm, while trying to make up time on the Porsches, was not encouraging; but the experience of driving at Sebring was something not to be missed after having come all this way, so Sherm agreed. Getting the feel of the car, Sherm spun it out on the first lap; but soon he got the feel of things and started cutting the times down on the Porsches. It was then that disaster struck after ten hours of racing. Sherm tells what happened.

The engine blew just after I had passed the start-finish line and gotten off the strip. I was always in pretty good shape and so I thought, well, I'll push it. It was right hand drive and on the left side of the road. I was trying to push it and of course I was partly on the road and these cars were coming out of the night. I had two of them sideways when they spotted me. I pushed it probably a mile and a half and I was pooped. Trying to get around the hairpin with that locked differential with one wheel sliding was tough! I finally stopped. The mechanic had come over by then but of course he couldn't touch the car. I cranked it over and it just went clunk, clunk, clunk. It tried to start, but it acted rich and I thought that if I could lean the carburetors out, I thought I could get it started. I got hold of the jets and of course, the jets wouldn't run. I turned to the mechanic and said, 'You know if you get me a jet wrench and just drop it here, I think I can get this thing to run.' He got me one and nobody saw it. It was dark anyway. I got the jets leaned out and it started. It knocked like crazy. You could tell the piston was gone and the rod was just flopping around. The longer it ran the less noise it made as the rod hewed out a path in it. The oil pressure was zero. I took off and drove about a quarter of a mile and it seized. I sat there and let it cool down and started it up again. I got it back to just about the start-finish line and parked it. I guess they pushed it over at the finish of the race.

Number 30 did in fact finish the race and placed 45th overall. Not a great achievement, but it did finish. Car number 28 was more fortunate and finished second in class, followed by number 29 which was third in class. Once again a Porsche won the class.

The end of the race was punctuated with a bit of humor as Gus Ehrman removed his pants in the pits and wrung them out to his wife's eternal embarassment. Those fresh air holes which were drilled in the toeboards also admitted water to the extent that the driver's compartment was literally flooded! The race results were as shown below:

Car	Drivers	Laps	Class Position	Overall Position
28	Ehrman/Saidel	155	2	27
29	Parkinson/Dalton	145	3	34
30	Pickering/Flaherty/Decker	121	—	45

Californians Jim Parkinson (left) and Jack Flaherty show off the Twin Cam engine.

The trunk of number 40 showing the spare tire arrangement and the heavy duty fuel pump.

Sebring 1960

For the 1960 race, BMC entered three MGA Twin Cam roadsters and three Austin Healey 3000s. The Donald Healey Motor Company also entered two Austin Healey Sprites, one in the 1100 cc Sports Category and another special one for the Four-Hour Grand Touring Car Race, which was to be held on Friday, March 25. This year the Twin Cams would sport aluminum hardtops in place of the coupe body to save on weight. There were many other changes made to the team cars which were indicative of the types of modifications made by the factory to the Sebring cars for all the years MGAs were run there. Bumpers were removed front and rear for lightness. A pair of powerful driving lights were installed up front and a signal lamp was located on the roof to signal the pits. The hood was secured with a single leather strap and an external hood release was located just to the left of the radiator grill. To the right of the grill was a cold air intake for the carburetors, with the air outlet located in the right front fender. The air scoop

The instrument panel came in for some extensive modification, presumably to keep obstructions away from the driver's hands. Top row of switches from left to right: wiper, starter (push type), on/off ignition and fuel pump, lights, unknown, rubber plug, panel light dimmer. Bottom row: windscreen washer, choke, left driving lamp, horn, right driving lamp, plug and generator charge indicator lamp. Instruments from left to right: fuel, water temperature/oil pressure, 8000 rpm tachometer with telltale at 7000, 120 mph speedometer.

The interior showing the competition deluxe seats, stock steering wheel and competition seat belts. Switch atop dash on extreme right controlled the roof light.

located on the hood was not for the engine, but rather to provide cool air to the driver's compartment. Under the hood was a basically stock Twin Cam engine. Modifications included two inch carburetors, some attention to gas flow in the heads and a careful strip down, inspection and reassembly. An extra water cooling pipe ran to the center of the cylinder head where a quick release oil filler cap was employed. The engine sported an oil cooler mounted in front of the radiator. For reliability, all engine nuts and bolts were drilled and wired. Fuel was delivered from a 20 gallon (17 Imperial gallon) tank via twin trunk mounted electric fuel pumps similar to those used in Jaguars of the time. A separate fuel line was run inside the passenger compartment to the carburetors. The gas tank was equipped with a quick release cap modified so that it could be sealed. The electrical system came in for some attention as well. The headlamps were replaced with Lucas Le Mans 24 high power lights. Lucas SLR 576 clear lens driving lamps, complete with black vinyl covers to protect them against flying stones when not in use, were mounted. The generator and voltage regulator were of heavier duty specification than standard. A single 12 volt battery was used. With a eye toward the rain laden Florida sky, two-speed windshield wipers were installed. In the interest of safety, a windshield washer, seat belts and fire extinguisher were fitted.

The right hand drive interior was equipped with the more comfortable competition deluxe seats. The dash came in for some extensive modifications. The standard tachometer was replaced with a large 5 inch model with tell-tale. This tachometer did not have a generator light built in it so a generator lamp was added to the lower left of the tachometer. The starter pull switch was removed as well as the fog lamp and lighting switches. The

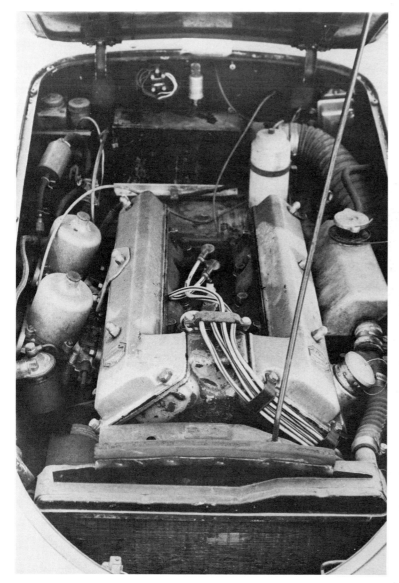

The engine compartment of car number 40 looks much the same today as it did in 1960, just dustier! Lyle York, owner of number 40 and Chairman of the MGA Twin Cam Registry, has devoted years to locating other Sebring cars and collecting information on them. By the way, the heater has been added on Lyle's car.

The bracket held a water bottle for the driver's use during the hot turns at the wheel. Internally routed cables and lines can be seen just below the bracket. The regulation "FIA suitcase" fit behind the drape to the right.

holes were filled with rubber plugs. The fog lamp and lighting switches were moved to a panel inserted where the speaker grill is normally found and a fuel pump/ignition switch was also located on the panel. The switches may have been moved to prevent interference with the driver's hands. The fuel pump/ignition switch replaced the standard key ignition switch. A solenoid starter was employed with a push type starter switch located just above the fuel gauge. A small panel located in a portion of the space where the heater control panel fits held a cable control knob which manipulated the flapper control on the cold air intake for the driver's compartment. On the top right-hand corner of the dash, an on/off switch was mounted to control the signal light mounted on the roof. The portion of the body immediately behind the seats was modified to accommodate the standard "FIA suitcase" which was required by regulation. The side curtain holder was also modified with two zippers to accept the suitcase. On at least one of the cars a bracket for holding a water bottle was mounted behind the driver's seat and a drinking tube ran up to the driver.

A close-ratio gearbox was provided. Chassis modifications were minimal. A front anti-roll bar and high rate front springs were fitted and Dunlop made some special radial racing tires available to the team. The cars were finished in British Racing Green, what else!

The MGA team was a truly international mixture of Canadian, British and American talent. Car number 38 was driven by the British team of Ted

Rubber cushions taped over the headlamps, number 39 is ready to race.

Lund and Colin Escott who would be joining forces again later that year at Le Mans. The Canadian pair, Ed Leavens and Fred Hayes, drove car number 39. Two Californians. Jim Parkinson and Jack Flaherty, were assigned car number 40. In addition to the three race cars and a practice car, a fifth car, identical in specification to the race cars, was sold to a Canadian dealer.

At exactly 10 a.m. 65 drivers sprinted across the concrete to their cars and the silence was broken as 65 eager engines roared to life. Amid the noise and smoke the team of three MGAs were off cleanly; however, the team was not to remain intact for long. Only 2-1/2 laps had been completed when the British crew were brought to rest with a broken valve spring. The remaining two entries were dogged by cracked brake cross-over lines which required several pit stops. The problem was attributed to the rough surface of the track. The Canadian entry was running about 35th with the American team leading slightly in 30th position during the early stages of the race. Unfortunately, the American car, number 40, received more than its share of brake troubles and the Canadian pair pulled ahead. The main competition in the GT Class for cars under 1600 cc were the Porsches, which were well suited for long distance racing. It soon became obvious to the Canadians that they had no chance of catching the Porsches, so they concentrated on beating the Americans who were nipping at their heels. The last thing a team manager wants is to have his only two entries racing each other in a long distance race like Sebring. Marcus Chambers, the BMC team manager, noticed that his instructions were not being taken seriously, so he simply stopped giving the drivers their lap times in order to keep them from driving the cars too hard! Grinding into the night, the Canadian team of Ed Leavens and Fred Hayes drove number 39 to a 3rd place finish in class, predictably behind the two Porsches and 12 laps ahead of car number 40, driven by the Americans, Jim Parkinson and Jack Flaherty. Average speed for number 39 was 69.11 mph and number 40 averaged 64.08 mph.

The race results were as shown below:

Car	Drivers	Laps	Class Position	Overall Position
38	Lund/Escott	2	—	DNF
39	Hayes/Leavens	160	3	24
40	Parkinson/Flaherty	148	4	29

It was BMC policy to sell the Sebring cars after the race so that they might stay on in the U.S. and Canada and continue to provide favorable publicity for MG in amateur races. Because of this policy, Sebring race cars have collected their own dedicated following in America and Canada. In the case of the 1960 Sebring team cars, four persistent enthusiasts have at last realized their dream of owning a Sebring MGA. Car number 38 is owned by Steve Woodyard from Washington, D.C. Car number 39 is owned by Dave Nicholas in Houston, Texas. Lyle York, founder and chairman of the Twin Cam Registry in the U.S., is the proud owner of number 40 and resides in Anderson, Indiana.

Fittingly, the fifth Sebring MGA Twin Cam which was sold to a Canadian dealership is now owned by a Canadian, Robin Barker from Brantford, Ontario. The practice car has had a rather checkered career. Starting off rather normally, the car was raced for three years until its second owner moved to Florida, taking the car with him. The owner then became involved in a "fishing survey for the Dominican Republic," which sounds suspiciously like a CIA cover story! He and his partner in the "survey" set sail aboard a 60 ft. schooner with the Twin Cam lashed to the deck. As luck would have it, the ship was caught in a bad storm in the Caribbean and the boat and Twin Cam sunk. The two intrepid "surveyors" drifted ashore in a lifeboat. Unfortunately the shore was owned by Fidel Castro and the pair spent the next five months in a Cuban prison before returning to the states! This story sounds far fetched, but no one has been able to refute it yet.

The remaining four cars are playing a part in a story almost as interesting. The owners are now in contact with each other and are planning to enter the four cars as a team in the 1981 vintage car race at Sebring, bringing the story full circle some 21 years after they originally ran.

Sebring 1961

The team for 1961 consisted of two 1600 Mk I Deluxe coupes, surely two of the rarest and most desirable of all MGAs. The engines were prepared under the supervision of Eddie Maher at Coventry while the bodies and chassis were done at Abingdon. Specifications for the cars were similar to

Ready for action, the two MG entries await the start. The British team of Peter Riley and John Whitmore with South African Bob Olthoff as reserve driver, drove number 43. The American team of Jim Parkinson and Jack Flaherty were assigned number 44 which was distinguished by its white taped valence panel for easy identification.

those in preceeding years. A small tin of shock absorber fluid was connected to keep the front shocks topped up in the same manner as the 1960 and 61 Le Mans MGA Twin Cam coupes. Preparation of the cars was completed very late and as a result the cars were rushed from Southampton to America in style, on the *Queen Elizabeth.*

Scrutineering went smoothly on Tuesday of race week. Marcus Chambers had made sure all the parts were properly homologated. Practice on Wednesday was not particularly fast as there was a stiff 15 mph headwind blowing. Additionally, the cars were suffering from too soft a suspension on the front, and the rear wheels were consequently lifting on hard cornering. A quick phone call to BMC Canada and the anti-roll bars from last year's race were on the way to Sebring.

Number 44 on its way to a first place class win successfully rising to the Sunbeam Alpine challenge. The MG bridge is seen in the background.

As in 1959, the team of MGAs was accompanied by a team of Austin Healey Sprites. MGA car number 43 was driven by the British team of Peter Riley and John Whitmore. Bob Olthoff, a South African, was the reserve driver. Car number 44 was driven by the Californian team of Jim Parkinson and Jack Flaherty.

For the 1961 race, MG's chief competition came from the Sunbeam Alpine team. The Porsches which won handily in 1960 were entered in the Sports category while the MGAs were in the GT category. The Sunbeams had shown great promise during trials at Silverstone and they were quick to exploit this in the motoring press and on British television. This competition surge by the team from Coventry put MG on notice to prove its racing reputation. The effect was to strengthen the resolve of MG departments concerned. A concerted effort was put forth with great cooperation from all departments to mount the best effort possible. When the cars reached Sebring, the Sunbeam and MG fans were already warmed to the occasion with much good humored discussion regarding the merits of their respective marques.

Pre-race practice showed the MGAs to be every bit the equal of the Alpine's lap times. However, the MGAs had two trump cards, less tire wear and a more efficient pit crew. Tests during practice showed the brakes could go the distance without a change and the tires would only have to be changed once. The Sunbeams, with their smaller diameter 13 inch wheels, would require more frequent tire changes, giving MG a big advantage in the pits. The pressure fueling system, first tried in the 1959 race, also added to the efficiency of the MG pit crew. The performance of the cars and the advantage enjoyed in the pit stops instilled the team with the confidence that they were up to the Sunbeam challenge.

Race day dawned clear and warm with a track temperature of 85°. Knowing this was a long race, the MG crew held to their plan, letting the Sunbeams go out with the initial lead, lapping about four seconds a lap faster than the MGAs. At the end of two hours the two Sunbeams led the two MGAs by one minute 42 seconds. This rather substantial lead lasted until the third hour when the cars had to come in for fuel. Peter Riley came in first and handed over MGA number 43 to John Whitmore, taking on a load of fuel in just 69 seconds while the first Sunbeam to pit needed a change of tires as well as fuel, taking two minutes nine seconds for its stop. Shortly afterward Jim Parkinson brought in number 44 for its first pit stop, turning it over to Jack Flaherty in a dazzling 54 seconds, while the other Sunbeam took an interminable four minutes 11 seconds. Following the pit stops the order was now MGA (number 44), Alpine, MGA (number 43), Alpine, Alpine with the MGA leading the closest Alpine by 46 seconds. Shortly afterward the third Sunbeam dropped out with engine trouble, which left the two MGAs to do battle with the two Sunbeams. In light of the longer lasting tires and shorter pit stops and a near even lap time, the MG crew was confident of their chances for victory. The two Elvas in the class were never really in the running. As the race wore on the MGAs began to increase their lead on the Alpines, indicating their lap times were quicker. At the four hour mark the two MGAs were first and second in class with the lead MGA holding a lead over the third place Sunbeam of one minute 28 seconds. At the sixth hour, the MGAs came in for fuel and tires and returned to the track settling down to lap times around four minutes five seconds. The lead over the Sunbeams continued to grow to nearly five minutes as the end of the twelve hours approached. An eleventh hour pit stop for fuel (no driver change) and an easy hour's drive earned the MG team a first and second in class over the Sunbeams and Elvas in the Grand Touring 1600 cc Class. The lead MGA, number 44, also managed fourth overall in the Grand Touring Class. Thus ended the MGAs most successfulyear at Sebring, having met the challenge of the Sunbeam Alpine team in head-to-head competition. Interestingly, the winning MGA was found to be 10 mph faster after the race than when it started. In the case of this MGA, racing definitely did improve the breed!

Race results are as shown below:

Car	Drivers	Laps	Class Position	Overall Position
43	Riley/Whitmore/Olthoff	173	2	16
44	Parkinson/Flaherty	175	1	14

John Whitmore, Bob Olthoff and F. Morrell brace against the winter cold during testing at Silverstone in preparation for the 1962 race. The cars were 1600 Deluxe coupes and had few modifications from the previous year's winning design.

Sebring 1962

For 1962 the MG team consisted of three 1600 Mk I deluxe coupes. It was decided to run the 1600s again because of the ability to run in the under 1600 cc class. The recently introduced 1600 Mk II had an engine displacement of 1622 cc, just over the class limit. The cars were prepared similarly to the previous years, however every other radiator slat was removed from the radiator grill to improve cooling.

The 1600 cc GT Class was much larger than in 1961 when the MGAs won first and second in class. No less than four Porsches, four Sunbeam Alpines, three T.V.R.s, an Elva, and a lone Osca 1600 were entered along with three MGAs. Marcus Chambers left BMC in the fall of 1961, so he was not along for the 1962 race. The MG team was entered as "Ecurie Safety Fast" with Jim Parkinson and Jack Flaherty back to try for a repeat class win driving number 51, Andrew Hedges and Jack Sears piloted number 52, and John Whitmore and Bob Olthoff with F. Morrell as reserve driver drove number 53. Bob Olthoff was a reserve driver on the 1961 team and John Whitmore was a veteran from the 1961 team as well.

The team cars at speed exhibit a bit of oversteer at the limit.

Friday's weather had been downright inhospitable with rain and heavy clouds dampening the racing spirit, but Saturday morning dawned clear and warm with a friendly blue Florida sky overhead. The MGAs could hardly hope to compete with the Porsches, but with the many British entries in the 1600 GT Class, the race promised to be a good one among the British entries. From the start Jim Parkinson was driving number 51 as though he had his sights set on a repeat class win. For the first ten laps he led the T.V.R.s and Sunbeams around the course, but as the Florida sun began to make its presence felt on the MG's cooling system the T.V.R. of Cuomo and Jacobs slipped past. The Cassel/Lane Porsche dropped in the opening laps with engine trouble. The first of the British 1600 GT entries to drop out was the Sunbeam Alpine driven by Ken Miles and Lew Spencer. Miles had rearranged the Alpine's body work earlier, sideswiping an Osca, and was finally put to rest with a broken connecting rod about two hours into the race. Shortly after the first pit stop around 1 p.m., the Cuomo/Jacobs T.V.R. came to rest with engine problems along with the Elva Courier of Smith/Whims, which suffered a broken crankshaft. Shortly after 2 p.m., Parkinson's MGA came into the pits for a clutch adjustment and quickly rejoined the chase. By three o'clock, the order in the 1600 GT Class was Porsche (75 laps), Sunbeam (72 laps) followed by the rest of the class field. At six o'clock the lone Osca 1600 dropped out with a blown head gasket. As darkness approached, the Goodyear blimp provided a unique illuminated scoreboard as it drifted serenely overhead. The T.V.R. of Bolton/Rothschild was soon out with a broken axle, leaving the top contenders in the class as Porsche, Porsche, the Harper/Proctor Alpine and the Donohue/Signore T.V.R. leading the Payne/Shepard Alpine and the Sears/Hedges MGA by a lap. With the end in sight, the Payne/Shepard Alpine developed a serious engine malady. A subsequent check in the pits revealed a rather large hole in the crankcase! At that point there was nothing to loose by soldiering on, which he did, finishing the race well down in the standings. When the checkered flag fell at 10 p.m., the order in the 1600 GT class was the Dan Gurney/Holbrook Porsche (188 laps), the Straehle/Edgar Porsche (182 laps), the Harper/Procter Alpine (173 laps), the Sears/Hedges MGA (172 laps), the Parkinson/Flaherty MGA (171 laps), and the Whitmore/Olthoff MGA (169 laps). Of the 15 cars in the 1600 GT Class that started the race, only eight finished. Although the MGAs didn't finish among the top three in their class, they were the only team to finish intact. In looking back over the six years and 17 MGAs which raced at Sebring, perhaps the most outstanding accomplishment was that only one car failed to go the distance. Quite a tribute to the MGA's reliability.

The race results were as shown below:

Car	Drivers	Laps	Class Position	Overall Position
51	Parkinson/Flaherty	171	5	17
52	Hedges/Sears	172	4	16
53	Whitmore/Olthoff/Morrell	169	6	20

So ended six years of racing at Sebring for the MGA. They had been cooperative ventures among the Americans, Canadians and British. Initially the impetus came from a small group of enthusiastic American SCCA amateur racers but the fever quickly spread to Canada and Great Britain resulting in the factory teams. Those six years started off successfully enough with the capturing of the team prize in 1956 and 1957 with locally sponsored teams. The factory teams in 1959—62 brought a bit of professionalism to the effort, but the greatest contribution was the bringing together of American, Canadian and British drivers and crews in a truly international effort with the MGA, whose greatest following was from these three countries. Running against almost overwhelming competition from Porsche, the MGA teams soldiered on until the right combination was found in the 1961 team when a one-two class win was posted. Admittedly, the Porsches' absence helped! All but a few of the twenty-odd Sebring MGAs have survived and they continue to provide excitement and interest for MGA enthusiasts in Canada and the United States.

The MGA competition program included an important effort in rallying, with both men and women drivers—represented here pictorially.

So there you have it, the major MGA competition thrusts at the Bonnevile Salt Flats and endurance racing campaigns at Le Mans and Sebring. Some were more successful than others but they all shared a common bond. The cars were carefully prepared, looked great, ran well and spread the name of MG around the world; but most importantly, they were there competing.

In addition to the factory teams, there were private entries which ran in some very prestigious events. A team of four MGA 1500s belonging to the Fitzwilliams racing team await the start of the Mille Miglia road race.

Nancy Mitchell, left, and Joan Johns are jubilant after their Coupes des Dames in the 1957 Leige-Rome-Leige Rally. Nancy was the Ladies' European Rally Champion in 1956 and 1957.

John Gott and Chris Tooley blast through Ora, Italy during the 1957 Leige-Rome-Leige.

For many the thrill of amateur competition leads to a professional career. Here Sherm Decker savors a moment of victory with his wife and mechanic, Hugh Francis. Sherm went on to drive at Sebring for MG and later at Daytona for Carroll Shelby.

P.J. Simpson (driving) and J.O. Blaksley await the start of Mille Miglia at Brescia in one of the four MGA 1500's belonging to the Fitzwilliams racing team. This grueling thousand mile race over public roads runs down the Italian boot and back again. Note the competition windscreen, 60 spoke wire wheels and the absence of headlamp stone guards.

In addition to factory teams, there were private entries which ran in some very prestigious events. The MGA 1500 above is shown participating in a Scotland to Australia marathon. The route ran from Scotland through England, France, Switzerland, Italy, Yugoslavia, Bulgaria, Turkey, Iran, Afghanistan, Pakistan, India and Ceylon (Sri Lanka) to Australia.

Chapter 7

Restoring Your "A"

As each 'layer' was peeled off the layer beneath appeared worse than the one above until it was finally admitted that a frame-up rebuild was needed.

In the meantime, catalogues from numerous MG specialists in England and the U.S. poured in and even more parts orders were sent out. Unfortunately it proved to be a long wait until some of the orders showed up and as usual the part needed first was the last to arrive.[1]

To Buy Or Not To Buy?

The MGA is no Bugatti. To some this may suggest an uninteresting, dull performing, commonplace, poor automotive investment. To those people who get their kicks spending megabucks on undriveable museum pieces I state emphatically, "Thank you for leaving the MGA to those of us with modest incomes and bulging enthusiasm!" To anyone who has been in the market for a used sports car classic the past few years, the skyrocketing prices for some models has been depressing. The entry of investors and collectors has pushed the price of many cars artificially high and beyond the reach of most mortals. There are, however, some refreshing cars left at reasonable prices for those of us willing to seek them out. The MGA is one of them. The lines of the MGA are among the best expressions of British sports car design during the heydays of the late fifties and early sixties. The engines, unfettered by EPA regulations, provide sprightly performance with the added advantage of excellent gas mileage. There were 101,081 MGAs produced between September 1955 and June 1962, more than any other sports car up to that time. Because of these large numbers, the cars are available at reasonable prices along with the spare parts to keep them on the road. Reasonable cost, classic lines, solid performance, excellent gas mileage, availability of spare parts at a price that won't make you wince and most of all *fun*!

Choosing A Model

The first place to start on the road to MGA motoring is with the selection of a car. Buying a car which is already in good to excellent condition is one way to go; however I personally don't recommend it. Unless you know the owner and car intimately or are a skilled appraiser of a car's condition, it is all too easy to get roped in by a slick reconditioning job. A new paint job, interior, top, tires and a steam cleaned engine can hide a badly rotted chassis and body covered over with undercoat, and a sick engine and transmission, doctored with oil the consistency of molasses. No sir, for me I'll take the one over there in the corner with the tattered interior, bald tires, flaking paint and an under carriage and body covered with road grime, not fresh under coating! Being better able to judge the real condition of the car is just one advantage to buying a car which hasn't been reconditioned. By reconditioning or restoring the car yourself you will know exactly what you have, it will be the exact color combination you want and best of all it will be YOUR car because you built it. The expense involved in reconditioning or restoring an MGA can usually be recovered by the added value these improvements will make to the selling price of the car.

The 1500 roadster was the most popular MGA model.

The Twin Cam coupe in 1600 body style was a rare model incorporating many production improvements over earlier Twin Cams.

The 1600 coupe offered a combination of performance, style and luxury that many find appealing.

Choice of a model depends on what you want out of the car. The 1500 and 1600 models were made in large quantities, offer modest performance, parts are readily available and the cars are to be found everywhere at reasonable prices. There were nearly twice as many 1500s as 1600s made; however the 1600 provides a substantial improvement in acceleration and braking. The 1600 Mk II is relatively rare, there were roughly seven times as many 1500s as 1600 Mk IIs made. It had the best acceleration of the MGAs with the exception of the Twin Cam. Speaking of rare, the Twin Cam is definitely that. With a total production of 2,111 units, there were roughly 29 times as many 1500s as Twin Cams produced! The Twin Cam is a complicated, finicky beast which will drive you crackers if you aren't the patient, mechanically oriented type. If you qualify, the Twin Cam will provide you with brilliant performance, handling and braking. Its rarity and desirability will guarantee an appreciating value.

The 1600 Mk II roadster was relatively rare and marked the end of the MGA production.

Among the rarest of all MGAs, the 1600 Mk II Deluxe is highly desirable from almost any viewpoint.

The ultimate in rare MGAs are the 1600 Deluxe and 1600 Mk II Deluxe, which is a long way of describing a Twin Cam without the Twin Cam engine. Approximately five-hundred 1600 and 1600 Mk II Deluxes were produced from left over Twin Cam bits after the Twin Cam line was closed down. To many the Mk II Deluxe is the ultimate MGA, combining the excellent braking and handling of the Twin Cam with the more docile (read easier to maintain) 1600 Mk II engine. If you can find a 1600 Mk II or 1600 Deluxe coupe, buy it! These are the rarest of all MGAs. Speaking of coupes, these models offer a degree of comfort above the roadster and because they are rarer the price is commensurately higher. Having narrowed down your choice of models, what do you look for in a car to determine if it is a sound purchase?

The Hunt

The first point to keep in mind when looking for your "A" is that the car is going to be at least seventeen years old. Mileage at this point is not a consideration unless it is exceptionally low and if it is the owner had better be

1500, 1600, 1600 MkII

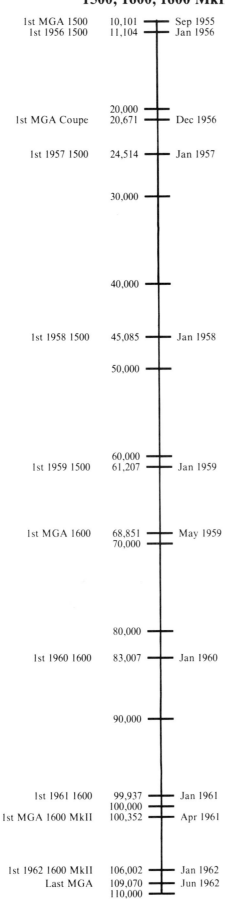

1st MGA 1500	10,101	Sep 1955
1st 1956 1500	11,104	Jan 1956
	20,000	
1st MGA Coupe	20,671	Dec 1956
1st 1957 1500	24,514	Jan 1957
	30,000	
	40,000	
1st 1958 1500	45,085	Jan 1958
	50,000	
	60,000	
1st 1959 1500	61,207	Jan 1959
1st MGA 1600	68,851	May 1959
	70,000	
	80,000	
1st 1960 1600	83,007	Jan 1960
	90,000	
1st 1961 1600	99,937	Jan 1961
	100,000	
1st MGA 1600 MkII	100,352	Apr 1961
1st 1962 1600 MkII	106,002	Jan 1962
Last MGA	109,070	Jun 1962
	110,000	

MGA Production

These two graphs can be used to see just where your MGA fits into the MGA production record. The graph on the left is used for 1500, 1600 and 1600 Mk II cars and the one below is used for the Twin Cam Models. The graphs are linear with respect to production numbers; however, the dates are not necessarily evenly spaced. The numbers are chassis numbers which are found on the data plate afixed to the firewall in the engine compartment in front of the heater. The dates on the right hand side of the graphs indicate the date the car was produced, not the date it was to be sold. The first car of the model year had a production date of around October for US sales and November for domestic sales. For instance, a car with chassis number 24,000 is a 1957 1500 even though it was produced in December 1956.

Twin Cam

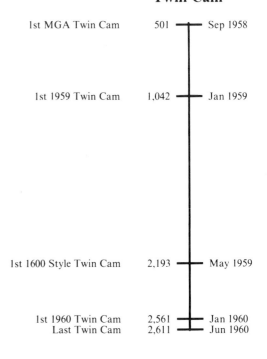

1st MGA Twin Cam	501	Sep 1958
1st 1959 Twin Cam	1,042	Jan 1959
1st 1600 Style Twin Cam	2,193	May 1959
1st 1960 Twin Cam	2,561	Jan 1960
Last Twin Cam	2,611	Jun 1960

able to document the fact. Running gear repair and replacement may be an all consuming consideration on a three year old used car but on a car seventeen years old plus the chassis and body are the areas that deserve the most attention. Believe me, replacing an engine is a lot easier than replacing the chassis! If you are planning to run your car on the street and recondition it as you go along, as opposed to putting it up on blocks for two years and slavishly restoring it for display at shows, you should look for a car in fair to good condition which will provide you with a mechanically reliable base from which to operate while the reconditioning process takes place. On the other hand, if you are planning a frame up restoration the mechanical condition is less important, however the chassis and body had better be in good shape or you will have a nightmare of welding and body work ahead of you!

Before leaving on your car hunting expedition, take the time to assemble a few tools to aid your inspection. A flashlight to look in those dark places where rust lurks and a Phillips screwdriver suitable for probing weak areas are your best tools in the search for rust. Check with the owner first before using the screwdriver and if he says no, walk away. If he says yes, use it, don't just peck around! A small magnet is handy for discovering body putty. A compression gauge and sparkplug wrench are the best tools for evaluating the condition of the engine. If you don't own a compression gauge by all means buy one. They are only a few dollars at your local auto supply store and worth every penny. An eyedropper is useful for inspecting the hydraulic fluid for contamination and a putty knife and rag will be useful for removing crud in search of demon rust, serial numbers and so on.

Check It Out

Found that dream car? Okay, let's give her the once over! Start with the chassis. When Syd Enever designed the MGA he specified a heavier gauge metal than was the normal practice in those days for chassis construction. What this means for us is that the MGA chassis has a better chance of weathering the ravages of rust than most of its contemporaries. Thanks Syd! The most common points to check are along the frame rails inside the car where rain water will collect between the floorboard and the chassis side rail. Lift the carpet along the rail and use that screwdriver! While you've got your head stuck under the steering wheel, check the point where the bulkhead support joins the frame just forward of the door. Flip the seat forward and check the area where the floor boards meet and the rear floor

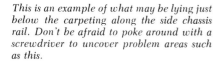

This is an example of what may be lying just below the carpeting along the side chassis rail. Don't be afraid to poke around with a screwdriver to uncover problem areas such as this.

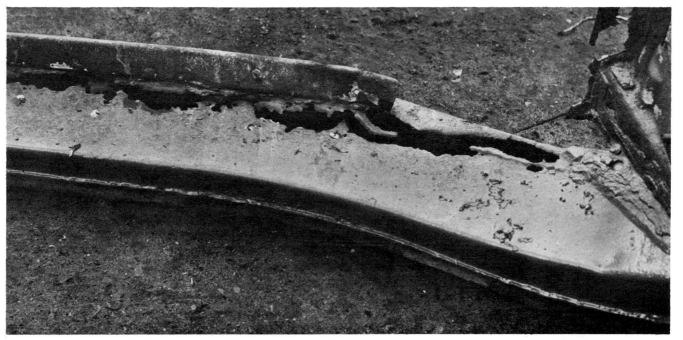

The rear portion of the frame is relatively rust free also. It's the center section that bears close scrutiny.

brace is welded to the frame. This area can also be checked from under the car. Open the door. Holding from the open end, try to move it up and down, paying particular attention to the hinges. If there is movement here check closely to see if it is the hinge which is loose or the chassis support to which it is attached. If it is the hinge, no big deal. If it is the chassis support...look out! While the door is still open, check the area where the lock is anchored. If there is movement of the lock or the door jamb, indicating the U-shaped chassis support is rusted, look no further. The repair of this area is prohibitively expensive on a car such as the MGA. Underneath the car, look at the battery boxes to see how much of them has been eaten away by rust and battery acid. Notice I said how much, not if. These boxes rarely survive intact! Check the area where they join the frame cross member for rot. Most

The point where the "goalpost" support joins the chassis side rail is also vulnerable.

Weakened or completely rusted out sections of the floorboard supports are not uncommon. Fortunately they are easily fixed.

likely candidates for body rot are the rocker panels. Don't forget to run your hand between the frame and the inside of the rocker to check for weakness from within. Replacement of the rocker panels is relatively easy and there are any number of firms which can supply them at a reasonable cost. The "dog leg" of the rear fender where the front part of the fender joins the rocker panel, the lower rear portion of the front fender and the gas tank (including the straps holding it in place) are all prime places for rust to form. Now we're ready to look the running gear over.

Check the springs for broken leaves on the rear and the rear axles for looseness by jostling the rear wheels. The rear axle is virtually unbreakable. Put the car in fourth gear, crawl under it and slowly try to rotate the driveshaft. If you hear a clicking sound, the U-joints are bad. Check the dif-

The area just forward of the doors is another place where water collects and rust begins. This hole lies on the outside of the frame rail.

This bottom view shows how the area behind the seats can rust out. Often water in the passenger compartment will drain to this area.

ferential and shocks for leaks while you're under there. Bounce the rear bumper checking for proper damping of the rear shocks. They should stop the car after one or two cycles. The rear shocks almost never go bad. Check the front shocks in a likewise manner. These do go bad often and are expensive to replace. If the car has wire wheels, take the Phillips head screwdriver and tap the spokes. They should sound the same note. A dead note indicates a loose or broken spoke. Slide under the car and check the front shocks for leaks.

The engine and transmission will normally have a liberal coating of engine oil if they have been in use for any length of time. Check for freshly greased fittings, especially the lower kingpin. The rubber boots on the steering rack should be intact with no tears and clamped in place. Shock mounting bolts often work loose so check these and look out for elongated holes in the shocks. The lower A-frame pivot bolts also deserve a check for tightness of fit. Jack each front wheel up and try to wiggle it from side to side. Any looseness here indicates worn tie rod ends. Now try to rock the wheel from top to bottom. Looseness here indicates a problem with the king pin and/or extreme wear of the lower A-frame pivot bolt. Using the sparkplug wrench you brought along, remove all four sparkplugs and check them for oiling, carbon deposits, burned electrodes etc. Many of the sparkplug manufacturers have handouts which explain how to read a sparkplug to get the most out of the information which they offer, which is considerable. With the sparkplugs out, take the compression tester and insert it into the sparkplug hole. Have a friend turn the engine over with the starter (remember to leave the ignition off). Watch the gauge carefully. It should pump up quickly to a maximum reading (8-12 revolutions) of about 120 lb, plus or minus 10 lb in all cylinders for a pushrod engine. 185 lb, plus or minus 10 lb is normal for a Twin Cam. A low reading here indicates worn

If movement of the door hinge is evident when the open end of the door is moved up and down, better check closely. You may have a mess like this on your hands! In this case the chassis support is completely rusted away.

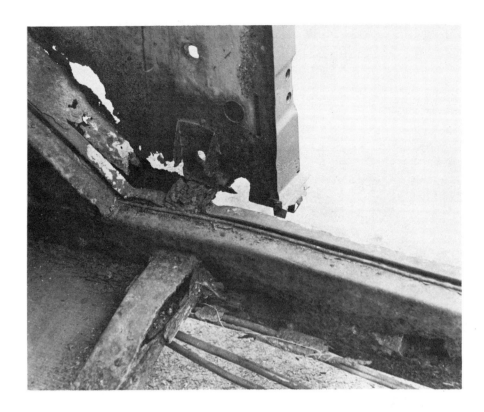

If the door lock shows movement, the chassis support may be as badly rusted as this one. If so, forget about buying the car!

The area just aft of the front wheel splash guard is a good candidate for rust problems.

piston rings or valves. Squirt some oil in the sparkplug holes and repeat the test. If the reading improves, the rings are probably at fault. If not, the valves are suspect. Check the transmission and engine oil dipstick for proper level and contamination by water, gasoline, dirt or metal particles. Believe it or not, you are now ready for the road test!

Start the engine up and allow it to run a bit while you check out the gauges, lights, horn etc. The steering should be free from play. If the wheel isn't cracked where the "banjo" style spokes join the rim, the car is the exception rather than the rule. Most of them are cracked. Warm the car up properly while you get the feel of the machine. Steering should be light. If not, the steering U-joints may need cleaning or the rack is in need of a lube job. Listen for excessive noise from the gearbox especially in the indirect gears.

The trunk floor in this car is little more than rust held together by road grime! The trunk floor is prone to rusting, particularly if the trunk has been leaking. The gas tank and its support straps are also susceptable.

Stripped to the bone, the MGA chassis reveals its substantial construction.

Shifting should be light and precise. Try a couple of fast shifts to check out the synchros, especially in second gear. The clutch should engage smoothly, without slip. Is the clutch noisy with the pedal depressed? If it is, the throwout bearing is probably shot. A two-bit part which is expensive to get at. Does the car feel tight or is it a rattle-box? The engine should respond crisply to throttle inputs. If you have the occasion to turn down a hill, take your foot off the accelerator on the way down and when you reach the bottom, floor it while looking in the rearview mirror for the tell-tale blue smoke indicating an oil burner. The brakes should operate smoothly with no pulling (assuming dry linings) or squealing. The former could indicate brake fluid on the linings and the latter could point to brakes worn down to the rivets. A slight amount of squeal in disc braked cars at low speed and light pedal pressure is not abnormal. Watch the water temperature gauge for overheating and notice the oil pressure. Pressure at idle should be no lower than 25 lb while 50 lb and over should be indicated at highway speeds. These readings are for engines at running temperature. On the Twin Cam a figure of 20 lb at idle and 45-55 running is good. Before shutting off the car, allow it to idle down. The idle speed should be constant at about 850-1000 rpm. If the idle is much above this, and the idle adjustment screws are backed off all the way, worn throttle shafts on the carburetors are the probable cause. Put the car in gear and gradually let off the clutch while holding the car in place with the brake

Some body parts are more expensive than others. The grill for the 1600 Mk II is expensive and hard to find. Unfortunately, they are very often the victim of inconsiderate "park by ear" motorists.

until the clutch just begins to engage. Push the pedal in just a bit and hold it there. If the clutch starts to engage, either the master cylinder needs rebuilding or the slave cylinder on the clutch is bad. Set the handbrake or run the front bumper up against an immovable object (gently please!) and gradually release the clutch with the engine running at 2000 rpm with no load. The clutch should be strong enough to kill the engine. Restart the engine, let it idle down and shut it off. "Dieseling" may indicate advanced ignition timing, worn carburetors or hot spots in the cylinder head. Check under the car for oil leaks and at the wheels for evidence of leaking brake wheel cylinders. Open the hood and take a sample from the master cylinder with the eye dropper. Check for evidence of contamination, especially black rubber particles which spell deteriorating rubber parts within the master cylinder. The level should be just beneath the filler neck. Also look around the front of the master cylinder for signs of a leak.

Check the radiator and hoses for leaks. Using a rag to protect your hand, slowly remove the radiator cap. It should hiss slightly, indicating the pressure cap and radiator sealing are working properly.

This ought to give you a good idea of the mechanical and structural condition of the car. The rest is up to you and your wallet!

From Rags To Riches

Let me begin by saying that this chapter is not intended to be a comprehensive guide to refurbishing your MGA, but rather to outline the general procedure of a restoration or reconditioning and point out some specific areas which apply to the MGA in particular. Do your homework before you begin by reading up on the mechanics of the restoration/reconditioning. A workshop manual is a must. There are any number of books on bodywork, painting, upholstery etc. After you have decided your intended course of action, sit down and decide what you can really afford! Having planned your project, you will be in a better position to gauge your progress and press on to the finish (no pun intended!).

A new owner of a used sports car classic who intends to improve its appearance and running ought to decide whether he wants to *restore* or *recondition* his car. These words are often used interchangeably by some unscrupulous dealers and unknowing owners but a *restored* automobile is generally attained by tearing the car down to the frame and rebuilding every blessed nut and bolt to as good as or better than new condition. This is in contrast to a *reconditioned* car which has been made mechanically and

Any painting done in the engine compartment is going to require a lot of preparation so be patient! The ideal time to tackle this job is when the engine is out.

This beautifully restored Twin Cam was the result of five years of hard work. Investing the time to pay attention to detail separates a truly great restoration from the rest of the field.

cosmetically sound without all the elaborate and costly work of a chassis-up restoration. This doesn't mean the one is any better than the other, just that they were built by their owners for different purposes. Reconditioned cars are generally owned for use on the road primarily and at shows occasionally. A restored car is generally used sparingly on the road but comes into its forte at the car show where it bears its soul to an admiring public. Needless to say a determining factor here is expense. Many young first time sports car buyers are discovering the MGA as their fathers did twenty years ago, and while their enthusiasm is boundless, their pocketbooks are not. The majority of MGA owners also share this distinction and it is to them that this section on reconditioning is dedicated.

Reconditioning

The most important place to start with the reconditioning procedure is to make sure the mechanicals are right before proceeding with the body. The best way to accomplish this is to drive the car to determine where the faults lie. For the most part, this will be an enjoyable task! While you are engaged in rebuilding the wheel cylinders and secretly wishing you were repainting your wheels, remember that faulty brakes can kill you and wreck the car while a frumpy looking car doesn't hurt anyone or anything. Work your way through the car starting with the brakes, then steering and front end and save the expensive items like the engine and transmission for last.

Having gotten the car into shape mechanically, you are ready to tackle the body and chassis. Begin with the chassis. Any reconditioning of a car should start with cleaning and the chassis is no exception. Use a high pressure hose, car wash wand, brushes etc. to remove road grime and mud. a good soaking with "Gunk" or some other grease dissolving agent will help remove sludge build-up. Now that you can see most of the chassis, attack any rust spots you find with a wire brush, steel wool or sandpaper to remove *all* the rust. Prime the bare area with damp-proof primer and paint with a polyurethane paint. If you decide on undercoating, remember it can trap moisture as well as keep it out. A good way to protect the chassis if you don't have the time for the above procedure is to simply take a brush and some old engine oil and brush it on to the chassis, rust and all. The oil will serve to isolate the metal from the air, thus arresting the oxidation. Take care to keep the oil off rubber parts and remember to renew it from time to time.

The next area of attention should be the engine compartment. Take care to cover the distributor and carburetors to protect them from water. Use a lot of "Gunk" or similar grease remover, brushes, steel wool and lots of patience! The latter will become difficult when you start to paint the engine and the engine compartment sheet metal. This is a tedious process and difficult to do properly. If you have the engine out, the job is much simpler!

Having put the mechanical, chassis and engine compartment in shape, you are ready to tackle the body. Begin by exposing the rusted areas. The worst areas may show rust through the paint while other areas may indicate rust with bubbled paint. In any case, the rust must be completely removed. In some instances the metal will have to be completely removed leaving a gaping hole in the process. Take heart that whatever the size of the hole, it will be smaller than if you had left the rust alone! Fiberglass patches will work fine in repairing most gaps in the bodywork. However, for originality and resale value, it is advisable to use quality steel repair panels whenever possible. If you are going to remove paint, use a water soluble paint remover. It will be much easier to clean the surface afterward. Wirebrushing works fine on chassis, suspension etc. Chances are the rocker panels will need replacement. Chisel off or drill out the spot welds and pop rivet or spot weld on the new rockers. There are several sources for these in steel or fiberglass, but metal is recommended. Save yourself a bundle of money by preparing the body for the paint shop. Unless you have the equipment and are adept at auto painting, save the heartbreak of runs and thin spots to the paint shop. Acrylic lacquer provides a good combination of durability, ease of mainte-nance and beauty. One drawback is that a considerable amount of rubbing on your part may be necessary to bring out the full luster of the paint. But then again, this is part of the joy of ownership, isn't it? Don't forget to remind the paint shop that the doors, trunk and hood are aluminum and may require a special primer. DuPont 100S is a good all around primer for all surfaces on the car, including aluminum. Otherwise a zinc-chromate primer is required on the aluminum surfaces.

The interior is one of the most visable areas of your car. Care and money spent here are wise investments. Although a local shop could conceivably do a decent job in fabricating door panels and carpet sets from scratch, you would most often be better off buying ready made kits from a reputable specialist.

Original Wilton wool carpeting is expensive and most owners opt for nylon cut pile which looks almost the same and is only a fraction of the cost. In either case, look for carpet sets which have felt or jute backing. These will wear better and reduce road noise.

Now that you have completed the reconditioning process you can enjoy a good looking, good running car which should give you many years of motoring entertainment. Happy MGAing!

Restoration

Anyone attempting to restore an automobile needs to have patience and dedication to excellence fortified by a good memory to see the job through to its successful completion. Working on a time schedule is asking for trouble. The work area should be sheltered from the elements and outside disturbance such as theives and neighborhood children, though not necessarily in that order! As in the reconditioning process, sit down and make up a plan of attack before you start, being realistic about what you want and can do. Start with working out the mechanicals first before you begin disassembly of the body and chassis. A great aid in reassembly, and in documenting your work for insurance and future sale of the car, is to take black and white photos of all stages and areas of the restoration. This will help nudge your memory and save a lot of hand wringing over where that @#$% part goes! As you disassemble the parts, try to label major items and keep the fasteners with that part in a small plastic bag. The MGA is an easy car to disassemble; all major panels are bolted, not welded, into place. The biggest plus in the case of a frame up restoration is that the MGA is the last MG to be built which has a separate chassis and body which allows complete access to

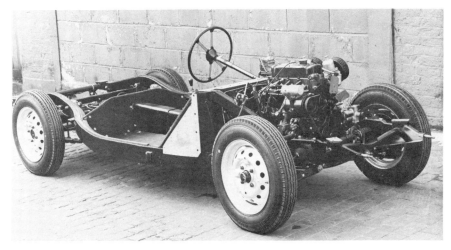

One of the big advantages of the MGA over the MGB is the ability to separate the body from the chassis. When you are done with your work on the chassis, it should look like this. Restorers take note of the details shown here and in photographs elsewhere in this book.

the hidden recesses of the chassis and body. Take off all the body panels, disconnect the electrical wires, hydraulic lines etc, remove the bolts holding the body and chassis together and you are ready to remove the body, with the help of a friend of course! Really not too bad.

The most thorough way to remove rust and crud is to either sandblast or dip the body panels and chassis. Sandblasting is very effective and inexpensive compared to the dipping process, however experience with sandblasting is essential as excessive heat buildup or too large a grit will result in warped body panels. This problem is not nearly so critical with the chassis and suspension items. Remember that the sand, all of the sand, will have to be removed before you begin painting. Believe me, you don't want a dust storm to be raised from all those hidden recesses when the painting begins! Dipping the panels at your local "strip joint" is an excellent way to remove the ravages of time. A major advantage of dipping is that it does not remove any of the metal, as does sandblasting, with no attendant problem of panels warping. The panels will come back looking like new, but the price may be high, certainly higher than sandblasting. Consider the price, your time and the benefits and make your own choice. Aluminum panels can be dipped, though not every dipping facility can do it. Aluminum requires a two step process which naturally costs more.

Another alternative to dipping is to strip the panels with a water soluble paint stripper. The water soluble paint remover allows an easier clean up prior to priming or application of body putty. Incidentally, the lead versus body filler controversy appears to be a moot point these days with the availability of improved body fillers. Body putty is much easier for the amateur to work with then lead. Removal of old undercoating is a real job, however gasoline will help dissolve it. Use a good quality metal preparation prior to priming. Use a good quality primer such as DuPont 100S, which is suitable for both steel and aluminum. There are a number of specialized frame paints available, DuPont Frame Paint being one of them. A good quality polyurethane enamel will also work well. Choice of body paint is a personal preference, however acrylic lacquer offers advantages of high gloss, smooth finish and easy application. It does require a lot of rubbing out after application.

Replacement of the floor boards is a must. Use exterior or marine plywood. Protect the finish with several coats of good quality polyurethane enamel on all sides, and don't forget the edges! You are bound to run into a few stubborn nuts in your disassembly. The chrome plated, round head bolts which hold the bumpers to the bumper brackets are particularly vulnerable to freezing up. Use a nut breaker on these recalcitrant nuts. The lever action type is preferable over the screw type because of its ease of use. Speaking of nuts and bolts, consider replacing the old ones with stainless steel fasteners. While you have the car all over the garage floor, do yourself a favor and replace the wiring harness, preferably with the cloth braided type. They are available from several suppliers at a reasonable price. The installation of a new wiring harness will reduce future breakdowns and guard against dangerous electrical fires. Use the old harness as a guide and rewire one connection at a time to save confusion. Be careful the harness doesn't lay between chassis and body contact points or places where the suspension might rub the harness. Soldered connections where applicable will last longer than the push-on connections.

The original interior was carpeted in cut pile wool mohair carpeting over jute padding. However, nylon cut pile is a cost effective and popular alternative. Seating surfaces and some passenger compartment surround moldings such as the door trim and the small curved pieces were covered in leather on most cars. The remainder of the seats, door panels, kick panels and passenger compartment surround moldings were vinyl covered, as is the side curtain pouch draped behind the seats. All convertible tops were made of vinyl. The first production tops came with a single rear window. In 1957, an improved three window design was introduced. Today, even on early cars, the latter design top is preferred. In addition, a handsome (and expensive) 3-ply canvas top is available from a few of the leading distributors. "Armor All" is a marvelous liquid suitable for use on vinyl, wood and leather to keep them looking like new. Keep in mind that use of

48 spoke wire wheels add to the elegance of this coupe.

"Armor All" on leather will make any re-dying very difficult or impossible because of the protective layer. Be sure and keep the "Armor All" off metal parts. Motorcycle visor plastic cleaner works well to remove scratches from side curtains and the top windows.

Back To The Basics

In deciding what color scheme to follow, it is a good idea to start with the original plan and then decide whether a change is desired. Needless to say, for the person interested in competing in concours d'elegance, following the original scheme is essential. If you have a 1500 model, the identification plate will be of some assistance in determining the original exterior color, otherwise you will have to do a bit of poking around to find the real truth. A good place to look is under the dash. Almost nobody paints under the dash! The original paint was nitrocellulose lacquer with Conolly leather seating surfaces. The accompanying charts map out the various color combinations available for each MGA model. Some comments on the charts are appropriate. Piping was carried out in the color specified wherever piping was applied, i.e. on the doors and passenger compartment surround molding. Tyrolite Green was only used on the MGA 1500 for the first couple of years. Afterward Ash Green was used, probably starting with the introduction of the Twin Cam model in September 1958. Interestingly, neither color was what is commonly called British Racing Green and only the 1500 body style offered a green color. Likewise, Orient Red was only offered on the 1500 body style while Mineral Blue was reserved solely for the 1500 coupe body style. Color schemes for the Twin Cam followed those of the appropriate 1500 or 1600 model upon which their body was based. Engines were painted dark red. Ditzler DQE 50782Y is the modern day equivalent. Having said all that, I should caution that just because the factory specification states that is the way things are to be done, it doesn't mean the factory always followed the specifications! MG was famous for the occasional special!

Whitewall tires were a popular accessory.

MGA 1500 & Twin Cam Roadster Color Scheme

Paint Upholstery

Description	Color Scheme									
Body	Orient Red	Orient Red	Glacier Blue	Glacier Blue	Ash/TY Green	Ash/TY Green	Old Eng White	Old Eng White	Black	Black
Dash (1500)	Orient Red	Orient Red	Glacier Blue	Glacier Blue	Ash/TY Green	Ash/TY Green	Old Eng White	Old Eng White	Black	Black
Wheels	Silver	Silver	Silver	Silver	Silver	Silver	Silver	Silver	Silver	Silver
Hard Top	Black	Black	Black	Black	Black	Black	Black	Black	Black	Black
Seats	Red	Black	Grey	Black	Grey	Black	Red	Black	Red	Green
Seat Piping	Red	Red	Grey	Grey	Grey	Green	Red	Off White	Red	Green
Door Panels, Kick Panels, Rear Quarter Panels and Passenger Compartment Surround Molding	Red	Black	Grey	Black	Grey	Black	Red	Black	Red	Green
Spare Wheel Cover	Grey	Grey	Grey	Grey	Grey	Grey	Grey	Grey	Grey	Grey
Top and Side-Screens	Black	Black	Ice Blue	Ice Blue	Ice Blue	Ice Blue	Black	Black	Ice Blue, Black	Ice Blue, Black
Tonneau Cover	Black	Black	Ice Blue, Black	Ice Blue, Black	Ice Blue, Black	Ice Blue, Black	Black	Black	Black	Black
Carpeting	Black	Black	Black	Black	Black	Black	Black	Black	Black	Black
Door Seals	Red	Red	Black	Black	Black	Black	Red	Black	Red	Black
Dash (Twin Cam Only)	Red	Black	Grey	Black	Grey	Black	Red	Black	Red	Green

MGA 1500 & Twin Cam Coupe Color Scheme

Paint Upholstery

Description	Color Scheme									
Body	Orient Red	Orient Red	Mineral Blue	Mineral Blue	Ash/TY Green	Ash/TY Green	Old Eng White	Old Eng White	Black	Black
Wheels	Silver	Silver	Silver	Silver	Silver	Silver	Silver	Silver	Silver	Silver
Seats	Red	Black	Grey	Black	Grey	Black	Red	Black	Red	Green
Seat Piping	Red	Red	Grey	Blue	Grey	Green	Red	White	Red	Green
Door Panels, Kick Panels and Rear Quarter Panels	Red	Black	Grey	Black	Grey	Black	Red	Black	Red	Green
Door Panel Piping	Red	Red	Grey	Blue	Grey	Green	Red	White	Red	Green
Door Capping, Dash Panel and Parcel Rail	Red	Red	Grey	Blue	Green	Green	White	White	Black	Black
Dash Top and Parcel Shelf	Red	Black	Blue	Black	Green	Black	Red	Black	Red	Green
Dash Trim Roll and Door Seals	Red	Black	Blue	Black	Green	Black	Red	Black	Black	Black
Roof Lining	Off White	Off White	Off White	Off White	Off White	Off White	Off White	Off White	Off White	Off White
Carpeting	Grey	Grey	Grey	Grey	Grey	Grey	Grey	Grey	Grey	Grey
Spare Wheel Cover	Grey	Grey	Grey	Grey	Grey	Grey	Grey	Grey	Grey	Grey

MGA 1600 & Twin Cam Roadster Color Scheme

Paint Upholstery

Description	Color Scheme									
Body	Chariot Red	Chariot Red	Chariot Red	Iris Blue	Alamo Beige	Dove Grey	Old Eng White	Old Eng White	Black	Black
Dash (1600)	Chariot Red	Chariot Red	Chariot Red	Iris Blue	Alamo Beige	Dove Grey	Old Eng White	Old Eng White	Black	Black
Wheels	Silver	Silver	Silver	Silver	Silver	Silver	Silver	Silver	Silver	Silver
Hard Top	Black	Black	Black	Black	Black	Black	Black	Black	Black	Black
Seats	Red	Beige	Black	Black	Red	Red	Red	Black	Beige	Red
Seat Piping	Red	Beige	Red	Light Blue	Red	Red	Red	White	Beige	Red
Door Panels, Kick Panels, Rear Quarter Panels and Passenger Compartment Surround Molding	Red	Beige	Black	Black	Red	Red	Red	Black	Beige	Red
Spare Wheel Cover	Grey	Grey	Grey	Grey	Grey	Grey	Grey	Grey	Grey	Grey
Top and Side-Screens	Beige	Beige	Grey	Blue	Beige	Grey	Grey	Grey	Grey	Grey
Tonneau Cover	Beige	Beige	Grey	Blue	Beige	Grey	Grey	Grey	Grey	Grey
Carpeting	Black	Black	Black	Black	Black	Black	Black	Black	Black	Black
Door Seals	Red	Red	Red	Black	Red	Red	Red	Black	Black	Red
Dash (Twin Cam Only)	Red	Beige	Black	Black	Red	Red	Red	Black	Beige	Red

MGA 1600 & Twin Cam Coupe Color Scheme

Paint Upholstery

Description	Color Scheme									
Body	Chariot Red	Chariot Red	Chariot Red	Iris Blue	Alamo Beige	Dove Grey	Old Eng White	Old Eng White	Black	Black
Wheels	Silver	Silver	Silver	Silver	Silver	Silver	Silver	Silver	Silver	Silver
Seats	Red	Beige	Black	Black	Red	Red	Red	Black	Beige	Red
Seat Piping	Red	Beige	Red	Light Blue	Red	Red	Red	White	Beige	Red
Door Panels, Kick Panels, Rear Quarter Panels, Door Capping, Dash Panel, Parcel Rail, Dash Top, Parcel Shelf, Dash Trim Roll and Door Seals	Red	Beige	Black	Black	Red	Red	Red	Black	Beige	Red
Door Panel Piping	Red	Beige	Red	Light Blue	Red	Red	Red	White	Beige	Red
Roof Lining	Off White	Off White	Off White	Off White	Off White	Off White	Off White	Off White	Off White	Off White
Carpeting	Grey	Grey	Grey	Grey	Grey	Grey	Grey	Grey	Grey	Grey
Spare Wheel Cover	Grey	Grey	Grey	Grey	Grey	Grey	Grey	Grey	Grey	Grey

MGA 1600 II Roadster Color Scheme

Paint Upholstery

Description	Color Scheme									
Body	Chariot Red	Chariot Red	Chariot Red	Iris Blue	Alamo Beige	Dove Grey	Old Eng White	Old Eng White	Black	Black
Wheels	Silver	Silver	Silver	Silver	Silver	Silver	Silver	Silver	Silver	Silver
Hard Top	Black	Black	Black	Black	Black	Black	Black	Black	Black	Black
Seats	Red	Beige	Black	Black	Red	Red	Red	Black	Beige	Red
Seat Piping	Red	Beige	Red	Light Blue	Red	Red	Red	White	Beige	Red
Door Panels, Kick Panels, Rear Quarter Panels and Passenger Compartment Surround Molding	Red	Beige	Black	Black	Red	Red	Red	Black	Beige	Red
Dash	Red	Beige	Black	Black	Red	Red	Red	Black	Beige	Red
Dash Top	Red	Red	Black	Black	Red	Red	Red	Black	Black	Black
Spare Wheel Cover	Grey	Grey	Grey	Grey	Grey	Grey	Grey	Grey	Grey	Grey
Top and Side-Screens	Beige	Beige	Grey	Blue	Beige	Grey	Grey	Grey	Grey	Grey
Tonneau Cover	Beige	Beige	Grey	Blue	Beige	Grey	Grey	Grey	Grey	Grey
Carpeting	Black	Black	Black	Black	Black	Black	Black	Black	Black	Black
Door Seals	Red	Red	Red	Black	Red	Red	Red	Black	Black	Red

MGA 1600 MK II Coupe Color Scheme

Paint Upholstery

Description	Color Scheme									
Body	Chariot Red	Chariot Red	Chariot Red	Iris Blue	Alamo Beige	Dove Grey	Old Eng White	Old Eng White	Black	Black
Wheels	Silver	Silver	Silver	Silver	Silver	Silver	Silver	Silver	Silver	Silver
Seats	Red	Beige	Black	Black	Red	Red	Red	Black	Beige	Red
Seat Piping	Red	Beige	Red	Light Blue	Red	Red	Red	White	Beige	Red
Door Panels, Kick Panels, Rear Quarter Panels, Door Capping, Dash Panel, Parcel Rail, Parcel Shelf and Dash Trim Roll	Red	Beige	Black	Black	Red	Red	Red	Black	Beige	Red
Door Panel Piping	Red	Beige	Red	Light Blue	Red	Red	Red	White	Beige	Red
Dash Top	Red	Red	Black	Black	Red	Red	Red	Black	Black	Black
Door Seals	Red	Red	Red	Black	Red	Red	Red	Black	Black	Red
Roof Lining	Off White	Off White	Off White	Off White	Off White	Off White	Off White	Off White	Off White	Off White
Carpeting	Grey	Grey	Grey	Grey	Grey	Grey	Grey	Grey	Grey	Grey
Spare Wheel Cover	Grey	Grey	Grey	Grey	Grey	Grey	Grey	Grey	Grey	Grey

During the course of its production, the MGA accumulated quite an extensive list of accessories. As is often the case with imported cars, the list included many dealer installed items which were approved by the factory. The listing of accessories was broken down into "normal" and "competition" items. Many of the competition items were sold as parts for the ambitious owner to install himself. As the MGA line progressed some of these accessories were incorporated as standard equipment while others were dropped altogether.

To assist in maintaining authenticity and hopefully shed some light into this little explored corner of MGA history, the following pages will describe the various accessories offered on the MGA. Where prices are available, they will be provided, however in many cases these are simply approximations due to currency fluctuations, labor costs etc. Exact times of introduction are difficult to pin down as some accessories were offered at the beginning of a model year while others were simply added as the production allowed. With those thoughts in mind, here are those "oldies but goodies!"

Rear axle assembly, 4.55:1 — This is the first option listed in the accessory material schedule for the MGA and was available at the beginning of the production run as a factory installed accessory. Since the speedometer gets its drive from the transmission, a speedometer with different gearing from normal was fitted at the time to compensate for the faster rotation of the transmission gears. This axle had a pronounced effect on acceleration and was popular with club racers, especially when coupled with the close-ratio gearbox. This was the only optional rear axle offered as a "normal" accessory. Other axle ratios were available, however they were offered as competition accessories. The cost was approximately $27 or £10 2s 6d in July 1958.

Wire wheels — The management at MG felt wire wheels were passe, but offered them anyway for their nostalgic appeal. The thinking was that *Dunlop* wire wheels would soon pass away in favor of the stronger, more easily maintained disc wheels. On this point management was wrong! Wire wheels, admittedly archaic, are still a popular option. Both painted and the increasingly popular chrome *Dunlop* wire wheels are still currently produced today by Wheels India, Ltd. Their efficiency has been somewhat diminished by safety regulations which "clipped" their ears in some countries. "But wait a minute!," you say, "Those regs didn't come along until the late sixties, well after the MGA's lifetime." That's almost right. During the time of the MGA, West Germany had a regulation which eliminated the ears on the knock offs, necessitating the addition of a "hub cap spanner" to the tool kit in order to remove the knock off. The original 1500 model wire wheels were 48 spoke and tended to be a bit weak, especially when subjected to over-enthusiastic driving. Today, most people opt for the stronger 60 spoke alternative. Wire wheels increase the track somewhat while providing additional cooling for the brakes and speeding up wheel changes. As a side benefit, they kept a thriving market of wheel-wrights busy tuning wheels and replacing spokes! They still may be expensive (as much as $150-200 each or £75-100 today) and a pain in the neck to maintain, but they sure do look good. These were not available on the Twin Cam model.

White wall tires — Seen in virtually all the ads, these were the rage in the late fifties. These wide white side walls could be yours for about $35 or £13 in 1961. These were not offered on the Twin Cam.

"Road Speed" tires — These black sidewall tires were offered as a dealer installed option for the enthusiast driver looking for a high performance tire. These tires were standard equipment on the Twin Cam model and 1600 Mk II cars exported to West Germany, however they cost you an additional $45 or £17 on any other model. If the four wheel disc brake option was added on the 1600 or 1600 Mk II models, "Road Speed" tires were part of the package. The tire also offered a larger cross-section, 5.90 x 15 vs 5.50 x 15 for the standard tire.

The telescopic steering wheel requires a wrench for adjustment.

The factory luggage carrier is of robust construction.

The original tonneau cover had a zipper which was offset slightly to the passenger side. The reinforcement tab at the end of the zipper was leather.

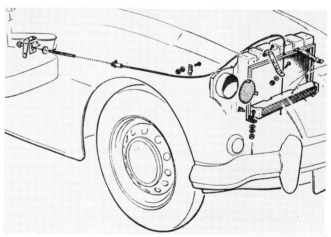

The radiator blind was operated from the driver's seat and was mounted in front of the radiator.

Rim embellishers — These chrome plated wheel trim rings were offered on disc wheel equipped 1500 and 1600 models only as a dealer installed option. Not a very popular option, they were dropped prior to the 1600 Mk II and therefore are as scarce as hen's teeth today!

Adjustable steering column — This was a very popular accessory. Although offered as a factory option on the 1500, 1600 and 1600 Mk II models, it is rare to find a U.S. car without one. It was standard equipment on the Twin Cam. It offered three inches of adjustment, with the assistance of a wrench to slacken the pinch bolt. The cost in 1957 was a modest $6 or £2 6s 8d.

Luggage carrier — This dealer installed luggage carrier looks hefty enough to carry Aunt Mary's piano! Part of its visual strength stems from the two broad metal straps which distribute the weight over a broad area of the trunk lid. No doubt an important consideration with the aluminum construction. As a consideration for the paint finish, the carrier was supplied with two strips of rubber to place between the mounting straps and the trunk lid.

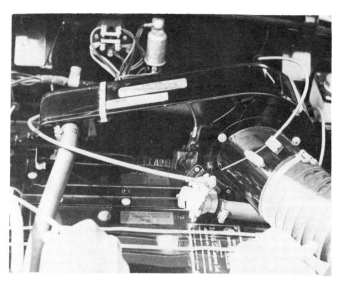

The heater in the Twin Cam was a mirror image of the one used in the standard cars. The heater water control valve, seen here at the base of the heater, was mounted on the engine block on other models.

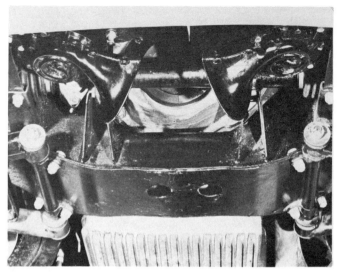

The twin horns were mounted just aft of the front valence panel.

The medium wave-shortwave model radio.

The medium wave non-push-button model radio.

Tonneau cover—This ever popular option was offered as a factory accessory on all models (except the coupe of course!). For many dyed-in-the-wool enthusiasts it served as the sole concession to weather protection. Actually it works quite well. At speeds above 35 mph or so the wind carries most of the rain over the passenger compartment, just don't stop for any lights! Offered at $35 or £13 in 1961. Some had their fasteners mounted in the wooden passenger compartment surround molding while others mounted in the body sheet metal. Most after market tonneaus are done in black, however only the 1500 body came with a black tonneau with certain body colors.

Radiator blind—I have never personally seen one of these on an MGA but they must have been somewhat popular because they were offered on all MGA models from beginning to end. Designed to block off cold air from the radiator using a venetian blind type device the engine was able to warm up quickly and stay that way. As a side benefit, the heater was able to produce its warm but feeble zephyrs more quickly. The device was controlled by means of a knob mounted high on the kick panel, behind the dash on the driver's side. This was a dealer installed option which entailed quite a bit of labor to install.

Heater kit—This ever popular accessory remained an option throughout the MGA's lifetime. Because of the different water flow arrangement on the Twin Cam, its heater was a mirror image of the standard heater. With its one-speed blower and all too easily breakable bakelight control panel, this heater provided a marginally acceptable level of heating above 20°F. Below that temperature the situation was hopeless, resulting in roasted toes and a frozen nose. Admittedly, the hard top option with sliding

The attractive and powerful Lucas fog lamp.

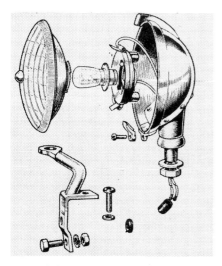

An exploded view of the fog lamp. Notice the lamp bracket. The lamps were mounted behind the bumper guard, between it and the headlamp.

sidescreens helped considerably. On some models the blower control was incorporated into the "Air" control while on others it was activated by pulling out on the "Temperature" control knob. Available at $65 or £16 32s 6d in 1957.

Cold air ventilation kit—This dealer installed option merely provided fresh outside air to the toeboard of the passenger compartment. No heating or demisting equipment was included. Controls consisted of a blower switch mounted on the dash next to the push-pull air control.

Twin horns—A two-toned way to announce your arrival! Available on all models for only $6 or £2 1s 3d. Dealer installed.

Fog lamp—The wiring for this accessory was already in place on every MGA model complete with a fog lamp switch on the dash (marked with an "F"). The spare red and yellow lead located behind the grill on the right side provides the necessary electrical hook up. The lamps were Lucas 55128A Type SFT and were mounted behind the front bumper over-riders. Starting in January 1959, a relay harness was fitted on cars destined for the U.S. This was a dealer installed option.

Radio—If you think today's auto manufacturers offer a large variety of optional radios, consider that in 1955 MG offered no fewer than six different radios! HMV radios came in two push-button models, a medium wave and a long and medium wave model. These two models were also available without push-buttons. A medium wave-shortwave high output and a low output model were also offered.

Windscreen washer kit—This was a factory installed option, available on all models for about $8 or £3 in 1958. A knob marked *push* was used to activate the washer system. It was mounted on the dash beneath the fuel gauge and connected to an unbreakable bottle fastened to the bulkhead in the engine compartment and had two nozzles affixed to the scuttle. The system worked on an air pressure system that was simple, inexpensive and light weight. There were two types: a large and a small cap reservoir (changed mid-1600).

Competition windscreen—For some odd reason this seemingly competition fitting was offered as a "normal" dealer installed option on all models. Resembling a cut-down version of the standard windscreen, it had an aluminum frame and perspex instead of glass. It stood 6-1/2 inches high and allowed the car to slip through the air more easily. Cost was a rather stiff (for the times) $89 or £35.

Wing driving mirrors—These were offered as a dealer accessory on all models. They were mounted on the top of each front fender about midway

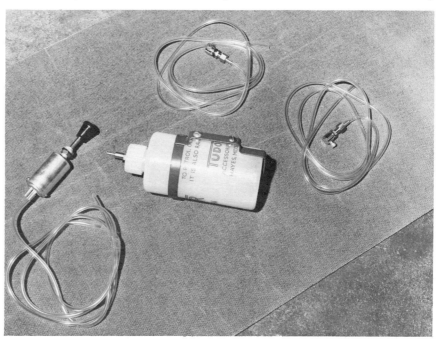

The windscreen washer employed two jets and a hand pump mounted on the dash. The later style is shown.

The competition windscreen on an early proto-type. Production models more closely resembled the standard windscreen.

Lucas wing mirrors were offered singly or in pairs. A dealer installed item, their placement was not always consistent.

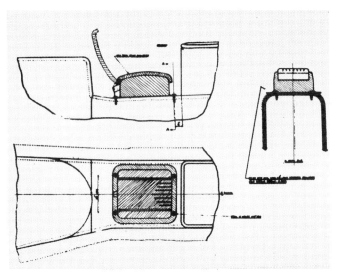

The radio speaker mounted behind the grill in the center of the dash. However, it didn't mount up flush to the grill, but rather mounted some distance behind and was angled downward as seen here.

Blueprint showing ashtray location and design which remained the same through much of the MGB model run.

Early model hardtops were aluminum. Its design inspired the coupe model.

Later models were available in fiberglass. A vinyl covered hardtop is shown here.

forward and afforded good rearward vision to either side, provided you had them adjusted correctly. This usually required an assistant as the mirrors were mounted too far forward for a normally equipped person to reach! They were of Lucas manufacture; model 406/1/29A for the right side and model 406/1/41A on the left. A single "Wingard" type 1C fender mounted mirror was also offered.

Ash tray—Offered as a dealer installed item, the ash tray was mounted between the arm rest and the gear shift on the driveshaft tunnel. It was chrome and black and sold for a paltry $3 or £1 4s 10d in 1955. It was available on all models.

Hard top assembly—A fiberglass hardtop was offered as an option on all MGA models, starting with the 1500 model in early 1956. Its introduction preceded that of the MGA coupe by several months and in fact offered the inspiration for the coupe's design. You could have your hardtop in any color, providing that color was black! On the later models, the hardtops were vinyl covered. There were a few aluminum hardtops made but these were for competition cars. In fact, the very first hardtops were made for the Alpine Rally in 1956 so the cars could compete in the GT class. Truly a competition bred accessory! To take full advantage of the weather protection of the hard top, sliding sidescreens were sold with it. Rearward vision was also improved with an extraordinarily large rear window. So large in fact that it incorporated two bars to brace the window against suction created by high speed motoring, just as on the coupe. A dealer installed option, the hardtop added a hefty $275 or £106 to the tally sheet.

Sliding window assembly—These plexiglass sidescreens were especially designed to go with the hard top option. Together they provided weather protection approaching that of the coupe. The frame of these early sidescreens was vinyl covered and they were offered as an option on the 1500 and early Twin Cams. With the introduction of the 1600, these windows were standard equipment.

DeLuxe sliding sidescreens—These later type sidescreens boasted a polished aluminum frame and a rubber gasket which could be trimmed to provide a tighter seal than the older style sidescreens. These new style sidescreens were offered on the 1600 models beginning in early 1960 and on 1600 Mk II models as an option over the standard vinyl covered sidescreens.

Badge bar—In late 1956 the badge bar option was offered as a dealer installed accessory. Mounted above the front bumper, it afforded the owner an appropriate place to proudly display his car club badges, a long standing British tradition. This option was available on all MGA models.

Cigar lighter—The cigar lighter was introduced as an option on the Twin Cam model and later offered on the 1600 and 1600 Mk II models. Mounted in the dash, between the radio and the adjacent gauge, the cigar lighter was a dealer installed option.

Competition deluxe seats—These seats were offered for the first time in September 1958, with the introduction of the Twin Cam model. They were available on the 1500 model after September 1958 and the 1600 and 1600 Mk II models. These seats offered a larger, better padded location from which to pilot your MGA. Additional lateral stability was also an advantage, contributing to the "competition" aspect of the Competition Deluxe seats. They were definitely a factory installed option as the floor boards were made differently to accept the modified seat rails! It was possible for these seats to be installed by the dealer, however. On the 1500 body style they were available in the following color combinations:

Seat Color	Piping
Red	Red
Green	Green
Grey	Grey
Black	White

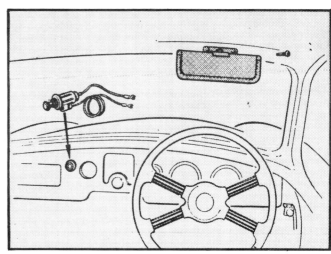

Sidescreen shown on the bottom was optional on 1500 and early Twin Cam models. The upper deluxe style side curtain was available from 1960 onward.

The badge bar doubles as a grill guard.

The cigar lighter was a dealer installed option which is seldom seen today. The lighter was mounted between the radio and the adjacent gauge as shown.

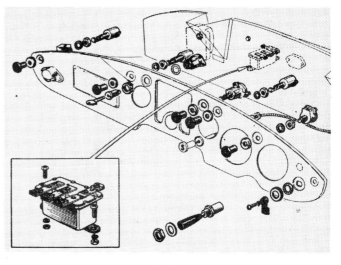

The competition seat substantially increased passenger comfort and is rarely seen on cars today.

The headlamp flasher switch is shown here at the right side of the instrument panel just above turn signal switch. The relay for the flasher is shown in the inset box and was mounted on the firewall.

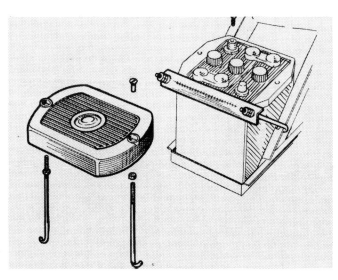

The battery covers afforded a measure of protection for the exposed batteries.

The sun visor was available on the coupe only, mounted singly or in pairs.

The anti-roll bar, similiar to this one, replaced the earlier optional Andrex friction shocks in controlling body lean.

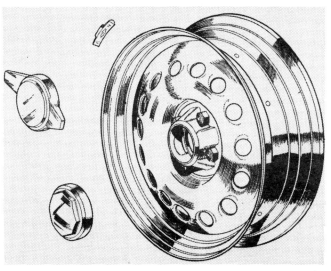

The knock-off disc wheels were a distinguishing feature of four wheel disc braked cars.

Black	Red
Black	Green
Black	Grey

On the 1600 and 1600 Mk II body style the selection was simplified:

Seat Color	Piping
Red	Red
Beige	Beige
Black	Red
Black	Blue
Black	White

The four-wheel disc brake option was actually a completely different chassis left over from the Twin Cam production. Shown here is a rear brake caliper.

These seats are quite rare, especially on models other than the Twin Cam, however they offered good value at a cost of $25 or £9 18s 9d in September 1958. These were the last additions to the 1500 option list.

Headlamp flasher switch—This rare option was offered beginning with the 1600 model and late model Twin Cams, continuing on the 1600 Mk II. The switch was mounted on the dash, above the turn signal switch where it could be within finger tip reach from the steering wheel. Cost was a paltry $6 or £2 16s 8d.

Anti-roll bar equipment—This option was offered beginning with the 1600 model and late model Twin Cams and later on the 1600 Mk II. This was a competition oriented accessory, replacing the Andrex shock absorbers which were in fact offered as competition items. The anti-roll bar was a dealer installed item, adding $60 or L23 to the price sticker.

Battery covers—This option was introduced with the 1600 model and late model Twin Cams. It was also offered on the 1600 Mk II. These dealer installed items provided additional weather protection for the exposed batteries.

Oil cooler—An engine oil cooler was offered on all models, however the Twin Cam was the only one to offer it as a non-competition accessory, part way into its production run. Under most conditions the engine oil cooler was unnecessary because the larger sump capacity of the Twin Cam engine eliminated much of the heat buildup in the oil. A factory installed option, the oil cooler cost $35 or L13 10s in 1958. Eventually the oil cooler was to become part of the standard equipment on cars sold for export after chassis number 102,737 during the 1600 Mk II production.

Sun visor—A flip-down, upholstered sun visor could be purchased and mounted by the dealer on one or both sides of the wind screen on the coupe model. This option was available on the Twin Cam, 1600 and 1600 Mk II models.

Close-ratio box power unit—This power unit combination was offered as a factory option on the 1600 late model Twin Cams and the 1600 Mk II. Interestingly, the close-ratio box was used quite early in the MGA's history on the EX 182 cars at Le Mans but didn't become available on production models until the 1600 model in 1959. First gear was quite high, making for some difficulty getting off the line cleanly, but the closely spaced gears allowed the driver to keep the engine working within the power band. This was a popular option with club racers, especially in combination with the 4.55:1 rear axle ratio. When the close-ratio power unit was fitted, the engine number plate was stamped with the letters "DA" under the engine serial number.

A Comparison of Gearbox and Rear Axle Combinations:

Gearbox Ratio Comparison:

Gear	Close-ratio	Standard ratio
1st	2.45:1	3.64:1
2nd	1.62:1	2.214:1
3rd	1.268:1	1.374:1
4th	1:1	1.1:1

MPH per 1,000 RPM Comparison (Std=Standard ratio, CR=Close ratio):

Gear	3.7:1 Std	3.7:1 CR	3.9:1 Std	3.9:1 CR	4.1:1 Std	4.1:1 CR	4.3:1 Std	4.3:1 CR	4.55:1 Std	4.55:1 CR
1st	5.8	8.6	5.4	8.0	5.0	7.5	4.8	7.1	4.6	6.9
2nd	9.5	13.0	8.9	12.2	8.3	11.3	7.8	10.7	7.6	10.4
3rd	15.3	16.6	14.3	15.5	13.3	14.4	12.6	13.6	12.2	13.2
4th	21.0	21.0	19.7	19.7	18.3	18.3	17.3	17.3	16.8	16.8

MPH per 6,000 RPM Comparison (Std=Standard ratio, CR=Close ratio):

Gear	3.7:1 Std	3.7:1 CR	3.9:1 Std	3.9:1 CR	4.1:1 Std	4.1:1 CR	4.3:1 Std	4.3:1 CR	4.55:1 Std	4.55:1 CR
1st	34.6	51.4	32.5	48.2	30.2	44.8	28.5	42.2	27.7	41.1
2nd	56.9	77.8	53.4	73.0	49.6	67.8	46.9	64.1	45.5	62.2
3rd	91.7	99.4	86.0	93.2	79.9	86.6	75.5	81.9	73.4	79.5
4th	126.0	126.0	118.0	118.0	110.0	110.0	104.0	104.0	101.0	101.0

Use these graphs and table to determine engine and car speeds at various rpm for the close-ratio and standard ratio gearboxes.

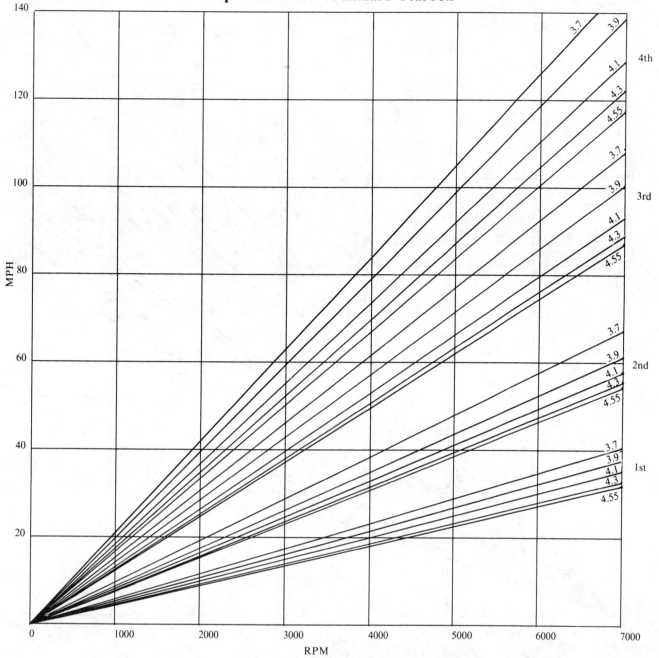

Disc brakes all round including center lock disc wheels and Road Speed tires—Not only is this the longest winded accessory title, but it also was the most expensive ($500) and complex (190 part changes) of all the options offered on the MGA. This option could be ordered on the very late 1600 models and the 1600 Mk II models. Basically, the package came about as an expedient way to use up left over Twin Cam chassis. See the 1600 Mk II chapter for a complete description.

Wheel discs—A set of four "Ace Mercury" louvered wheel discs could be yours for the asking on the 1500, 1600 and 1600 Mk II models. Did anyone actually order these dealer installed items?

Now we get into the competition accessories which were not normally listed in the sales brochures because those who needed them knew enough to ask. Many of these options were sold as parts over the counter for the owner to install, so there was often some duplication with dealer or factory installed items of similar description. This listing includes most, but not all, major competition accessories.

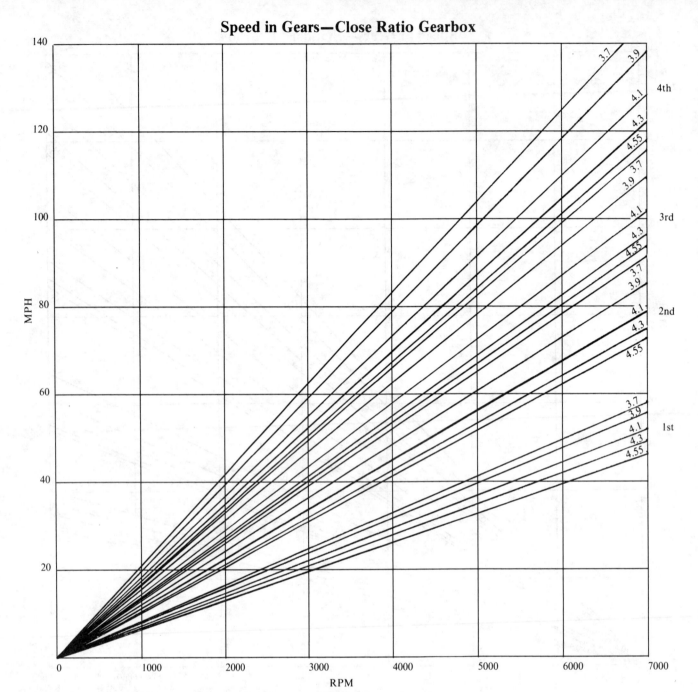

3.9:1, 4.1:1, 4.55:1 crown wheel and pinion—All the parts the serious racer needed to adapt the rear axle ratio to match that of the track's character. These were available on all MGA models for a pretty stiff price of $100 or £40 for the 3.9:1 set, $68 or £26 for the 4.1:1 set and $37 or £14 for the 4.55:1 gear set.

4.875:1 and 5.125:1 crown wheel and pinion—This was a continuation of the axles offered on the 1500. These became available when the high-revving Twin Cam came on the market and were subsequently withdrawn with the demise of the Twin Cam. Admittedly, 6,000 rpm didn't go too far with the 5.125:1 axle!

15 x 4.1/2J 60 spoke alloy or steel rim wire wheel—These 60 spoke wheels offered additional strength for the stress of competition which would quickly prove too much for the standard 48 spoke wheels. Surprisingly, wire wheels are quite heavy and the alloy rim was designed to offset some of the weight picked up by the additional spokes. These wheels were offered on the 1500, 1600 and 1600 Mk II models. The alloy rim version sold for $119 or

£46 in 1961, while the steel rim model was more modestly priced at $38 or £15 in 1961.

Petrol gas tank, 20 gallons—Designed with the long distance racer in mind, this tank was also used by factory teams at Le Mans and Sebring. Offered on all MGA models for $104 or £40.

Petrol gas tank, 15 gallons—A smaller version of the 20 gallon tank for $59 extra cost! Available on all MGA models for $163 or £60.

Petrol gas tank, 17 gallons—Available only on the 1600 Mk II. The above measures are Imperial Gallons.

Bonnet hood straps—A pair of leather straps with buckles to hold the hood shut as a sort of back-up system for the hood latch. Certain to cause anxiety on the part of the crew member trying to open the hood in haste during a pit stop! Cheap at $5 or £2 each! Available on all MGA models.

Andrex shock absorbers—A friction type adjustable shock absorber mounted only on the front suspension to assist the standard hydraulic shocks control body sway and bounce. Available on early 1500, 1600 and Twin Cam. Not available when the anti-roll bar was mounted. Cost was $48 or £20 in 1961.

Competition brake shoes—These heavy duty linings offered better fade resistance than stock linings. Available on late model 1500 only.

Oil cooler—This competition oil cooler cost $94 or £38 in 1961 and was available on late model 1500s, 1600s and 1600 Mk IIs.

Polished cylinder head assembly—The latest word in cylinder head gas flowing done by the factory enabled the engine to breathe more deeply. Offered on late model 1500 and 1600 models.

Steering wheel woodrim Italian style—This handsome riveted wood-rim wheel with alloy spokes added just the right sporting touch to the helm. Its greater rim thickness provided a better grip and best of all the rim didn't break where the spokes joined it like the standard wheel. A pretty steep $84 or £32. Offered on late model 1500, 1600, 1600 Mk II and Twin Cam models.

Close-ratio gears—These were offered only on the Twin Cam model as

a set for $121 or *L*48.

High setting hydraulic damper valves—These gave a firmer, more controlled shock absorber action without the addition of Andrex shocks. Available only on the late Twin Cam models.

Competition brake pads—These heavy duty pads for the Dunlop four wheel disc brake set up on the Twin Cam improved on an already excellent braking system.

Valve spring, inner/outer—Available for the 1600 Mk II only, these stiffer springs allowed higher revs before valve float set in. Cheap at $11 or *L*5.

Inlet manifold with 1-3/4 inch carburetor—The hot intake set up for the 1600 Mk II only. The carburetors would run you $113 or *L*42 and the manifold was $23 or *L*9.

Wide overlap racing camshaft—The perfect combination with the bigger carburetors, this cam was available on late model 1600 Mk IIs only.

Blanking sleeve/thermostat by-pass—Still available today as a racing part, this was one of the last items to be added to the MGA's option list on the later 1600 Mk II models only. Besides being a racing part, it also helps your street engine run cooler in the summer time by replacing the thermostat and allowing full water circulation with just the proper amount of restriction. Works so well, BL made it a dealer retrofit on the "Rubber Baby Buggy Bumper" 1974-1/2 MGB which ran into cooling problems due to the huge bumper over-riders!

Modified cylinder head—As many found out, the 1622 cc engine ran better and better the more the compression was raised. Apparently the fac-

tory shared this opinion and offered the option of raising the compression ratio to 9.8:1 by shaving 0.040 in. off the cylinder head. Available on late model 1600 Mk II only.

Accessory Availability

Accessory	1500	Twin Cam	1600	Mk II	Remarks
Rear Axle Assembly, 4.55:1	X	X	X	X	
Rim Embellishers	X		X		
Adjustable Steering Column	X		X	X	STD on Twin Cam
Luggage Carrier	X	X	X	X	
Tonneau Cover	X	X	X	X	
Wire Wheels	X		X	X	
White Wall Tires	X		X	X	
Road Speed Tires	X		X	X	STD on Twin Cam
Radiator Blind	X	X	X	X	
Heater Kit	X	X	X	X	
Cold Air Ventilation Kit	X	X	X	X	
Twin Horns	X	X	X	X	
Fog Lamp	X	X	X	X	
Radio	X	X	X	X	
Windscreen Washer Kit	X	X	X	X	
Competition Windscreen	X	X	X	X	
Wing Driving Mirrors	X	X	X	X	
Ash Tray	X	X	X	X	
Hard Top Assembly	X	X	X	X	Late 1500s
Sliding Window Assembly	X	X			STD 1600 & Mk II
DeLuxe Sliding Sidescreens			X	X	Late 1600
Badge Bar	X	X	X	X	Late 1500
Cigar Lighter		X	X	X	
Competition DeLuxe Seats	X	X	X	X	Late 1500
Headlamp Flasher Switch		X	X	X	Late Twin Cam
Anti-roll Bar Equipment		X	X	X	Late Twin Cam
Battery Covers		X	X	X	Late Twin Cam
Oil Cooler (non-competition)		X			
Sun Visor		X	X	X	Coupe only
Close-Ratio Box Power Unit		X	X	X	Late Twin Cam
Disc Brakes All-Round Including Center Lock Disc Wheels & R.S. Wheel Discs			X	X	Late 1600
3.9:1, 4.1:1, 4.55:1 Crown Wheel and Pinion	X	X	X	X	Late 1600
4.875:1 and 5.125:1 Crown	X	X	X	X	

Accessory	1500	Twin Cam	1600	Mk II	Remarks
Wheel and Pinion					
15 x 4.1/2J 60 Spoke Alloy/Steel Rim Wire Wheel	X		X	X	
Petrol Tank, 20 Gallons	X	X	X	X	
Petrol Tank, 15 Gallons	X	X	X	X	
Petrol Tank, 17 Gallons				X	
Bonnet Straps	X	X	X	X	
Andrex Shock Absorbers	X	X	X		
Competition Brake Shoes	X				Late 1500
Oil Cooler (competition)	X		X	X	Late 1500
Polished Cylinder Head Assy.	X		X		Late 1500
Steering Wheel-Woodrim	X	X	X	X	Late 1500
Close-Ratio Gears		X			
High Setting Hydraulic Damper Valves		X			Late Twin Cam
Competition Brake Pads		X	X	X	4 WHL Disc
Valve Spring-Inner/Outer				X	
Inlet Manifold with 1-3/4 inch Carburetor				X	
Wide Overlap Racing Camshaft				X	Late Mk II
Blanking Sleeve/Thermostat By-Pass				X	Late Mk II
Modified Cylinder Head				X	Late Mk II

Chapter 8

Clnbs

Almost every post brings me letters from MG owners. Some bear a near-by postmark, others are from distant parts of the world. Some relate experiences during lengthy tours, others tell of successes and failures in high-speed events. That is my life... [1]

Cecil Kimber

The best part about MGs is the people who drive them. The MG has earned a reputation for being an honest, straighforward, forgiving car and the same can be said of MG owners. MG owners tend to be enthusiastic about their cars and naturally enjoy sharing their enthusiasm with other MG owners. MG people have been doing this through clubs all over the world since 1930 when the first meeting of the MG car club was held.

Roy Marsh ran an ad in *The Light Car & Cyclecar* in October 1930 asking that anyone interested in forming an MG car club come to his house on a certain date and talk about it. Five persons, including Mr. Marsh, attended that first meeting from which sprang the MG Car Club. Present at that meeting was the redoubtable John Thornley who was selected as Honorary Secretary of the fledgling club. The club began to grow rapidly and took up much of John's time. He made trips to the MG works nearly every week, and soon he began to hint to Cecil Kimber that the works ought to take over responsibility for the running of the club or hire him to run the club. After some persistence, Kimber hired Thornley to run the club. Thus began a long association between the MG Car Company and the MG Car Club, an association which lasted until 1969 when British Leyland cut its ties with the club.

The MG Car Club has done quite well since then. It is the largest car club in the world, with more than 50 centers all over the globe. One of the chief means by which the club keeps in touch with its far flung members is through the club magazine, *Safety Fast*. *Safety Fast* was not the original title of the club magazine. The first magazine was published in May, 1933, and was called *The MG Magazine*. This was quickly followed in April, 1935, by a new monthly magazine called *The Sports Car*. In 1959, John Thornley called in noted MG historian F. Wilson McComb to produce *Safety Fast*.

Activities of the MG Car Club include rallies, club racing, technical discussions and just plain socializing. Each center has its own special assortment of events, tailored to its members' special wants and needs. The three biggest club events in England are the jamboree at Beaulieu, the races at Silverstone and the hill-climb at Wiscombe Park. Whatever the activity, members are drawn together to enjoy one another's company, be they internationally acclaimed race driver or first time sports car owner. The tie that

This boisterous group is enjoying itself at the "Hare and Hound Natter," an MGA Register sponsored event.

Somehow even the most dignified MG events have a way of loosening up! Here Nancy Mitchell, Ladies European Rally Champion 1956 and 1957, concentrates on extracting the optimum performance from her mount at an MG Car Club dinner.

MG and Triumph are longtime rivals. This photo taken at the Karlshoza track in Sweden shows the MGA about to overtake a TR.

MG drivers are usually eager to participate in a rally. This was taken during the "Highland Rally." The MGA is atop "Rest and be Thankful" hill. Is the fellow next to the TR wishing he'd bought an MGA instead?

binds them together is what really matters. Those interested in joining the MG Car Club should contact their local center, or write to: MG Car Club Ltd., 67 Wide Bargate, Boston, Lincs. PE21 6SG, England.

The MGA has risen in popularity in recent years and with this renewed interest, MGA registers and clubs have been organized in the same fashion as the "T" type registers.

MGA Register

The MGA Register of the MG Car Club was constituted in October, 1970 after no small amount of convincing the parent club that an MGA Register was wanted and needed. The idea to form the register began at the "Natter & Noggin" held at the Phoenix Public House in Hartley Witney early in 1970. In order to demonstrate their resolve, the MGA owners decided to crash the Beaulieu Concours, an event which was organized by the T Register for T-types and earlier models. Dennis Ogborn, one of the chief instigators of the MGA Register, describes what occurred. "The day duly dawned and some 40 MGAs appeared on the scene. . .and not exactly received with enthusiasm! However, we were allowed to form a row outside the rope marking the boundary of the field. . .in those days it was held in one of the fields of the Estate. It got the message across that there were enough eager types who wanted a Register, and were obviously not going to quietly 'go away.' "

Following the meeting at Beaulieu, a committee consisting of George Ward, Ian Andrew, and Dennis Ogborn was formed to seek official recognition of the register at the council meeting in October, 1971. The creation of the MGA Register was approved, and the three MGA enthusiasts named above were designated the committee to organize the register. Dennis Ogborn was the first register secretary.

The register, or any register for that matter, is a club to which the car,

Racing MGAs has become very popular in England and the MGA Register is in the thick of it. Here a Twin Cam coupe and 1500 roadster battle it out in the wet at Silverstone.

Vic Ellis, well known garage owner and MGA buff, pilots his coupe during the Six Hour Relay at Donnington.

Not all MGAs look as stock as Vic's. This highly modified racer was also entered in the Six Hour Relay race at Donnington.

not the owner, belongs. The main purpose of the register is to preserve the existence of a particular marque or model through a registration of the cars, a mutual exchange of technical information, location of spares and in many cases the joining together to have certain parts remanufactured. Naturally, all this activity requires a good bit of socializing! The activities of the MGA Register include a racing championship for the Fitzwilliam Trophy, a Concours Championship for the Byrne Trophy, a Register Rally and an Annual Dinner and Disco. The Register has an excellent magazine called *MGActivities*. *MGActivities* has been published on a bi-monthly basis since 1971 and is available on subscription from the publishers, Snowball Press, 14a Cross Street, Reading, Berkshire RG1 1SN, England. The register has grown rapidly, registering over 1,000 MGAs by 1980 and welcomes new members. Membership information can be obtained by writing to the Register Chairman, Stu Holley at 12 Sweet Briar Close, Shaw Clough, Rochdale, Lancs 0L21 6NX, England.

NORTH AMERICAN MGA REGISTER

The North American MGA Register was organized in the summer of 1975 on the occasion of the 50th anniversary of the MG car. Started by a small group of enthusiasts from the United States and Canada, the Register has emphasized the U.S.–Canadian partnership in its activities which include local, regional and national GTs (Get-Togethers). Members come together to talk about MGAs and to have a good time. The annual GTs are held in a different area of the U.S. or Canada each year, giving all members the opportunity to attend.

In the first twelve years of its existence, NAMGAR has registered over 3,200 MGAs and variants throughout North America and worldwide. We publish a bi-monthly newsletter, *MGA!*, which contains technical, historic and general-interest items for the MGA enthusiast. We encourage members to contribute articles for publication in our newsletter.

Our primary purpose is to register and track MGAs. Owners may join NAMGAR or simply register their cars if they prefer. The club emphasizes the fun aspect of MGA ownership, encouraging its members to enjoy their cars as originally intended.

For membership information, contact:

Jack Kurkowski
76 Blossom Lane
Mooresville, IN 46158 U.S.A.

NAMGAR members enjoy their MGAs. Here MGAs gather at a national get-together held at the Indianapolis Motor Speedway. A chance to drive around the historic track is an experience to remember for a lifetime.

The interests of NAMGAR members vary. Here is a Sebring racer preserved in its original condition.

Some MGAs are registered with NAMGAR by their original owners; others are acquired in baskets and brought back to life. Most NAMGAR MGAs are not the subject of ground-up restorations, however, but are lovingly maintained and driven by their owners.

 **A TYPE OWNERS HOLLAND**

MGA Type Owners Holland

Holland has always been a "hot-bed" of MG activity, and the MGA enthusiasts are no exception. The MGA Type Owners Holland was organized on 1 October, 1974, and quickly grew to over 150 members in its first five years of existence. The MGA, MG T-Type and MG Car Clubs are joined together to form a federation of MG Clubs in Holland. This joint organization sponsors two main events each year. A well attended race meeting is held at the famous Zandvoort Race Circuit during the summer months and a night rally is held in the fall. A monthly meeting is held in various locations throughout Holland where Dutch enthusiasts enjoy each other's company and cars, joining in a short rally with a dinner afterward. Those interested in joining the MGA Type Owners Holland can contact Rutger Booy at Lepelaarsingel 106, 3136 Vlaardingen, The Netherlands.

 **TWIN CAM GROUP**

MGA Twin Cam Group

The Twin Cam Group was organized in 1965 by Mike Ellman-Brown, who is currently Chairman of the Twin Cam Group. Mike has had a long association with MGs and it will be remembered that he purchased the last MGA Twin Cam. The driving force behind the Twin Cam Group's formation was the dwindling availability of spares. With the blessing of the MG Car Club, Mike advertised in major motoring publications, soliciting members. Since then the group has grown to an annual membership around 100; however, over the first fourteen years 330 members and 587 Twin Cams have been registered in eighteen different countries. The club provides many services for its members, including the publication of the *Twin Cam Guide* with annual addenda. *The Twin Cam Guide* is a comprehensive compilation of articles and technical information of interest for the Twin Cam owner. The register maintains a listing of cars and their owners, as do all the registers. A complete spares and technical service is provided, an advantage which is becoming increasingly important to the Twin Cam owner. The register is active in competition events, fielding a team of cars for a national six hour relay race, enforcing MGA Twin Cam Motor Sport Competition regulations and providing judges at Concours d'elegance events.

Prospective members can contact the club General Secretary, Phil Richer, 9 Grenville Way, Shitley Bay, Tyne & Wear NE26 3JJ, England.

The MGA Twin Cam Registry is a U.S. based group which saw its beginning in 1968 when two dedicated Twin Cam enthusiasts, Lyle York from Anderson, Indiana and Jim Treat from Minneapolis, Minnesota got together and organized the register. Membership soon grew to 200 members and a regular newsletter was published. Through the years the newsletter has been cut back to an annual issue, keeping members informed of the latest events. In its first ten years of existence, the register has grown to 769 members.

Its activities include the publication of an annual newsletter, including a list of register members, providing a spares service and working with other MG Car Clubs to further the interest in the Twin Cam. Lyle York, current Register Chairman, was instrumental in organizing the 1979 tour of EX 181 to the United States, and arranging for its stopover at the Indianapolis Motor Speedway Museum. This was the first visiting exhibit at the museum, an event which was marked by a jointly sponsored gathering of the North American MGA Register and the MGA Twin Cam Registry. Those interested in joining the Register should contact Lyle York, 5105 Kingswood Lane, PO Box 1068, Anderson, Indiana 46011, U.S.A.

The AMERICAN MGB ASSOCIATION

"You chose an MG, an excellent choice. You experience motoring pleasure far above what the average motorist will ever dream about."

Since 1975, the American MGB Association has been keeping the tradition very much alive. They are the official registry for MGB's, MGB-GTs and MG Midgets in North America. Headquartered in Chicago, the AMGBA has over 2000 members throughout North American and the rest of the world!

Not all are ace mechanics or MG historians — although they do have some of these people who are more than happy to share their knowledge with their fellow members. AMGBA members come from all walks of life but they all have one thing in common — "The Magic of MG."

If you've ever had trouble finding a good mechanic, parts, or if you ever wanted to learn to do some of your own repairs and maintenance, the AMGBA can steer you in the right direction. The AMGBA *Octagon* is their official publication. Each issue contains technical information, interesting articles and photographs from AMGBA members the world over.

Each year a different city within the U.S. is chosen to host their annual national convention. This convention draws hundreds of MGs from all over the USA and Canada and provides an informal weekend of fun and camaraderie for members and their families. In addition, there are many regional conventions and get-togethers held throughout North America. The *Octagon* keeps AMGBA members informed of all such events.

The annual membership is $20.00, for which you receive their national quarterly magazine, *Octagon*, along with free classified advertising privileges, parts discounts, local chapter news, technical advice and much more. For more information contact:

The American MGB Association   (312) 843-3898
PO Box 11401
Chicago, IL 60611

The NEW ENGLAND MG 'T' REGISTER

The New England MG 'T' Register is an international organization dedicated to the maintenance, preservation and enjoyment of T-series and vintage MG's. It supports the active use of these cars and encourages the exchange of technical, historical and social information through the pages of its bi-monthly publication, *The Sacred Octagon*, which contains articles, photos, drawings, spares information, advertisements and other material of interest to the membership.

The Register has over 4500 members and 40 local chapters located throughout the USA and Canada. Two large meetings are scheduled each year, one in early summer, the other in the fall. These meetings are called the *Gathering of the Faithful* or GOF. The GOF is an informal, low pressure, social-type weekend, where T-Series enthusiasts meet and talk MG's. The GOF features photo contests, model displays, funkhanas, ralleyes, etc., with the high point being the car display. The members attending, vote for their favorite cars in each class, and awards are given. In 1989, the Register will celebrate 25 years of serving T-Series and vintage MG owners from all over the world.

One need not own a pre-1955 MG to belong to the Register. Full membership is for T-types, Y-types and selected variants such as the Arnolt as long as powered by original type engines. Vintage membership is for pre-1940, non T-type cars. Associate membership is open to anyone with a strong interest in MG's. The annual membership is $25.00 for which you receive The Sacred Octagon 6 times per year, and MG Magazine 4 times per year. If you would like an application form and additional information, please write:

MG
Drawer 220
Oneonta, New York 13820

Acknowledgements

This work would have been impossible without the assistance and encouragement of a long list of contributors. To them goes my heartfelt thanks for sharing with me a portion of their busy lives so that this book could be as complete and accurate as the MGA deserves.

First and foremost I am greatly indebted to my family who have put up with this nonsense for the past two and one-half years. Writing this book has been personally very important to me and their understanding and patience made my concentration on the project possible.

When I first started on this project I sought the advice of Dick Knudson who has written so many excellent books on the MG. He was kind enough to share with me information and sources which proved to be invaluable. One of the major sources he introduced me to was Henry Stone.

Henry Stone has been with MG since 1931 working most of the time in the Experimental and Competition departments. He has contributed mightily to the competition chapter, lending an historical perspective which might otherwise be lost. He and his wife, Winnie, were kind enough to spend several evenings with me sharing the history and atmosphere of MG.

John Thornley, General Manager of MG from 1952-69, and his wife Anne, graciously shared nearly two days with me. John's account of the management dealings behind the production of the MGA and straightening out the origins of the Twin Cam engine were major contributions in insuring the accuracy of this book. I am especially grateful for his writing the foreword.

Marcus Chambers, who was Competition Department head for BMC from 1954 to 1961, provided me with many original documents and photos. His insight into the relative position of the MGA with respect to the other BMC products at the time helped put the MGA in the proper historical perspective.

Don Hayter and Terry Mitchell from the Design Department provided me access to design office records which filled in some important gaps in the MGA story. Their recollections of the design history of the MGA shed a brighter light on the behind the scenes activity that made the MGA what it was.

Anders Clausager from BL Heritage was my host for two days, which he took out of his vacation, escorting me around the Cowley photographic offices and the MGA factory.

John Wright and Reid Willis contributed substantially to the restoration chapter. John spent five years restoring the magnificent black Twin Cam roadster seen in this book and Reid has owned his red Twin Cam roadster since buying it new in 1958. *English Restoration* newsletter was kind enough to share with me the results of an MGA owner survey which provided the basis for identifying common trouble spots in the MGA.

Sherm Decker provided me with a great story about his bittersweet experience with MGAs in racing as well as allowing me to use a number of photographs from his collection.

A special thanks to Jeff Bloxham of *Autosport* magazine for allowing me to use their photographs.

Two Canadians, Gord Whatley and Robin Barker, were a great help to me in putting together the story of the EX 182 and Sebring cars. An Australian friend, Ian Prior, also contributed to the Sebring story. Lyle York, who is the "Godfather" of the Sebring MGA owners, offered additional insight regarding the various Sebring efforts and the Twin Cam.

To the MG groups goes a big thanks for essentially writing the clubs chapter. Contributors include Dennis Ogborn and Peter Slip of the MGA Register, Len and Ruth Renkenberger from the North American MGA Register, Phil Richer of the Twin Cam Group, Rutger Booy from the MGA Type Owners Holland and Lyle York of the MGA Twin Cam Registry.

Last, but not least, I owe a huge debt to my good friend Ray Burt who graciously invited me to spend my time in England with him sharing his apartment, food and knowledge of the country. Ray is by no means an MG enthusiast or even a car buff but his hospitality contributed in a big way to making this book possible.

There were many others who contributed and I apologize for not including them but their efforts are greatly appreciated and certainly not forgotten.

Second Printing

The first printing of "MGA - A History & Restoration Guide" sold out in just over three years, confirming my belief that there are a lot of fellow MGA enthusiasts out there!. The book you are holding would not have been possible without the herculean efforts of Cecelia Bruce, one of the owners of Scarborough Faire, who just about singlehandedly took this project from start to finish, overcoming dozens of unanticipated obstacles and setbacks.

Initially, the idea of a second printing seemed to be a relatively straightforward and simple project. But alas, just as in an MGA restoration, the task at hand was far more difficult than originally anticipated. The original printing plates had been destroyed, greatly complicating the second printing process. The film negatives could have saved the day, but they turned out to be second generation copies. Whatever original textboards that were still available were turning various shades of yellow or brown. About the only thing Cecelia had to work with was an original copy of the book with my corrections penciled in the margins.

Few people would have resisted the temptation to simply make new negatives and plates from a corrected first edition book; but, Cecelia insisted that you have the best possible product and not have to settle for a second rate job in the second printing.

This pursuit of excellence did not come easily or cheaply. Custom software had to be written to convert the text diskettes to a format readable on Scarborough's phototypesetter. Several attempts were necessary, yet this was only partially successful. The most discouraging aspect, however, was that the original photographs, which I had painstakingly borrowed from several collections all over the world had to be recovered or substituted.

Cecelia rose to this challenge, and several trips to England followed. For two or three days on end, Cecelia laboriously poured through hundreds of file drawers filled with uncatalogued photographs. The "restoration" is complete and copies of my book are once again "on the street"; my hat is off to you, Cecelia. Well done!

Glossary

Glossary Of British—American Motoring Terms

British Term	American Term
Accumulator	Battery
Axle Shaft	Half Shaft
Bevel Pinion	Small Pinion
Big-End Bearing	Rod Bearing
Bonnet	Hood
Boot	Trunk
Bulkhead	Firewall
Capacity	Displacement
Change Speed Fork	Shift Fork
Control Box	Voltage Regulator
Core Plug	Freeze Plug, Expansion Plug, Welch Plug
Crownwheel	Ring Gear
Damper	Shock Absorber
Differential Gear	Sun Wheel
Differential Pinion	Planet Wheel
Draglink	Side Tube, Steering Connecting Rod
Dynamo	Generator
First Motion Shaft	Clutch Shaft, Main Drive Pinion, Drivegear
Gearbox	Transmission
Gear Lever	Shift Lever
Gudgeon Pin	Wrist Pin
Hood	Convertible Top
Lamps	Lights
Layshaft	Countershaft
Mixture Control	Choke, Strangler
Oil Sump	Oil Pan, Oil Reservoir
Propeller Shaft	Driveshaft
Saloon	Sedan
Scraper Ring	Oil Control Ring
Screenwasher	Windshield Washer
Silencer	Muffler
Spanner	Wrench
Sparking Plug	Spark Plug
Starting Handle	Crank Handle
Stub Axle	Swivel Axle
Swivel Pin	King Pin
Track-Rod	Cross Tube
Tyre	Tire
U-Bolts	Spring Clips
Windscreen	Windshield
Wing	Fender

Footnotes

Footnotes to Chapter I

[1] Kenneth Ullyett, *The MG Companion*, (Burbank: Autobooks, 1960), p. 35.
[2] Lord Montagu and F. Wilson McComb, *Behind the Wheel*, p. 130.
[3] Walter Groves, "The Morris-Oxford Light Car," *The Motor*, 17 December, 1912, p. 978.
[4] Ullyett, *The MG Companion*, p. 28.
[5] Ullyett, *The MG Companion*, p. 35.
[6] Doug Nye, "Abingdon Modern-The History of the MGA," *Automobile Quarterly*, vol. XVII, no. 1, First Quarter 1979, p. 33.
[7] Nye, "Abingdon Modern," p. 34.
[8] Nye, "Abingdon Modern," p. 37.
[9] Ullyett, *The MG Companion*, p. 80.
[10] Ullyett, *The MG Companion*, p. 80.

Footnotes To Chapter II

[1] "Road Testing the MG 'A' ," *Road and Track*, October 1955, p. 40.
[2] John Bolster, "John Bolster Tests the MGA," *Autosport*, October 21, 1955, p. 494.
[3] "The MG Series-MGA Two Seater," *The Motor*, September 28, 1955, p. 299.
[4] "MG Model 'A'," *Road and Track*, November 1955
[5] "Fast and Friendly," *The Autocar*, 2 March 1956, p. 189.
[6] Griff Borgeson, "SCI Road Test: The MGA," *Sports Cars Illustrated*, January 1957, p. 16.
[7] Borgeson, *Sports Car*, p. 16
[8] "Road Testing the MG 'A', *Road and Track*, October 1955, p. 41.

Footnotes to Chapter III

[1] Kenneth Ullyett, *The MG Companion*, (Burbank: Autobooks, 1960), p. 119.
[2] "The New Twin Cam MG," *The Motor*, July 16, 1958, p. 911.

[3] "MG Twin Cam MGA," *The Autocar*, July 18, 1958, p. 89.
[4] "DOHC MG-A," *Road and Track*, November 1958, p. 24.
[5] *Sports Car Quarterly*
[6] Richard L Knudson, *MG International*, (Surry, England: Motor racing Publications Ltd, 1977), p. 119.

Footnotes to Chapter IV

[1] Kenneth Ullyett, *The MG Companion*, (Burbank: Autobooks, 1960), p. 96.
[2] Ullyett, *The MG Companion*, p. 96.
[3] "The MGA 1600," *Autosport*, October 9, 1959, p. 49.
[4] "MG-A 1600," *Road and Track*, October 1959, p. 34.
[5] "The MGA 1600 Two Seater," *The Motor*, September 2, 1959.
[6] "MGA 1600," *Sports Cars Illustrated*, October 1959, p. 24.

Footnotes to Chapter V

[1] "More Power for the MGA," *The Motor*, June 28, 1961, p. 826.
[2] "MG MGA 1600 Mark II," *The Autocar*, July 21, 1961, p. 93.
[3] "MG-A 1600 Mk II," *Road and Track*, 1961
[4] "More Power for the MG A," *The Motor*, June 28, 1961, p. 826.
[5] John Christy, "MG-A Mk II Competition," *Sports Car Graphic*, May 1962, p. 61.

Footnotes to Chapter VI

[1] Reprint from *MG Magazine*, British Leyland Motors, 1979.
[2] Ibid, 1979.
[3] John W Thornley, *Maintaining the Breed*, 2nd ed., (London, England: Motor Racing Publications Ltd., 1956), p. 165.
[4] Thornley, *Maintaining the Breed*, p. 167.
[5] Jonathan Wood, "Le Mans MGA," *Thoroughbred and Classic Cars*, January 1957, p. 16.
[6] Thornley, *Maintaining the Breed*, p. 168.

Footnotes to Chapter VII

[1] Chris Harvey, *MG: The Immortal T Series*, (Oxford, England: Oxford Illustrated Press Limited, 1977), p. 171.

Footnotes to Chapter VIII

[1] Kenneth Ullyett, *The MG Companion*, (Burbank: Autobooks, 1960), p. 24.

Credits

Autosport
Barker Collection
Bray Collection
British Leyland
Chambers Collection
Decker Collection
Herson Collection
MG Register
MGA Register
MacKenzie Collection
R A Cover
R P Vitrikas
Stone Collection

Recommended Reading

MG Sports Cars, by Peter Garnier
MG: The A, B & C, by Chris Harvey
Postwar MG & Morgan, by John Blake and Henry Rasmussen
The T-Series MG Collector's Guide, by Graham Robson
MGA, MGB and MGC: A Collector' Guide, by Graham Robson
The Magic of MG, by Mike Allison
MG: The Sports Car America Loved First, by Richard Knudson
Tuning & Maintenance of MG Cars, by Philip H Smith
The 'T' Series MG, by Richard Knudson
MG 1911 to 1978, by Peter Filby
The MG Workshop Manual, by W E Blower
MG by McComb, by F Wilson McComb
Car Graphic MG (text in Japanese, 115 illus)
An MG Experience, by Dick Jacobs
MG 1946-62 (text in French)
MG Sports—the 6 Cylinder Cars
MG Sports Sedan Guide, by Stone
More Healeys: Frog-Eyes, Sprites and Midgets, by Geoffrey Healey
The New MG Guide, by John Christy & Karl Ludvigsen
Safety Last, by Captain G E T Eyston
William Morris, Viscount Nuffield, by R J Overy
The Classic MG Yearbook 1973, by Richard Knudson
MG World/75, by Richard Knudson and John Lavery
MG International 1977, by Richard Knudson
MG Owner's Club Yearbook 1979
MGA 1600 (Mk II) Owner's Manual
MGA Twin Cam Workshop Manual
BLMC Engine Emission Control Workshop Manual Supplement
The MG Workshop Manual
Clymer MGA, MGB, MGB/GT Service, Repair Handbook 1956-76
Autobook MGA, MGB, 1955-68

Index